ENTANGLED

ON RECORD
1969-1976

MARTIN POPOFF

ENTANGLED

ON RECORD
1969-1976

MARTIN POPOFF

WYMER
PUBLISHING
Bedford, England

First published in 2024 by Wymer Publishing, Bedford, England
www.wymerpublishing.co.uk Tel: 01234 326691.
Wymer Publishing is a trading name of Wymer (UK) Ltd.

Copyright © 2024 Martin Popoff / Wymer Publishing.

Print edition (fully illustrated): **ISBN: 978-1-915246-62-2**

Edited by Agustin Garcia de Paredes.

The Author hereby asserts his rights to be identified
as the author of this work in accordance with sections
77 to 78 of the Copyright, Designs & Patents Act 1988.

All rights reserved. No part of this publication may be
reproduced or transmitted in any form or by any means,
electronic or mechanical, including photocopying, or any
information storage and retrieval system, without written
permission from the publisher.

This publication is sold subject to the condition that it shall not,
by way of trade or otherwise, be lent, re-sold, hired out or
otherwise circulated without the publisher's prior consent in any
form of binding or cover other than that in which it is published
and without a similar condition including this condition
being imposed on the subsequent purchaser.

Printed and bound in Great Britain by CMP, Dorset.
A catalogue record for this book is available from the British Library.

Typeset/Design by Andy Bishop / Tusseheia Creative.
Cover design by Tusseheia Creative.
Cover photos © Alan Perry Photography.

TABLE OF CONTENTS

Introduction	7
From Genesis to Revelation	9
Trespass	37
Nursery Cryme	67
Foxtrot	93
Selling England by the Pound	123
The Lamb Lies Down on Broadway	151
A Trick of the Tail	187
Wind & Wuthering	217
Contributor Biographies	245
Special Thanks	248
About the Author	248
A Complete Martin Popoff Bibliography	249

ENTANGLED
GENESIS
ON RECORD
1969-1976
MARTIN POPOFF

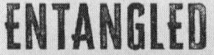

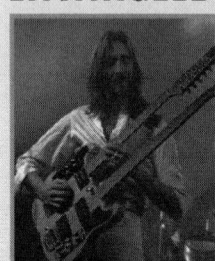

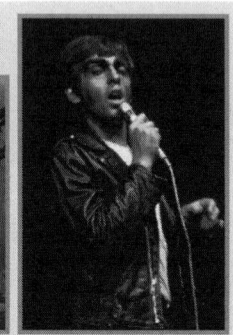

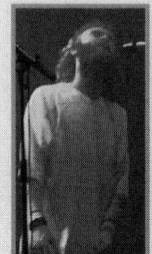

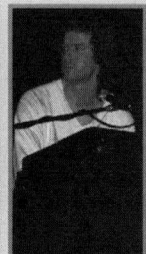

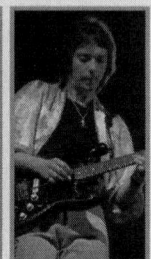

INTRODUCTION

Welcome, folks, to a book about a band I've wanted to write about for a long time, and absolutely in this format. And the answer to why Genesis and my tested and successful assembled panel format are such a great fit for me is the following: I have a pile of friends who are smart Genesis experts, and I was eager to enter into dialogue with them to help me look at this band in a myriad of new ways beyond my own experience. And what is my experience? Well, as I kick the dust up about repeatedly in my pointed questions to these guys, I've always found Genesis to be the progressive rock band at the hub of the prog bike wheel, the band with the least distracting eccentricities, the band with no distance down various spokes toward the tire. Go beyond, I suppose, and you are no longer a prog band. But like I say, Genesis is the hub.

In tandem, I've always considered Genesis the most British of prog bands, heck, maybe the most British of bands period, even beyond Queen and The Beatles (but maybe not The Kinks or The Jam). Arriving at that sentiment, I guess, is a feedback loop to the idea of progressive rock being ridiculously British, or more pointedly, English. This is because of lots of things, including classical music influence, Moody Blues, hill and dale.

So I wanted to test those theories, but I also wanted to get a sense of that fanatical Genesis fandom, where certain of the band's songs are seen as some of the greatest masterpieces in rock. I also wanted to talk to some people who were not afraid to try to describe what Peter Gabriel's *The Lamb Lies Down on Broadway* story is all about, or to comment with authority on Jonathan King, John Burns, David Hentschel or time signatures.

As you may have figured out by now, this book looks at the eight studio albums Genesis put out up to and including Wind & Wuthering, when guitarist Steve Hackett left the band. It's a cut-off point I found sensible, allowing for a book of similar length fashioned upon *And Then There Were Three* through to the end of the catalogue, *Calling All Stations*.

So yes, we begin with the outlier that is *From Genesis to Revelation*, and then move on to the proper—but pre-Phil Collins and pre-Steve

Hackett—album known as *Trespass*. Are the next three somewhat of a set? Our intrepid experts and their detailed descriptions (and incessant opinionizing) should have you confused but ultimately leaning one way or another. We then arrive at 1974's aforementioned *The Lamb Lies Down on Broadway,* a double album, an opaque concept album, and the last for Peter Gabriel at the mic and, in this case, all the lyrics.

Are *A Trick of the Tail* and *Wind & Wuthering* of a set? Again, you may choose to ponder that question or not, as we look at each and every song. Very likely, through the enthusiasm of these guys, you'll wind up more concerned with checking out individual songs in isolation, as passages of music are heartily recommended for circling back upon.

Which is really my primary joy and job at doing these books—as much for myself and for you, the dear readers. The point is, I wanted these guys to play DJ, be pushers of Genesis' music, and send us to various points along the long songs crafted and executed with alarming regularity over the course of the first half of the decade. That, indeed, I believe we have accomplished together, emerging out the other side with renewed enthusiasm about giving these eight records repeated spins.

That's also been the mandate of the previous books in the series, which up until now consist of *Wild Mood Swings: Disintegrating The Cure Album by Album, Dominance and Submission: The Blue Öyster Cult Canon, Pictures at Eleven: Robert Plant Album by Album, Honesty Is No Excuse: Thin Lizzy on Record* and *Run with the Wolf: Rainbow on Record*. Heck, slowing down the writing of them (and man, these are a ton of work, because it's mostly editing and otherwise cleaning up robot-transcribed interviews) is all the stopping I do to play a certain song I've just had explained to me in a way I'd never previously considered, often in comparison to some other song by that same band or indeed someone else.

Anyway, I might have absorbed more of that with this book than any other, given how verbose this band is lyrically (and thus literarily) and how much depth and substance and texture there is to the music. I mean, fact is, this the first one of this series on a full-blown prog rock band, and a prog rock band that is, again, arguably, the gold standard of prog rock bands.

So without further pondering and promise, let's move past my introductory greeting and into the band's "Baroque pop" album made as teenagers and, somewhat illogically, touching off an immense career of progressive rocking.

Martin Popoff
martinp@inforamp.net; martinpopoff.com

FROM GENESIS TO REVELATION

March 28, 1969
Decca SKL 4990
Produced by Jonathan King
Engineered by Brian Roberts and Tom Allom
Recorded at Regent Sound Studio, Soho, London, UK
Personnel: Peter Gabriel – lead vocals, flute; Anthony Phillips – guitars, backing vocals; Tony Banks – Hammond organ, piano, backing vocals; Mike Rutherford – bass, guitar, backing vocals; John Silver – drums (except on "Silent Sun")
Additional musicians: Chris Stewart – drums on "Silent Sun;" Arthur Greenslade, Lou Warburton – strings and horn arrangements, conducting
All songs written by Genesis

Entangled: Genesis on Record 1969-1976

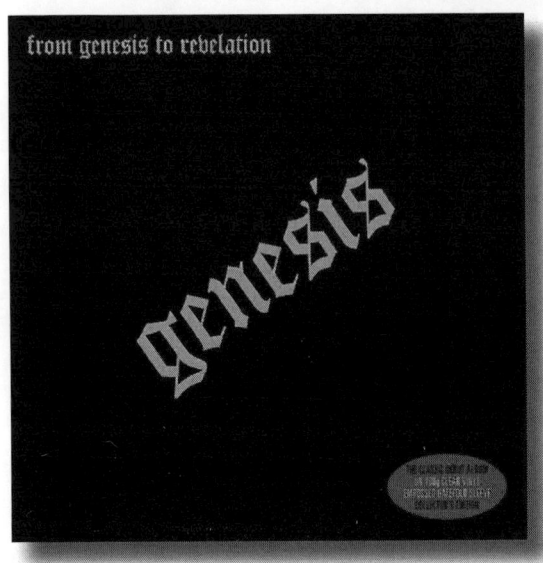

Side 1
1. Where the Sour Turns to Sweet 3:20
2. In the Beginning 3:40
3. Fireside Song 4:15
4. The Serpent 4:32
5. Am I Very Wrong? 3:25
6. In the Wilderness 3:20

Side 2
1. The Conqueror 3:36
2. In Hiding 2:35
3. One Day 3:15
4. Window 3:27
5. In Limbo 3:25
6. Silent Sun 2:15
7. A Place to Call My Own 1:54

Entangled: Genesis on Record 1969-1976

A *From Genesis to Revelation* Timeline

September 1963 – April 1965. At Charterhouse School, a public school in Godalming Surrey, UK, Tony Banks and Peter Gabriel soon welcome classmates Anthony Phillips, Mike Rutherford and Chris Stewart to the house of learning.

January 1967. After the split of school bands Anon and Garden Wall, the above lineup records a six-song demo tape at a friend's homemade studio.

August – December 1967. Under the auspices of former Charterhouse alumnus Jonathan King, the band record a series of potential singles at Regent Sound in Denmark Street, London, soon taking the name Genesis, instead of the proposed Gabriel's Angels.

February 2, 1968. Genesis issue "The Silen Sun," backed with "That's Me" as their first single.

May 10, 1968. "A Winter's Tale"/"One-Eyed Hound" is issued as a single.

August 1968. Drummer Chris Stewart leaves Genesis, to be replaced by John Silver. The band, all teenagers at this point, record enough tracks for an album over a ten-day period the same month.

March 28, 1969. Genesis issue their first album, *From Genesis to Revelation*. With manager and producer Jonathan King refusing to change the name of the band upon hearing that there's an American act called Genesis, a compromise is struck whereby only the album title appears on the cover. Coupled with the stark design, this causes the album to be filed under religious music, greatly curtailing potential sales.

June 27, 1969. "Where the Sour Turns to Sweet," backed with "In Hiding" is issued as a single.

Entangled: Genesis on Record 1969-1976

Martin talks to Daniel Bosch, Ralph Chapman, David Gallagher and Rand Kelly about *From Genesis to Revelation*.

Martin Popoff: Okay, guys, thanks for kicking this off with me and discussing this difficult outlier of a Genesis album. How would you frame what the guys came up with here on *From Genesis to Revelation*?

Daniel Bosch: Well, this was a record that they recorded while they were still at Charterhouse public school. They were still teenage school boys at this stage. They sent a tape to Jonathan King, who was a bit of a music impresario at the time, and who was also a Charterhouse school boy. And they basically got to make this record on their school holidays. And then it got released in March of 1969 and disappeared without trace.

Martin: Is it a folk album, a psych album, a wyrd folk album, just a pop album?

Daniel: It really doesn't sound like anything that was going on in 1969, let alone anything that would come from the rest of the Genesis catalogue. It's a real outlier, both, as I say, within the Genesis catalogue, but also within what was going on in 1969. You've got these strange folk songs, and then you've got these odd sort of psychedelic rock songs. But then it's got these string arrangements and horn arrangements over the top of it. The one thing I will say about this album overall, if I were to sum it up in one sentence, this is an album of some very young men whose ambitions far outside exceed their abilities. Their songs are quite ambitious, but the execution is just not there yet. They don't have the chops to actually pull the songs off for the most part.

Martin: Would you say there's a little bit of first and second album Pink Floyd to it? I mean, the guys themselves talk more about The Kinks and Beatles as influences.

Daniel: Yeah, I think so, but the big difference is that you have a lot of strumming acoustic guitars here, whereas Pink Floyd is mostly electric with a little bit of acoustic. But this is mostly sort of strummed acoustic guitars, almost like a folk version of The Who, with those strumming structures that Pete Townshend used to write.

Ralph Chapman: I'd say that *From Genesis to Revelation* is a Baroque pop record in the spirit of The Left Banke or elements of The Zombies. This is a Jonathan King production, and Jonathan King went to the same school and became successful. I can't remember who sought who out first, but I'm confident that Jonathan King got one of his first opportunities in the business working in management for The Zombies, and The Zombies were really quite a progressive pop band. But they had a very distinct singer in Colin Blunstone.

Martin: Has progressive rock started yet or not?

David Gallagher: If it has, nobody's calling it that, are they? And certainly there's just a sense, on the other hand, that it's being lumped in with psychedelia. People are trying new things, of course, but it's certainly not a movement unto itself. It's really just a spin-off of whatever The Beatles tend to be doing. So everybody's really just siphoning off from *Sgt. Pepper's*, from *Yellow Submarine*, from *Magical Mystery Tour* and the like. And with this baby band, certainly you can hear that they've been listening to a lot of pop music that we now have these different labels for. You can hear some Yardbirds across the record and things, but it's not an album where you can distinctly say, here's the birth of prog in the way that we could say that with King Crimson. You wouldn't make that mistake here. You wouldn't think that this band, particularly, would turn into anything major in the upcoming prog rock sphere.

Rand Kelly: There's a version of this album with 27 tracks in total, and Jonathan King does a 20-minute description of how he got everything going. Firstly, he talks about himself, of course, but then he talks about the band. They were just at this school and they were writing songs together. And they were two different groups. Peter Gabriel and Tony Banks were in a band, or trying to start a band, called Garden Wall, and then Mike Rutherford and Anthony Phillips were friends and they were doing a thing called Anon. And they just got together and started playing at school and writing songs.

And a friend of theirs happened to run into Jonathan King in London in an elevator or something. He was notable because he had a hit single called "Everyone's Gone to the Moon." So he had an in with the business, and somebody handed him a tape and he listened to the tape and he liked what he heard. So he just kind of took them under his wing and tried to nurture them into what he thought they would be good at. And the thing about it is that the timing is weird, because they're trying to sound like, "Go Now," The Moody Blues, with Denny Laine, and maybe the Bee Gees with less harmonies or The Buckinghams and there's no prog whatsoever. It didn't exist as a term, of course, but there's no adventurism in this music. It's just basically bland, inoffensive pop music, although it's really well done. It almost sounds bubble-gum. But I really like the Peter Gabriel vocals on it. Plus he plays flute. And the songs are good.

Martin: As a prog keyboardist and synth-player yourself, how would you frame who Tony Banks is at this early stage?

Rand: Tony Banks actually did play guitar a lot in Genesis and nobody really noticed that. He plays guitar and we'll talk about those key songs later, like "The Musical Box." But anyways, Tony Banks is basically just using a piano, grand piano, and an organ on this album. He doesn't have anything else. He hasn't got a Mellotron yet. They essentially fit in a small orchestra kind of thing, because there are some symphonic-type passages, but again, they're very pop-oriented.

Martin: What are your thoughts on this album cover?

Rand: All it said on it was *From Genesis to Revelation*. The original, Martin, didn't have that diagonal Genesis on it. They sent it out into the record stores and the people in the stores went, "File this under biblical" (laughs). Nobody was buying their record and people were going, "Have you heard that band, Genesis?" And you'd go, "No." And then you'll notice later ones say Genesis. But everybody thought it was like a narrative out of the Bible or something and it killed them until somebody figured it out. And then once Charisma got a hold of them, they straightened all that stuff out.

Martin: How would you describe Jonathan King's production job?

Ralph: It's quite good. They're recording at Regent. They had Tom Allom as an engineer who, of course, went on to great things. So these weren't boobs. And the big thing I think that that album suffered from is that Genesis couldn't find a drummer yet that was up to even the fairly low level the rest of the band was at. I read an interview somewhere with Jonathan King where he talks about deliberately burying the drums, which were played by Josh Silver. And that actually dates the record. It makes it sound like they utilised poor recording techniques. But we know that by '67, '68, even in that studio, records were being made where the drums are loud and vibrant and detailed. So I think that's just an interesting facet, and something they didn't face on *Trespass*.

Also, *From Genesis to Revelation* reminds me a bit of the career track that Cat Stevens was on, because he was another guy who tended to write very vulnerable, introspective lyrics. But he was paired in the '60s with Mike Hurst as producer, who was bent on turning him into a pop star. So it was laden with brass and strings and blah, blah, blah. And when Cat got sick, he got TB or whatever, and he goes into this isolation, when he emerges again, he emerges with a different producer. And the album *Mona Bone Jakon*, although there are strings on it, they're not used in that kind of larger-than-life way, but almost like a Nick Drake kind of thing, where he worked with Robert Kirby as a strings arranger.

Martin: Do you like the horns and strings arrangements on this record or not?

Ralph: You know, it's very hard to be critical of this album, because they served a purpose. It sounds churlish to go, "Well, I wouldn't have done that." Although I do say they didn't have a strong drummer, and the strings and horns hide a multitude of sins. But I don't think Genesis had any. The guys are 18-year-olds and didn't have any choice. So do I like it? Yeah, I like it for what it is. It's an interesting one-off, which is a term I use a lot. And lyrically it's substantial. But you have to dig a bit and you have to follow along. So I don't really have anything critical to say about it, because it is what it is.

Rand: I agree; it sounds really nice. It's a very crystal-clear production. Nothing's murky on it. You know, that could be because I know mostly the remaster. I didn't have the original when it first came out because I didn't know about it. I didn't find out about this band until *Foxtrot*. But yeah, he had access to the orchestra because he had that one big hit. They sort of looked up to him and he had some pull because you could make some money just with one hit back then. And "Everyone's Gone to the Moon" was a big hit worldwide. Everybody liked it. So everybody wondered, who is this Jonathan King guy? And of course he's full of himself. He thinks he's as good as Roy Thomas Baker or Eddy Offord or whatever.

Martin: All right, the entire Genesis canon begins with "Where the Sour Turns to Sweet." What kind of opener is this?

Daniel: I think it's a great opening track. I love how it starts just with Tony's piano and that clacking sound that sounds like finger snaps—very hip. As for Peter Gabriel's vocal. I said that their ambition outstrips their ability on this album, but the one exception to that is Peter Gabriel. Right out of the gates, he's a brilliant singer. Even as an 18-year-old, his voice is just so good right from the get-go. But the strings on this song are really sappy. And that'll be a recurring theme on this album; the string arrangements, for the most part, are really, really horrible. I understand why they put these arrangements on a lot of these tracks, because otherwise they would have been very bare-bones. But the actual arrangements are essentially easy listening-styled, muzak-like arrangements.

Martin: But that was a pop trope back then, right? You enter into the studio system and some guys show up with suits and ties and stuff and before you know it, you've got horns and strings.

Daniel: Oh, absolutely. But I mean, compare these arrangements with the sort of arrangements that George Martin was doing with The Beatles and there's no comparison. George Martin was a master arranger. I think the strings on this are arranged by a guy called Arthur Greenslade, and yeah, I'm not a fan of his work.

Ralph: On "Where the Sour Turns to Sweet," it almost sounds like Gabriel is channelling Colin Blunstone. There's a certain, I wouldn't say fake quality, but a very precise way of singing that is on some of these tracks that betrays a producer who was looking for, again, a Baroque pop band. I'm not by any means an expert on that sub-genre of pop music in the late '60s, but in many ways you could say it was an antecedent to prog in its musical ambition and its arrangements and its use of strings.

Arguably, there's a lot of antecedents to prog, and a lot of it goes back to The Beatles in the mid-'60s, '65, when George Martin and Paul collaborated on that string arrangement for "Yesterday." And even though that song was buried on side two of the *Help!* album, it really did start something that would, within two or three years, completely overwhelm one particular facet of the British pop scene.

And it's interesting too that with *From Genesis to Revelation*, there was the Baroque scene happening and the blues scene still happening, although it was starting to fade by the late '60s for a variety of reasons. But Genesis were almost never about the blues, perhaps because of people like Tony Banks and his formal training, or perhaps their upbringing. There's a myriad of reasons why their references are like Keith Emerson and possibly Rick Wakeman. I don't know a lot about those guys, but their references were not Howlin' Wolf; they were Rachmaninoff and the famous British composers like Malcolm Arnold and Benjamin Britten. Who else am I thinking of? *Norfolk Rhapsodies* by Ralph Vaughan Williams.

David: With "When the Sour Turns to Sweet," the career of Genesis beginning with ten seconds of click-clacking and piano-plonking like a Phil Spector-produced B-side—it's quite surreal. Jonathan King... let's not forget to mention that he became a convicted sex offender and it was a disgrace that Genesis had him on the official "making of" *after* he was released from prison, on their official career "making of" DVD.

But Jonathan King's production becomes an integral part of this song and never goes away after the trademarks are established. This opening track, with the strings and the horns and the choral vocals kicking in for the chorus, it's like... every single track on this record, to some extent, feels like there's a song hidden there, but it's just being so over-produced by an overbearing producer, that it kind of distils what may be there in the first place, and dissipates it, really, or evaporates it, I suppose. It's kinda the same thing in different parts of the distillery process. But regardless, that's the theme of the album. So if I begin to sound a bit repetitive saying "and the horns again," I hope people will understand. And if they've listened to the record, they certainly will understand.

Rand: "When the Sour Turns to Sweet" sounds like it could be like a rock song; it really does. But it turns into a really nice, mellow kind of pop song. Peter Gabriel was like, 18 years old and this is his first time at the microphone and I'm sure he was just head over heels. They were all happy as could be that they got this far, I imagine. But yeah, this first song, just coming out of the gate, has got a really cool intro with Peter going, "We're waiting for you/Come and join us now." It's quite intriguing.

Martin: "In the Beginning" is a little darker, and a little more up-tempo. I don't know; feels pretty psych to me, but then again, psychedelic rock is on its way out in 1969, isn't it?

Daniel: Yes it is, and I agree that "In the Beginning" is basically a psychedelic rock thing. You have these great, sort of weird noises generated on the guitar at the beginning, creating that vrooming sound, and then you get Mike playing the bass. Mike was not an accomplished bass player at this stage, but I like the bass playing on this song. And the lyric is really good. "Ocean in motion" and all that sort of thing. You get some nice guitar playing from Anthony Phillips. It's one of the highlights of the album.

David: Yes, "In the Beginning" is actually a really good song. This is one of the perfect examples of, just leave them alone please and they'll be able to produce something perfectly nice. Nothing on here is revelatory. Nothing on here tells me this band is going to be amazing. This song is just an example of wonderful poppy goodness. But there are certainly elements in here where you can hear promise, like the lovely bit of distortion on the guitar on those Anthony Phillips guitar stabs peppered throughout, where you think, yeah, they've certainly been listening to the Yardies. They may even have been listening to the slightly harder-edged tracks, not that there were many, by—I never get the name right—Dave Dee, Dozy, Beaky, Mick & Tich or whatever they're called. But certainly the Yardbirds of about 1966—*Having a Rave Up* Yardies loomed large over that track. It's not a bad attempt to replicate that sound at all. It's a good song, but not a great song.

Martin: Would you say that there's a bit of Syd Barrett in here?

David: A little bit, but it's not quite the same level of whimsy. Genesis don't evoke as much English tradition. And I always say English tradition for that, because it's much more of an English thing rather than a British thing in general. They don't have the whimsy, is the best way to put it. They don't have something that perhaps would link them more to the Canterbury scene, where there is a distinct Englishness. The sound of Englishness is across quite a bit of their catalogue in the early years, but not distinctly in a sense that would link Genesis to the whimsy of Syd's solo records, at least, and perhaps some of the Floyd singles.

Rand: "In the Beginning" is a bit of a rocker but it's just at the wrong time. I mean, this is the same year that Yes and King Crimson are doing their first albums. Crimson are taking the world by storm over there. It's like, holy crap, listen to what King Crimson is doing. But it's funny, even though this rocks, it's framed on acoustic 12-string. There's not a lot of actual electric playing. So yeah, it's a lot of acoustic on this one, acoustic piano and acoustic 12-string, even if it starts out with some strange feedback and weird effects. I like that one. It's the only tune that has any balls while the rest is sort of a one-trick pony given the strings and how Tony is quite limited in terms of playing mostly piano. There's a bit of distortion here, but it sure isn't "The Knife."

Martin: That idea of Baroque pop that Ralph brings up, I definitely hear with "Fireside Song," especially when it comes to the chorus, which sounds depressing and yet so mainstream at the same time.

Daniel: Yes, and it's another one brought down by those string arrangements. Still, at the heart, it's a lovely folky song. And I always loved the opening lyric of this song: "As daybreak breaks;" you know, using break twice there. But it's actually a fireside song because you could imagine the boys strumming their guitars playing this song around a campfire. And again, what a lovely, delicate vocal from Peter Gabriel.

Martin: But multi-tracked. There are a lot of harmonies and multi-tracked vocals all over this album, right?

Daniel: Yeah, absolutely. With both that and the string arrangements, they're trying to flesh out what were very bare bones tracks originally, sort of acoustic guitar, piano and a bit of drums. And they really needed something to fill them out, as it were.

Martin: And there's barely any drums as well.

Daniel: Yeah, and on these folky songs, you don't even get much in the way of bass. You really only hear the bass on the rock songs.

David: On "Fireside Song," Tony's parts were cut by that producer who should not be named, who didn't like complicated music. So again, we're kind of establishing that they perhaps had ideas and that they wanted to progress, even if they didn't know that what they had in mind was progressive rock music, and therefore be progressive music, before prog was a four-letter word. The producer himself was saying, "I don't like that, it's too arty, just cut it." Which is stifling them when they're at the very birth of a scene. Again, I don't think they're intentionally aiming for that scene. It's just perhaps an awakening amongst the young generation that we can push this. Why do we have to follow 12-bar blues and this kind of style? Why can't we incorporate classical and jazz and whatnot?

So there's an idea that a lot of different musicians are coming to this realization generationally, and Genesis are doing the same here, but they're being stifled by their own production team. They didn't like the producer, who, again, we should refuse to name, and who didn't like tempo changes, for example, which is why a lot this is very single-paced.

However, the intro to "Fireside Song" is a lovely introduction to Tony, the piano player. And the vocal line, you can even hear the proto version of "Dancing with the Moonlit Knight," which is quite something. It's the same vocal line that comes in at the start. Peter Gabriel's voice is nearly fully formed for a teenager who's barely started shaving. The harmony's extremely 1967. It seems like at any point, someone's going to chime in and tell me to wear flowers in my hair if I go to San Francisco. But it's the first of too many, "Oh, this is a bit too long" songs in the catalogue for me, at 4:16. Nonetheless, it's a pretty four minutes.

Martin: Amusingly, I can picture "The Serpent" as a proto-heavy metal song, but as usual, this arrangement and performance and production of it, again, keeps it quiet and stealth-like.

David: Yeah, and there's a drummer on this album, and we're only starting to realise it four tracks in, the rather wonderfully named John Silver. It's certainly not Long John Silver, given he was only here for the one record. But it's a very simple track, which, again, evokes more established bands. You can hear a little bit of The Zombies and you can hear Love. There are a couple of time signature changes which somehow got past the booth. The harmonies and the organ are almost being used as a blanket for the track rather than, in the case of the organ, being used for soloing purposes. And again, I'd shave a minute from the end. But it's fun and it shows a lot of talent, coming from a bunch of school kids.

Daniel: Apparently this morphed out of a song called "She Is Beautiful," which was the very first song that Jonathan King heard from them and that made him sort of prick up his ears and think he really liked these guys and say, "I'd like to do something with them." This is one where you actually do get to hear some bass guitar, as part of that sinister little riff there. And it's a great lyric on a cool, comparatively action-packed musical track. I do find that side one of this album is probably better than side two as far as consistency goes.

Martin: A descriptor we haven't used yet is "pastoral," which is what I get from the next track, "Am I Very Wrong?," although it's kinda ruined by the chorus vocal melody and associated key change.

Daniel: Yeah, "Am I Very Wrong?" is really gorgeous. Again, what a beautiful vocal from Peter Gabriel. It's one of the songs where I don't think the orchestral arrangement is too bad; it gels with the song a bit better than a lot of the other orchestral arrangements. You get Anthony Phillips doing a bit of a vocal in the second half of it, and he's definitely not a confident vocalist just yet. He would get better when he went into his solo career. But at this stage, there's a naivete to them, which is a word that applies to the album as a whole as well.

David: Lovely piano intro from Tony. But I definitely agree: the backing vocals are a bit cloyingly 1967 for my taste here. We're getting a little bit twee. It's almost like a parody of 1960s music. Frankly, they have such a different tone in the music from Peter's own desperate, yearning vocal, where I don't think the backing vocals add anything here. And that's really a theme of the album, where the strings and the horns and the choral backings don't add anything. They subtract, or they take away, potential. Which, you know, at this point, you could say the production is going for a Pretty Things "S.F. Sorrow Is Born" kind of style. But all it does is make a stillborn version of "S.F. Sorrow Is Born" because you don't have any of the end product of that masterpiece.

Martin: Going a year earlier than Pretty Things still, is there a comparison to be made with David Bowie's debut?

David: Yeah, I'd put it on a spectrum with that too, sure, although I like the Syd Barrett comparison better. I think David Bowie was a bit more of a magpie, looking for his place in the scene. And I think these are just curious schoolboys. Again, I don't think they have too much of a sense of where to go in the process of making this album.

Martin: Cool. Next is "In the Wilderness," and again, it's the production that hogs the spotlight.

Daniel: Yes, and it gets quite anthemic when it gets into the choruses. The verses are quite quiet, but the chorus is pretty wide spectrum, with that "Music, all I hear is music" refrain. The music almost swells to match the lyric; it's a nice touch.

Martin: Would you say, also in terms of legacy or throughline, that this album bears resemblance to what The Moody Blues were doing?

Daniel: Yeah, definitely, especially sort of *Days of Future Past*, because that had a real string section as well as the Mellotrons, which is what the Moodies were known for.

Ralph: That's a great musical hook on the chorus. You get to see how advanced they are as a songwriting unit. And I should preface all this by reiterating that this is the start of the songwriter collective experiment that Genesis never ever shook. So as a first statement on that, I think it shows a lot of promise and a lot of acute talent. "In the Wilderness" is one of the better examples of this, because it manages to pair a great hook in that chorus with a great lyric: "Music, all I hear is music/Guaranteed to please/And I look for something else/Raindrops pouring down the rooftops/Flowing in the drains/As the people run their lives/And their lives are run by time" Again, this is a 16-, 17-year-old kid writing this and it's such a keen, teenage, societal observations, very perceptive of the human condition. It's, as I say, a hooky song, but it's also probably Gabriel's strongest vocal, his most varied and dynamic vocal on the record. So "In the Wilderness" is one of these hidden gems on the record.

David: "In the Wilderness," with that lovely opening—Tony's piano and Peter's voice—it sounds wonderful just with the two of them alone. It tells me that the album could have been more like this. It may not have been a particularly progressive album. It's just piano and vocals and some mellow guitar in places and some low-key drums. But I'm pretty sure the songs are already there. I almost wish that the demos were the actual final product. My heart sinks.

It's like they're in the process of becoming. They're in the process of waiting. So rather than Genesis, it's pre-Genesis. It's not the genesis of Genesis. It's the proto-Genesis in a lot of ways. What happens before the birth of the universe? Nothing, apparently, if the wrong producers get a hold of them. However, you know, I really like the celebratory chorus of, "Music, all I hear is music." I mean, that's some fun, upbeat pop stuff that wouldn't be out of place if The Move had done it. And that's a compliment for music of this period. It's superior pop music more than anything else.

Martin: Side two of the original vinyl opens with a bubbly, joyous, almost evangelical pop rocker called "The Conqueror." Where does this one sit with you guys?

Daniel: There's a Noel Gallagher's High Flying Birds song called "If Love Is the Law" where it's basically an homage to "The Conqueror." Apparently, Noel is a big fan of this album. And there's one of these little touches, which I think is great. At the end of "In the Wilderness," they start playing that "Music, all I hear is music." bit on piano, softly and instrumentally, as the song fades out. Then you flip the record, and you start "The Conqueror" and it's playing that same theme, the "Music, all I hear is music," on a guitar this time, on an electric guitar, with a kind of a tremolo effect. But yeah, "The Conqueror" is a really great way to open side two. It's a rollicking song. But then side two begins to pale compared with side one.

Ralph: "The Conqueror" is another one I love, in part because of the mixing choices. It's about this larger-than-life fictional character, and reflecting the story, sort of, there's a large presence of backing vocals on it. But also, in the stereo mix—everything I'm gonna say is about the stereo mix—Jonathan King has Peter singing in the left and then the right and then on the left and the right. He's panning Peter left and right in the mix. This gives the sense of a crowd of people observing this person, while also of a voice narrating the story. It's just a really cool choice. And there's very period lyric choices, with the looking glass and the castle on the hill and the monuments and the empty grave, which are very evocative and rich.

But it's ostensibly, from what I can tell, a very mature comment on what I feel is that English condition of someone who seems very well put-together and assured and is celebrated by those around him who see something in him. But really, behind that, there's this empty, doomed existence. It's those kinds of universal themes that run through Gabriel-era and Collins-era Genesis, and they are evergreen. But they're also just very rich, poignant and humane.

One more thing about "The Conqueror" that is impressive is that you get to hear a 17-year-old Anthony Phillips turn in a really nice, tasteful lead guitar line that doesn't seem to be a pastiche of other guitar players. Like I say, this album is largely considered a Baroque sort of pastiche of a very inexperienced band attempting to emulate one particular sound of the day. But occasionally, like the lyrics, like Anthony's lead playing, there's a maturity here.

I read an article somewhere where Gabriel apparently went to see Otis Redding in the summer of '67 and became enraptured with him and the whole soul scene. So, as much as he might have been kind of invoking Colin Blunstone, he had a soulfulness, even at that age, even at 17, that permeates that record and grounds it. A lot of those lyrical flights of fancy are evocative, and are grounded by this thick, soulful voice which reaches in and grabs you. And that's an important part too. You can listen to the first Beatles record or the early Who stuff or all the great bands, and you can hear it. You can hear the signs of what's coming, if you listen closely. It's not so out of the blue. And I would say the same thing for Elton John. Even in his earliest recordings, you know what's coming.

David: "The Conqueror," I think, is a strong song. It's got a vocal line that oddly precedes John Hiatt's "Your Dad's Dead" by 20 years. Couldn't get that out of my head when I was listening to it; it's remarkably similar. But there's a very Dylan-esque quality to that vocal melody as well, distinctly "She Belongs to Me" from *Bringing It All Back Home*. And there's no way as teen musicians they didn't know that album inside and out in the '60s. Absolutely no way.

I have big issues with the mix in particular here, not just for the additions from the production point of view, but Anthony Phillips has been recorded a mile-and-a-half away from the microphones. It's just a bizarre choice. It's as though, again, we're stifling what is available in the band and not allowing anybody to reach their full potential. I understand the original idea from the producer to rename the band to Peter and the Gabriels or some nonsense and establish it as Peter's project. And you kind of get that sense, because clearly there's no interest in the band. The production is plainly focused on Peter and vocals and it's not highlighting anybody else's true skills. And that kind of shows in "The Conqueror"—Anthony's guitar is just horrendously mixed.

Rand: This song is a little more up-tempo, but like all of them, I feel like it's Tony and Peter who are prominent. Gabriel propels this album. His vocals are just absolutely gorgeous on every song. This is how I learned to sing, aping this guy. But if you could redo these songs and add a Mellotron instead of the orchestra, and maybe some Minimoog, it would sound much better. I might do that myself, cover this album but do it on Mellotron and Minimoog. I don't think anybody's ever done that. It might even turn it into a prog album, because there are progressive elements here. I mean, I think the songs are great, but unfortunately they're relying on acoustic guitar and piano.

Martin: Next is a short one called "In Hiding," and I'd just call it a pop song in 3/4 time, but given those sawing strings, we may as well call it a waltz.

Daniel: You know, there's "In Hiding," "One Day," "Window" and "In Limbo," and I mean, all four of those songs have a similar feel. They've still got beautiful vocals, by Peter Gabriel. But again, the rest of the band kind of struggles a little bit to fully convey the music that they want to convey. Remembering that these are songs written by teenagers, they're really well-written songs, but they're just not good enough musicians at this stage to make it all come together and pull it off. It's quite amazing how in 18 months, they went from this to *Trespass*, which is a much more accomplished album as far as their musicality goes.

David: "In Hiding," well, speaking of, it may as well be Anthony Phillips' guitar in hiding. But "I have a mind of my own/In hiding" sings Peter as we open, and that kind of sums up the record, really. Thankfully we'll get to explore that mind when *Trespass* kicks off. I mean, quite often if the guys in the band are asked about their debut, they will just refer to *Trespass* and completely ignore this. I think Tony Banks is the only one who kind of acknowledges this as being the debut by default.

Rand: I listen to this song and I'm remined that Peter's lyrics can be very positive-sounding. Plus he can sound sad and make you feel good. That's another thing I love about him. He literally is my favourite singer. Like on "In Hiding," for instance, "Turn me 'round/ Switch me on/Let me go/I have a mind of my own/In hiding." It's a beautiful song. I think girls would love this album, especially back in those days, because it's not offensive. There's nothing on here that they'd go, "Oh, God, what are you listening to?!" You know, like prog (laughs). There's no prog.

Martin: "One Day" uses the trumpet fanfare trope one associates with British pop from the '60s, maybe the Mod movement. But like Daniel says, the song itself is a variation on a theme, more of a set, especially given how many songs there are on this album now piling up.

David: Yeah, with "One Day," this time it's the horns' turn to ruin affairs rather than strings. Just because it worked for The Beatles doesn't mean everybody needs to go with it. I mean, it's a pretty acoustic song with an advanced vocal line. And it's a bit closer to something like Fairport Convention than pop. But when the horns come in, the choruses are just lost under a cacophony of sludgy, badly-recorded nonsense, which although we don't have Mellotron yet, it's as though somebody is badly using a Mellotron to just gouge everything down in a deluge of decadence, which has translated really badly. Utilizing horns and strings to give something a larger production and a more advanced flair now just sounds like you've killed the actual beauty of what could be here, in places. And this is one of those tracks, where there's an added folkiness, something that they didn't really explore much. This shows how they could have gone down that more Canterbury path.

Martin: And I suppose "Window" carries on with that.

David: Sure, and I love Tony's piano opening for that. It's becoming a theme where Tony gets to kick things off, and then it's completely lost in the track later on. It's so esoteric and interesting and boom, horns have completely ruined affairs. It was nice while it lasted—so long and thanks for all the effort, guys. Still, the horns are a bit more subdued on this track. It's a pastoral song—to use a word you brought up earlier—a very autumnal song, warm and inviting, again, quite folky. But it's been buried under so much production that I can only imagine these things sounded better in their early live gigs or indeed on any kind of demos they might have made.

Martin: "In Limbo" is another production tour de force, if the high bar is extravagance of production but on campfire songs. In other words, even though there's an actual drum kit here, augmented by percussion, there's still no strong rock 'n' roll beat.

David: In retrospect "In Limbo" would be quite a good name for the record. Let's starts with those bizarre clickity-clacks from the opening song, only here they clearly sound like handclaps. They are no more suited here than they were on "When the Sour Turns to Sweet." It's got some nice parts, strong vocal lines, rinky-dink piano, but so little that progresses without, once more, horns just completely taking over. There's gorgeous stuff underneath heavy-handed, one-note production. I mean, they're young here, of course, but they've got a lot more talent than the production lets them show.

"In Limbo," in particular, because it's quite an eerie track, it could be, if not Nick Drake—I don't think anything here is of that quality—but it could be Bill Fay or someone like that, for an early comparison. But not the way it's done here. Nick Drake did have the overproduced third album, but that was done very sympathetic to his music, in accordance with his music. Not just stick a choir on it, stick a string section on it, a mariachi horn section, get some hand-claps and hope for the best, which this album often seems to do.

Martin: Next is "Silent Sun," which is a bit more conventionally arranged, i.e. with a rhythm section.

David: Yeah, it's one of the more standard pop songs, but it doesn't really add up to much anyway. Genesis having a chorus relying on Peter Gabriel singing the word "baby" over and over again, it's quite a surreal thought. That's not really the raison d'être of Genesis. Leave that sort of thing to Justin Bieber. It's an odd feeling and frankly I don't encourage it. It's a bad attempt, really, to do something a bit more upbeat and mainstream. Think of something like Cat Stevens,

"Here Comes My Baby," that more mainstream version of what Cat was doing.

Ralph: When I started buying up the catalogue, that was the song I gravitated to off the debut. First of all, I just loved that title, "Silent Sun." As a 17-year-old, I thought, what does it mean? Silent sun? Well, the sun is a symbol of light and warmth and it gives life. We can't survive without the sun. But this sun, for whatever reason, in this imaginary world, is silent. It's taken itself out of whatever existence this person is dealing with. And I thought, that's so beautiful and poetic, such an arresting image to have, a silent sun.

So the lyric is insular and frustrated and yearning, again married to this irresistible chorus. And when I listened to "Silent Sun" then 18 years later, I'm listening to something like "In the Glow of the Night," which is again about images and atmosphere and melody. They are completely connected with each other. I also love the beginning of "Silent Sun," with the dramatic piano. And I don't know if that was a King concoction or a band concoction, but it's a very musical, alive, vibrant statement. I'm surprised no one's ever covered that one. Maybe they think it's too steeped in its era. But I just think it's irresistible melodically and very thoughtful lyrically.

Daniel: Yes, a beautiful song. It was their very first single. Tony Banks is on record saying that they wrote this song as a kind of Bee Gees pastiche. Because Jonathan King apparently was nuts about the Bee Gees and Robin Gibb in particular. We're talking about that early Bee Gees, which was lush, orchestrated, Beatle-esque pop. Not the disco stuff that they got known for in the late '70s. So they wrote this song to kind of please Jonathan King, and Jonathan liked it so much that he recorded it as the first single and it's a lovely, delicate song, very folky. Peter Gabriel's vocal has a bit of a Robin Gibb quiver in certain places.

Martin: "A Place to Call My Own" is omitted from the back cover of my Canadian London/Polygram vinyl copy of this record, although the lyrics are on the inner sleeve and it's properly showing up on the record label.

Daniel: Interesting. Well, it's almost a little coda of a song anyway. It's under two minutes long, there's no rhythm section and it's basically Peter Gabriel and Tony Banks on piano. It's a quietly understated way to close the album out.

David: On the first half of "A Place to Call My Own"—a full minute, for goodness sake—there's no horns and no strings and we do get to hear Tony's piano and Peter's voice unadorned with all the razzmatazz that's been forced upon them. But then the second half arrives and just ruins what's happened in the lovely first half. And that really is the theme of the whole record, that it's an album of two halves. Now, normally when you see that, you're referring to half good songs, half bad songs. In this case, it tends to be half the song rather than half the album. So the two halves tend to be the half of each song that is, ooh, that's nice, and then, oh my goodness, the strings and the horns have just ruined it. So it's a game of two halves, oddly, inside of each song.

Martin: Interesting; I like that. To summarise, where do you guys stand on the first Genesis record?

Rand: Well, here's the thing. "Fireside Song" and "The Serpent" and "Am I Very Wrong?" and "In the Wilderness," they're all kind of mellow ballads. I think they threw too many of those in a row. "The Conqueror" is pretty good. It's got this classic Tony Banks piano chord progression, and then "In Hiding" is really nice, a little waltz, as you say. "Window," "In Limbo" and "Silent Sun," those are all nice songs. But again, we're just talking about "not rock," you know? This is a pop album. It's Genesis, it's a good start, it's a pretty good pop album and I like it a lot, but it's not something I will listen to every week. You know, I might listen to this every four years or something, just to kinda get a little shot of the history of the band, remind myself of where they came from.

With respect to the drumming. John Silver, he basically gets the job done. I watched all the interview videos that I have on my copies of *Nursery Cryme* and stuff, and found out why they ended up getting Phil Collins. But like Peter says, the situation here was just like the next guy who ends up on *Trespass*. They went through three drummers in two albums and they just couldn't find anybody that was willing to go… well, into an adventurous place. And they weren't fast learners anyway. They just wanted to play the beat and sort of jam with the band. That's kind of how I play drums. I'm not a very good drummer. I can keep time, but I can't do anything fancy. I think they wanted somebody who could do something fancy.

There's not a lot of psychedelic about this album, in retrospect. Well, there's some phase-shifting on "In the Beginning," but that's just running a 12-string through some kind of pedal. But again, it's acoustic. There's only occasional electric guitar and it's not wild or noticeable. It's pretty subtle. Anthony Phillips can play good guitar. He's just not, I don't think, a great lead player. His forte is more rhythm guitar. You hear when he tries to play lead, like on "The Knife" from *Trespass*, for instance, but he didn't do it very often. And then then he quit the band after that.

Martin: Slightly off-topic, but do you know what kind of Hammond Tony Banks played?

Rand: After this album, for the *Trespass* rehearsals, he got his first Hammond, an L-122 or L100, something like that—I've seen both—and later a T102. I thought it was an M1. I've got one of those here right next to me, with draw bars on it and stuff. But his had like presets, which you can push and get different tones and stuff. What Tony was playing is set up more for somebody's house than like a rock 'n' roll band. I think that's the way to put it. The acoustic piano, that was his forte; that's what he's really good at. And that sounds nice on this album. That particular part of the sound picture is really well-produced.

Daniel: I mean, look, *From Genesis to Revelation* is undeniably British and it's undeniably unlike anything else in their catalogue. They would always sound very British, or certainly throughout the '70s. But this one has that sort of, as you say, I don't know how psychedelic the album is, but it definitely has that flavour to it that you find on, say, *Piper at the Gates of Dawn* or the very first David Bowie album from 1967. It's got that sort of Englishness to it, I think, yes. But as I said earlier, I'd qualify it.

Martin: And it's not wyrd folk?

David: No, and beyond genre, I'd frame it as a record for Peter Gabriel fans. It's more of an interesting document that says, here's what he was doing, more than any of the other guys. If you're a Mike Rutherford fan—and I'm sure there are some out there—then I don't think there's any reason for you to ever listen to this. If you're wanting to hear what Mike is sounding like, you're not going to hear much.

If you're a Tony fan, there's a little bit of piano, but I'm pretty sure there's a million different places to hear that. So it's of mild interest for the enthusiast, but really, you need to be quite the train-spotter if you didn't like some kind of '60s music to have any interest in what's happening here. I'm much more sympathetic to it than a lot of other people, who think music did kind of start in 1969 or 1970 and anything before that's far too primitive. I think I'm more sympathetic to it by default. But for a lot of people, I just couldn't recommend it.

Rand: You know, in the beginning, Jonathan King just fell in love with their sound, but he had no idea they were gonna do what they were gonna do, like on *Trespass*. He thought he was going to nurture this band and compete with The Magnificent Moodies and stuff like that. But then they changed. I don't think Jonathan King saw the psychedelic age for what it really was. I mean, he probably thought they'd turned into weirdos. Because he really wasn't like that. But Tony Banks and Michael Rutherford—because they're really the heart of Genesis all through their entire career—those two guys, along with Peter Gabriel, were thinking in terms of the music that was to come. *Trespass* was in a whole different dimension. At the beginning, I'm sure their first thought was, wow, we've got an orchestra. I'm sure they were absolutely thrilled that this guy had taken him under their wing. But then something happened between this and the next album (laughs).

Ralph: As we move on, the relationship between Jonathan King and Genesis became fractious. It's clear that they're kind of mutually using each other. And that's somewhat what *From Genesis to Revelation* is about. Genesis seized the opportunity to hear their songs put on tape, although it sold nothing. I believe it sold 650 copies or something when it was released.

But it's still a crucial part of their story, and yet deceptively so. Lyrically, some of the themes they begin to explore on that first record carry over, not just to *Trespass*, but through their whole career. You know, Roger Waters and other British composers like Pete Townshend explored this too, but there's something about a) the British education system at that point, and b) the culture. Maybe it's the stiff upper lip that betrays or hides an isolation and loneliness and a yearning. That whole British male thing where you don't show your feelings. And yet, even on something like *From Genesis to Revelation*, where they are kids, the lyrics are remarkably open about vulnerability. And I'm jumping the gun for a second to *Trespass*, but that first line, "I'm looking for someone/I guess I'm doing that" to me, is cut from the same cloth as "Silent Sun." So *Trespass* is not as much as an absurd leap as it's made out to be. It's a huge progression, but it's the same band.

Entangled: Genesis on Record 1969-1976

TRESPASS

October 23, 1970
Charisma CAS 1020
Produced by John Anthony
Engineered by Robin Geoffrey Cable
Recorded at Trident Studios, London, UK
Personnel: Peter Gabriel – lead vocals, flute, accordian, tamborine, bass drum; Anthony Phillips – acoustic 12-string guitar, lead electric guitar, dulcimer, vocals; Tony Banks – Hammond organ, grand piano, Mellotron, acoustic 12-string guitar, vocals; Mike Rutherford – acoustic 12-string guitar, electric bass guitar, classical guitar, cello, vocals; John Mayhew – drums, percussion, vocals
All songs written by Genesis

Side 1
1. Looking for Someone 7:06
2. White Mountain 6:44
3. Visions of Angels 6:52

Side 2
1. Stagnation 8:51
2. Dusk 4:13
3. The Knife 8:56

Entangled: Genesis on Record 1969-1976

A *Trespass* Timeline

September 1969. Having split with Jonathan King and Decca Records due to the commercial failure of the first album, the band splits up, with various members embarking upon further schooling. They reconvene, now with drummer John Mayhew, and begin playing live shows.

October 1969. Flaming Youth issue their one and only album, *Ark 2*, on the Fontana label. Drumming for the band but also doing some singing is Phil Collins.

October 26, 1969. Genesis play their first show, a private birthday party gig.

March 1970. After seeing the band at Ronnie Scott's in Soho, Tony Stratton Smith signs the band to his fledgling Charisma Records label, also including a management deal.

June – July 1970. The band, now regularly gigging in and around London, work at Trident Studios on tracks for their forthcoming second album.

August 8, 1970. Phil Collins, responding to an advertisement in *Melody Maker* looking for a drummer "sensitive to acoustic music," replaces John Mayhew as drummer for Genesis. Also, given that Anthony Phillips has left the band, due to extreme stage fright, Phil's mate from Flaming Youth Ronnie Caryle auditions at the same time. But after a week's break, at Mike Rutherford's behest, he is denied the gig.

October 23, 1970. Genesis issue their second album, entitled *Trespass*.

December 28, 1970. After playing shows as a four-piece, the band find themselves playing The Lyceum Theatre in London and making do with guitarist Mick Barnard. In attendance is strummer Steve Hackett, who is told by Gabriel that Barnard's days are numbered. Hackett auditions and is in the band the following month. Just previous to his joining, he had been in the band Quiet World, who issued an album in 1970 called *The Road*. Also in the band was Steve's brother John, who played flute and acoustic guitar.

January - April 1971. Genesis tour the UK, on and off with Lindisfarne and in support of Van der Graaf Generator. The three bands are label mates and the campaign is dubbed the Six Bob Tour.

May 1971. "The Knife" is issued in the UK and Germany as a picture sleeve single from *Trespass*, spread over two sides.

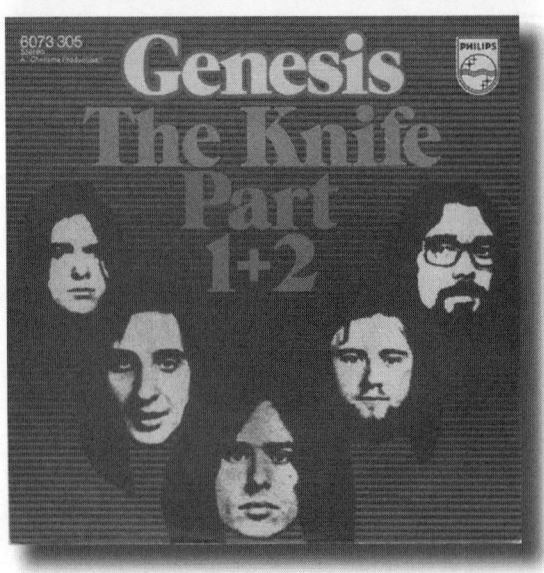

Martin talks to Ralph Chapman, Tate Davis, Rand Kelly, Jamie Laszlo and Pontus Norshammar about *Trespass*.

Martin Popoff: Here we are at *Trespass*, which is considered to be one of the sheerest leaps forward in rock, when we talk about debut albums to sophomore albums. Set it up for us. How has Genesis changed with *Trespass*? Interestingly, the band themselves call it the only album they played live before they recorded it.

Jamie Laszlo: Oh my God, well, *From Genesis to Revelation* isn't even proto-prog and now prog has happened and this record is squarely prog, so I guess Genesis skipped the proto-prog stage. But you have no Phil Collins; you have John Mayhew. You have no Steve Hackett; you have Anthony Phillips. But honestly, I don't care. I feel people get hung up on who is and who isn't playing on an album, and when it comes down to it, the question is, do you like what you hear?

Martin: All right, and like I say, given that this is 1970, albeit late 1970, they are absolutely one of the collectives that is inventing this new kind of music, progressive rock. They talk about Fairport Convention as an influence, as well as Procol Harum now.

Jamie: True, but you don't want to forget everything The Moody Blues have done up this point. As for Genesis in comparison, it's the same kind of lushness, but now we get sort of faster, busier, more muscular music and different time changes, along with more dynamics. But they absolutely borrow from The Moody Blues.

Tate Davis: On *From Genesis to Revelation*, you have a band that was really kind of obligated to do the whole psychedelic pop-type thing. Because the producer on that had the connection that they went to the same public school and wanted to give them a shot at recording something. They said sure, and then they were pressured, basically, into doing this psychedelic pop album.
    And then after that came out and didn't really do anything, they broke up. Then they got a different drummer—John Mayhew, replacing John Silver—and started writing these more elaborate, more mind-challenging type compositions that were sort of progressive in nature, in other words, stuff that really hadn't been done yet except

for, you know, King Crimson and Touch and other bands like that.

And really, what you get is a record that is completely an about-face for the band, and for the five people who got it when it came out, because that record wasn't really a huge seller either. They were probably like, whoa, this is different. So it was a huge change for Genesis at the time and a landmark album, just for the sole reason that it was that progressive in nature.

Pontus Norshammar: By 1969, they become sort of professional. They'd done the first album and it was very Jonathan King, a very sort of a poppy album. For the times, it's almost like *The Cheerful Insanity of Giles, Giles and Fripp*. It's like the pop end of things, but there's still this hint of progressiveness. What happens then is that they want to expand and go further. So they move into a cottage which is called Christmas Cottage. They go to the country and they write and they rehearse. I mean, Genesis foremost was a writing band. They started out as writers. They wanted to write for other people. So what happens is they then discover that they could expand, and they could do other things with the music.

So they have a great backlog of songs and they choose six of the best songs for the album. What they come up with is a transition album. I looked at some interviews, and they said they were inspired by The Nice and Fairport Convention. And they had two writing teams. It was Banks and Gabriel and then it was Rutherford and Phillips. And John Mayhew was a guy they recruited from an advert. He had been in other bands and had been more experienced; he was older.

And the writing teams, especially Rutherford and Phillips, were very into the acoustic sort of 12-string guitars. And I feel like that is a major theme on this record, that British folk thing where it's almost like, you know, stay out in the forest or the countryside or garden and contemplate life; it's sort of equivalent to that. And then you had Banks and Gabriel. One was the more classically trained and one was more into soul and things. So you got a mixture. They wanted to mix up different styles.

Martin: Who was into soul, Pontus?

Pontus: Gabriel was, which is why you get a bit of a soul influence on "Looking for Someone," with that bluesy vocal there. But they also wanted to experiment with heavier stuff and combine the two. So that is very much the Genesis of that era. And the funny thing is, as you alluded to, *Trespass* puts them in the tradition of bands that have this sort of second debut album. You have for instance, Moody Blues. The original debut is, of course, *The Magnificent Moodies* from '65. But everybody sees *Days of Future Past* as a major step forward, therefore a debut. You have Trapeze for instance; the first Trapeze album is very different from the hard rock albums that follow. You have David Bowie and even Elton John. Elton John does these recordings in '69, which don't go anywhere and he's not really focused; it's almost like proggy.

Martin: Warren Zevon.

Pontus: Warren Zevon is another example, yeah. And Van der Graaf Generator. You have *The Aerosol Grey Machine*, which doesn't appear in the UK at all. It's just an American record, and almost thought of as a solo album by Hammill. So this is where the guys in the band themselves think they start. Like I say, they wrote in a cottage and they generate a lot of songs and they choose the six that show up on the *Trespass* album and you get a very focused album, with one exception. I've always loved this album. I think it's a beautiful sort of early prog album. What we see here, I think, is prog rock being formulated. Yes, you can argue that the first real prog album is by King Crimson. But in a way, picking Genesis might be more accurate, with these folky and sort of anarchic leaps from one musical genre to the next, which will be their trademark through the '70s that inspires lots of bands, especially in Italy, especially in Sweden. There's Änglagård, and you have a band from Norway now called Jordsjö. And if you listen to most of the Italian bands, like PFM, there's influence from early Genesis, this record and *Nursery Cryme*.

Ralph Chapman: Let me start with a bit of context. So Genesis go from 13 songs on *From Genesis to Revelation* to six on *Trespass*. Just on that very surface level, it's a completely different band. But in the meantime, the back story is them going professional, disappearing to their roadie's parents' cottage and woodshedding these songs and going in a different direction. And I believe after *From Genesis to Revelation* was done, Jonathan King was at first interested, but could see the writing on the wall and lost interest in them.

But the *Trespass* story, to me, really starts with that process of them deciding to play live and holing up not just in the MacPhail family cottage but at Ronnie Scott's. I believe it was upstairs at Ronnie Scott's, that club in Soho, where Tony Stratton Smith, the owner of Charisma Records, saw them and elected to sign them. And why I think that's so crucial to *Trespass* and the Genesis story… I mean, they intertwine with each other, because Tony Stratton Smith was so active with his artists. I don't want to say that Tony Stratton Smith was benevolent, but anything he made, he poured back into his artists. If he made a lot of money on say, Lindisfarne, one of his acts, he'd use that money to support his other bands. So because they got Strat, they had a label, they had a proper budget, they had a proper producer in John Anthony, they had a booking agent, they had all these things that allowed them to just be musicians and artists eager to create. And it makes sense that when Stratton died in 1987, that sent shockwaves throughout the whole prog community.

Anyway, okay, so now they're at Trident Studios, and now they've got John Anthony. There's another thing that is kind of an inversion of the *Trespass* story, which is that John Mayhew was often brought up in an unflattering way. It's like they talk about the ending before they talk about the beginning. And I just want to talk a bit about the beginning of Genesis going out. They fire Chris Stewart and they fire John Silver. So they are completely aware that they need a drummer and they find this guy, John Mayhew, a little bit older than them and experienced as far as I know. And he was a carpenter. So he was able to bring more to the band than just his musical acumen.

But the big knock on John, before I get to that, is that he was a real drummer. Say what you want about him, but he was a real drummer, and all you've got to do is listen to that record; you know, John Anthony is not hiding him in the mix. His drums are front and centre. He was accused of not being able to bring creative ideas, but in my mind, listening to it, he could certainly execute them. So he wasn't Bill Bruford or Mike Giles or even Clive Bunker or those great prog drummers of the day. But he was still a very lyrical, powerful, musical player. So if he wasn't coming up with the ideas, like I said, he could certainly integrate what they wanted. I feel that's true speaking as a drummer myself, and as guy who adores Phil Collins above every drummer on the planet, save for maybe Ringo.

So I think *Trespass* succeeds in large part because, all of a sudden, you're hearing Genesis with a real drummer. And he's got a great sound and it's just not power. There's a lot of subtlety. There's the simple hits on "Looking for Someone" and all sorts of dynamics. Against what Jonathan King was about, although there are some dynamics on *From Genesis to Revelation*, with *Trespass*, we get the full extent of the classical influence. There is no form of music on the planet more dynamic, more about light and dark and shade and tempo than classical music, in my opinion. And you see Genesis really adopt those textures. I'm not saying they were the first or that's a staple of progressive rock. You know, Led Zeppelin were doing it. But it's really a big thing in progressive rock because it's classical-influenced, and classical-infused. And you're getting to hear that with this drummer who can navigate these big and small moments, these loud and quiet moments, with aplomb.

Also, *Trespass* is by a band no longer augmented by strings. Again, they're paired with a producer who's sympathetic to what they're doing. They've got a label guy who loves what they're doing, and he's put them in a stable. And as far as John Anthony goes, he was not only a great producer, but he also knew instinctively how to sequence a record. So what was previously just a collection of pop songs—without using that as a pejorative because it was of its time—compared with *From Genesis to Revelation*, *Trespass* was a completely different statement.

Martin: Rand, and what can you tell us about this album in context. Out of all of us, you're the wise elder!

Rand Kelly: Well, this is too early even for me (laughs). Okay, it's 1970 and everybody's doing these kinds of albums, although Yes was just coming out with *Time and a Word* and this is well beyond that. But I got into this album later. I was living in Sacramento and I'd just gotten out of the Air Force. I didn't even know about Genesis until I got out of the Air Force. And the first thing I heard was *Selling England by the Pound*. It had just got released. And I wasn't ready for that album. But then I went backwards and heard *Nursery Cryme* and then decided to try *Trespass*, a few months down the road.

Trespass really moved me. I love that album. And I didn't even know about *From Genesis to Revelation* at the time. I heard that much later. But when I heard *Trespass*, I was floored. And of course, when you buy an eight-track, you don't get any information. So you don't know who Anthony Phillips or Steve Hackett is. You have no idea. So I was listening to Steve Hackett and then I was listening to Anthony Phillips, but I thought it was the same guy. I didn't know. I love every song on *Trespass*, but it's not very well produced. I guess it has kind of a murky sound. I don't even think Steven Wilson was able to remaster that one. But it's definitely in need of some sort of an improvement because the songs are worth fixing. I probably love *Trespass* more than most Genesis fans. I am amazed at how people dismiss this record, but it's just such a step up from the from the debut. Instantly they were in a league with Yes, Pink Floyd, Emerson, Lake & Palmer and Jethro Tull and all these bands—*Trespass* just fits right in.

Martin: And what are your thoughts on this album cover? To me, it's kinda scary, in a fire and brimstone kind of way. Like a Trouble cover.

Tate: Right, nice (laughs). It's definitely gloomy and maybe self-reflective in nature. Not to get ahead of myself here, but I listen to a song like "Dusk" with the flute and keyboards and those lyrics and that cover looks like a representation of that story. Genesis are not known for having terrific album covers but they aren't the worst at it either. Except for maybe *Foxtrot* and *A Trick of the Tail*, I'm not gonna go around and tell people, oh, Genesis album covers are the greatest thing ever. That's no disrespect to the artists, but they're not as grandiose as, say, the Roger Dean covers for Yes.

Jamie: That cover's kind of like the Black Sabbath live album, *Live Evil*, where various bits of the lyrics are represented on there, like with the angel and the slashing knife and the people looking at the mountains.

Pontus: Yes, but also the amusing thing is that they don't seem to have learned their lesson about the religious album cover art from the first album to the second, do they? I mean this got filed in the religious section too, right? It's a mishmash, with the angel and people looking out into the sky and all that. And then there's a knife slash right through the record, right through the cover, and that idea came from either Peter or Tony, who wanted something a little edgier, not so mellow and nice. I think the best picture is in the gatefold, with that British countryside scene; it's sort of Tolkien-like.

Rand: It's a strange but beautiful cover, with that king and queen or whatever. It's a moody traditional painting, and then somebody's take a goddamn dagger and just sliced it right through, from right to left. So if you have the gatefold open, the knife ends up on the back cover. And then of course, you have a song called "The Knife." The whole thing looks Greek to me, like the Parthenon or something.

Martin: What are your thoughts on the overall production of the album?

Ralph: It's really good for late 1970, or actually mid-1970, for the making of it. It sounds like a 1970 Trident-recorded album. The drums have that Trident house sound. You can hear it on John Anthony recordings and all those guys who favoured Trident, like Roy Thomas Baker and Gus Dudgeon. They've all got this slightly overdriven unique tom sound that gives it a sameness. So the drums remind me of the first Queen album. But that slightly distorted, overdriven Trident house sound wears on me, I must say. But in many ways, yeah, it's a great-sounding record, although still dated. They would rapidly advance past this; they really came together later.

Martin: John Mayhew is really up in the mix. The drums sound really alive and aggressive.

Tate: Yeah, which is one of the reasons why *Trespass* is my favourite Peter Gabriel-era Genesis album, even though Phil's not on it. The production is really clear for 1970. Like you were saying about the drums, the drums are really upfront in the mix. I like hearing that. I'm not just saying that as a bias because I'm a drummer myself. It's not buried by the keyboards and the guitar being so prominent in the mix, which is a bit of a criticism that I have as you get into the early Phil Collins era. Sometimes I feel like Tony Banks is really, really up in the mix. All right, I love you, Tony, but I also want to hear Phil.

Rand: John Mayhew is a good drummer. Some people compare him to Phil Collins, but when I heard it, I didn't know who was who and I thought the drums sounded fine. I've never really paid much attention to drummers. If they can keep time, I'm happy. I'm not a very good drummer myself. But he did a fine job. I don't think he was let go because of his playing. I think he had issues with his life.

Martin: All right, into the album and wow, no kidding; "Looking for Someone" barely sounds like it's by the same band.

Ralph: Yes, and it's pretty much the blueprint of Genesis for me. It has everything. And that line, "Looking for someone/I guess I'm doing that," when you hear that, the first thing you hear is Gabriel. He's shed all his affectation. It's raw but there's clarity and there's that soul influence. And the lyrics represent a continuation of themes explored on the debut, of confusion, frustration, isolation. "Keep on a straight line/I don't believe I can." Very simple, evocative lyrics of, I don't know, the male condition of the young British man.

And then when the band crashes in—and they do—John Mayhew is front and centre. No one has done an objective appraisal of the drum work on that album. I know I'm talking a lot about that. But to me, his tom fills during that first eruption in "Looking for Someone" are so tasteful and exquisite. And beautifully paired with what Phillips is doing on the guitar, that stabbing guitar along with the aggressive organ of Banks. It's that atmosphere they would mine over and over and over again right up into something like "In the Glow of the Night"—very dramatic.

And if you listen to the left channel on "Looking for Someone," which is really where, on this song, they've stuck Anthony Phillips, I feel a sense of tragedy, not to overstate it. But this guy never really got his due. That's his only statement as an aggressive lead guitar player. He made some—and continues to make—great records. But that was the only moment you heard him. If he hadn't quit because of stage fright and illness or if he had died, I think people would have mined *Trespass* for every single moment. But instead, like Mayhew, he has suffered the indignity of being replaced by a monster in Steve Hackett, just like Mayhew was replaced by Phil. Now, arguably, Phillips was a much more capable player and certainly more of a songwriter than John Mayhew was, but it's the same kind of thing in that we take it for granted; we don't even really pay attention.

In the end, *Trespass* is viewed as a stepping stone album, and that's a shame. Again, in "Looking for Someone," there's just so much. There's that break around 3:20 with those punctuated bursts and the introduction of Pete as a flutist, and it's just so expansive and rich. It's really the only song you need to hear on *Trespass*, in terms of the legacy of that band and their embryonic roots. But then you're gifted with the rest of the record. But yes, in "Looking for Someone," you really get the sense that Anthony Phillips might have become a really interesting guitar player. Interesting is one of those banal words, but I'm a layman when it comes to guitar, so I can only say that.

Martin: How can you tell who's doing the 12-string guitars on this album, between him and Mike and Tony? Or can you?

Ralph: I don't think you can. I don't imagine Tony did a lot of 12-string on any Genesis record, although I think he's on "Entangled." But as you know, on *Trespass*, they were a band divided. It was Anthony and Mike and Tony and Pete as the writing teams, as progenitors of the song ideas. But essentially, they recorded their 12-string parts together to create a singular sound. I read somewhere that they would overdub and overdub, but they were so precise that they'd end up cancelling each other out.

Rand: I love "Looking for Someone," but it's a weird tune because it basically has no chorus. It doesn't seem to have any direction. It meanders from one thing to another all the way through. But I love it. They start with the title "Looking for someone/I guess I'm doing that," you know? So you could call that the chorus, but it's only three words (laughs). And the rest of the song, it's like going down a waterslide, where you go in all these different directions and stuff and then you end up in the pool, which of course is a completely different place than where you started.

Tate: With "Looking for Someone," the first second that someone in 1970 who bought this album put on the vinyl, the first thing that they're met with when they hear *Trespass* is Gabriel going "Looking for someone/I guess I'm doing that." Pardon my terrible Peter Gabriel impression. But no one had ever really heard singing like that before, I don't think, at the time, or very few people did. And from the very beginning of that song, from that little stanza alone, you can tell that this is going to be completely different than *From Genesis to Revelation*.

One thing I gotta say about Anthony Phillips and John Mayhew, just overall throughout this album—this is going to be a recurring theme when I talk about this—

they both do really, really well, I think, for an album of this nature. And granted, Phil Collins, when he joins for the next album, he's gonna make this band better, obviously, and same thing with Steve Hackett. But for the music on this album, I think they do a great job and I don't think that they get enough credit. Mayhew adds a lot of colours on the first part of the song with his cymbals. I love the gallop that they add in the middle of the song and the little hits that they make. And Peter's flute solo is terrific, if you would even call it a solo—maybe it's a flute flourish.

Lyrically, you're not really sure who Gabriel is looking for, or who the protagonist is looking for. I went over and read the lyrics a whole bunch of times and you know, I couldn't really interpret who they were looking for. I guess it could be a lover; maybe it could be a relative—I don't know. And John Mayhew's drumming on the song reminds me a lot of Mitch Mitchell, from The Jimi Hendrix Experience. You can hear that especially as the song builds, and kind of after the beginning as well. And the doomy outro, and the climactic build into the final triplet bass romp is just a really great way to end the song. The song does a great job at capturing the listener's attention at the beginning of the journey that is this album.

Jamie: First of all, I should say I'm a bigger fan of *Trespass* than a lot of other people. But with "Looking for Someone," you get Peter Gabriel's vocals right off the bat, and like Ralph says, just with that, "Looking for someone/I guess I'm doing that," you get the right amount of grit sprinkled with some heart and some soul. You know, the first three minutes of this song can almost be labelled as progressive soul, given the vocals and the prog-like structure. Then when it kicks into more proggy parts, the song doesn't become overly busy—it's complex without going off into any deep ends. Not that deep ends are bad, because they can be fun. It's just that I find myself sometimes drowning in the music when it comes to prog, and with "Looking for Someone" it's more like I'm swimming in the adult pool and I'm still able to touch the bottom with my feet. It's adventurous music while still remaining stable.

Pontus: "Looking for Someone" starts and you're right in the thick of it. It starts with Peter singing unadorned and they have the organ and you're in this mysterious place where you don't know what's going to happen next. As it turns out, we're about to go through so many sections. One minute it's very bombastic; the next minute it's very calm. But it sort of holds together. I mean, this is a young band. It has this pastoral thing going at the same time as it has the almost virile bombast. It's very light and shade, with the folk elements, the classical elements, the blustery rock elements.

Especially in the end, where you have the inspiration from The Nice, the early Keith Emerson, with that dramatic musical flourish for the climax. It works, and it works through all these sections, and it's very interesting, because it's never sort of verse, chorus, verse. There is, but it goes on different tangents all the time. So it's very much like you're entering another realm of rock in the sense that this is not a pop song. This is something else. And yet I don't really know if they knew what they were doing. They were just writing stuff.

Martin: Good production for the day, too, right? The guys liked John Anthony, found him funny, no arguments.

Pontus: Yeah, absolutely. I mean, I like the drums.

Martin: He's a powerhouse. He's a freight train.

Pontus: Yeah, absolutely. He really moves the songs forward and you hear him all the time. And if you compare it with Van der Graaf's second album, *The Least We Can Do Is Wave to Each Other*, which, like *Trespass*, was also produced by John Anthony, you get almost the same drum sound. You get a thick, sort of big, boomy presentation. And, of course, I mean, Phil Collins copied a bit of that aesthetic, because they liked it. But Phil had other ideas of what to do as well. Yeah, I like John Mayhew on this record.

Martin: Next is "White Mountain," and the temperature is about the same. But I can't help but think that in 1970, this was at the front edge of achievement.

Tate: Yeah, "White Mountain" is a great, great song that has a yin and yang. It has this really moody acoustic intro where Peter Gabriel is singing about a fox that lives over on a white mountain. It's snowy and he's going out and just kind of fending for himself. And then the fast sections provide the great musical accompaniment to the battle that he fights with a wolf, or at least what I think is supposed to be a wolf. And you know, all the blood that's shed with all the fighting is kind of tainting the white mountain in red, as they mention. Tony Banks adds a lot of colour with his beautiful keyboards on the song and then, like the last song as well, there's really great flute with a cool whistling outro as well.

Martin: And Mellotron for the first time with Genesis, right? There's Mellotron here, although I believe this is before Tony purchases one from Robert Fripp. That's the following year.

Tate: I believe so, yeah. And then Tony Banks would go on to do even better, with his keyboards, going forward. This was just the beginning. And even on *From Genesis to Revelation*, there's some good keyboard tones as well.

Jamie: "White Mountain" tells the story of two wolves, or a fox and a wolf, battling one another. One is named Fang and the other is named One-Eye. So instantly, it gives the feel of the type of animated children's story that can also be appreciated by adults. It reminds me of a short story; it could have been a short story that Rudyard Kipling would have written. He wrote *The Jungle Book* and *Riki Tiki Tabby*, so this would have fit right in with that. But with this story, you don't get the visuals of any of the animation that *The Jungle Book* and *Riki Tiki Tabby* had.

So the music has to paint that picture. And I think the 12-string guitars in the beginning paint a fine picture of a snow-covered mountain and the snow coming down. And when the wolves meet, the music gets very sinister-sounding, like something big is about to go down. And the last line of the song is, "One-Eye hid the crown and with laurels on his head/Returned amongst the tribe and dwelt in peace." And with the whistling afterwards, it gives a sense of peace within the vast mountain after the big battle. It's almost like it was an animated movie. It's almost like the camera's panning out during the whistling, as the animated movie ends, showing you the whole quiet mountain right before the end credits start.

Rand: I got to see "White Mountain" live actually, when Phil Collins was the lead singer. It was during the tour with Bill Bruford, the 1976 tour. And to introduce it, Rutherford went up to the mic and told this story about going up to a cabin or something and opening the door. He says they pulled this dusty rag off of this record, or pulled the record out of the cover, and said it was called "White Mountain." And then they went ahead and played it. It was incredible with Bruford on drums.

But yeah, it seemed like Mike was trying to play the role of a Peter Gabriel, because Phil wasn't really doing that stuff. So that was interesting. That was in Berkeley, California, by the way. But I think that's right. It was something about how he was wandering around in the woods and found a cabin and went inside and found a record player or whatever. And then he said something about picking up a record and it was called "White Mountain." Maybe I'm not getting it quite accurate, but it was like he was testing the crowd to see if they recognised that title. Because this is the *A Trick of the Tail* tour. It was like they wanted to see how many people knew about *Trespass* (laughs). And then Phil Collins sang it. But it was really good. It's got that line, "He, the usurper, must die." I didn't even know what a usurper was. I'm going, what the fuck is a usurper?

Pontus: "White Mountain" is like British folk meets Beatles. It starts with this Russian sort of melody and then it goes into a poppy tune. It has these sort of C.S. Lewis/Tolkien lyrics. There's some nice flute, and that appears on the whole of the album. Great use of flute in the quiet section, then followed by this doomy but quite mellow middle section. Then it goes back to the poppy structure. One thing that we will see with Genesis is that they are very accessible. They are melodic to a degree that King Crimson never was. They are very much into pop. So here's a link back to what they did with *From Genesis to Revelation*. They have that pop sensibility in them. You can always sing the tune.

Martin: I feel like the newly discovered prog fog continues, evenly, soberly, for the rest of the side, namely "Visions of Angels." Which is kind of ironic, because they had this one kicking around when they were doing *From Genesis to Revelation*.

Pontus: Yes, similar to what came before, "Visions of Angels" is a great pastoral ballad, strong chorus, with organ and piano that take the lead. It has a naive sensibility to it. It actually was written before the first album, by Anthony Phillips, and then Banks helped him out to finish it off. It has this sort of cool acoustic section into what I call the church section, where we're talking about angels, so we've got a lot of these big "aah-aah" angel choruses going. It's very early British prog and you can hear it's a young band, because everything doesn't fit together. But in a fun way, it does, right? It's not a train wreck at all.

Martin: Well. they're inventing a new kind of music, right? I mean, Peter reveled in combining genres, much to the disdain of the label.

Pontus: Yeah. You know, like the *Black Sabbath* album, everything wasn't set in stone. They have all these long jams and they are trying things out.

Tate: Like I was saying earlier about the album cover, you can listen to "Visions of Angels" and end up reflecting on certain things, because at least the way that I interpreted it, it's about a main character who's stuck in a blizzard and seems to hallucinate, seeing this beautiful angel who is kind of letting the world freeze over into a second ice age. The way I interpreted what Gabriel is singing, the protagonist is seeing this hallucination of an angel in a really deep blizzard, in the middle of Siberia or Finland or the Arctic Circle or wherever, and he's freezing to death. And he believes that the higher deity or somebody up there is just letting the world freeze. Or whatever deity that's letting the world freeze is just sitting there and letting it happen instead of actually doing something about it.

And then it just disappears. In the middle section of the song, the protagonist is looking for the angel that they saw and she's just nowhere to be found. And there's a great Mellotron-driven ending to the song with Mayhew putting on a clinic, as I tend to say whenever you have these drummers creating these drum barrages in a song. He's playing his ass off and I think it's a really good ending to the song. So yeah, "Visions of Angels" is a great tune.

Rand: "Visions of Angels" sounds like the heavens opening up. Because there are all these parts that just build and build and build and there's Mellotron in it. When he goes "Visions of angels all around," I can just lay on the bed and kind of float away. Like I say, it sounds like angels in the clouds.

Jamie: In "Visions of Angels," the piano starts off sounding like the beginning of an Elton John song. And that's what gives some of these early Genesis prog songs that singer-songwriter feel. It's a great balance between the two, I think. It's a beautiful song. It's a prog song that can go down easy. And maybe that's why this album isn't seen by fans as all that great—it's not challenging enough. But I think it's produced wonderfully. Allmusic.com gives this album two out of five stars, claiming it's too soft and wimpy and Gabriel's voice lacks power and competence. I don't hear that at all and I disagree with both of those statements. I think *Allmusic's* got it all wrong, if you ask me.

Martin: Okay, flip the original vinyl and you've got "Stagnation," which the band themselves consider the finest tune on the album. The pattern persists, where we have these semi-long songs or long songs and they all start mellow and then get busy eventually.

Tate: Yeah, and there seems to be this theme of ice, not just throughout this album but even throughout the early Phil Collins era. So I don't know if Mike Rutherford and Tony Banks just like writing lyrics about ice and snow and inclement weather, but I found that to be really interesting. "Stagnation" also perpetuates this pattern of reflection. It begins similarly to the previous track, with tender acoustic guitar and keyboards.

One thing I want to say, Mike Rutherford is a great acoustic guitar player. He knows how to write 12-string acoustic guitar lines that are engaging and that take you to a higher plane of existence. I am a sucker for hypnotic acoustic guitar lines, and Mike Rutherford is great at doing that.

So, anyway, "Stagnation" begins really well. Peter sings of a character that wants to wash away his past but the pool of water is stagnated and dirty. So he's got a reluctance to do so. Tony Banks' synth—this is my interpretation—offers a degree of reflection for the character as he's sitting by the pool of water. And then there's this really funky part too, that maybe is an expansion of that, which is really cool. And then the protagonist ends up drinking the dirty water because he's so thirsty.

I don't know; it's ambiguous as to whether the protagonist ends up with diarrhoea or not from drinking dirty water with all sorts of bacteria and nasty stuff in it. The listener has to draw that conclusion for themselves. So yeah, "Stagnation" is another great song that, like you said, kind of continues the pattern of not only having these really tender intros before picking up and then slowing down again, but offering a degree of self-reflection as well.

Martin: I asked this earlier, but how do we know when it's Anthony Phillips on the 12-string versus Mike Rutherford on the 12-string? Or can we tell? I mean, as Anthony explains it, he and Mike were pushing for the band to be hard sort of blues rock, so it's kind of ironic that they are doing this, much to the delight of Peter, it seems.

Tate: Yes, true. Early on, I don't think that there's an easy way to tell. I think that Mike Rutherford's 12-string has a bit more texture to it, as heard on songs like "Ripples," because on "Ripples"... it's like I don't even know how to describe it. I feel like I get more engaged with Mike Rutherford's 12-string guitar parts than those of a Steve

Hackett or an Anthony Phillips. That's probably the best answer that I have for that question. I'm of the impression that the 12-string guitar parts from Mike Rutherford are a bit more textured and a bit more, like, hypnotic.

Jamie: "Stagnation," I won't lie. This is a little bit of a personal thing and I don't know if you want to use it. I used to go to bars back in the day and come home very late. I don't anymore, but I used to. And I went through a long phase where I would come home late at night and I would put this song on or put this album on. And the ending where Peter sings, "I, I, I, I want to sit down/I want a drink, I want a drink" well, you would see a very discombobulated Jamie Laszlo dancing around the room singing those lines. And those lines worked perfectly for how I felt.

Because after the first six minutes of this song, where it's like chill time, and it leads up to that "I, I, I, I" part is always like a second wind for me—"I want a drink!" Maybe out of all the '70s albums, that's why I gravitate towards this one. I like to sing along with it. You know, I have the 5.1 SurroundSound DVD that came with my copy. And it shows the album cover on the TV as the music plays. But maybe for this album, they should have also included the lyrics along the bottom with a little sing-along ball that bounced over the words—just for me.

Pontus: Nice one, Jamie (laughs). I like this one too. I think it's the most successful song on the album and it points the way to where Genesis is going best. I wonder if it was the producer who might have gotten these songs and even shortened them, told them to use the best parts. Because they're long but not super-long. Maybe he said, "Oh, concentrate on that bit, take that bit out, make something out of this part."

But yeah, "Stagnation," for me, is the first sort of inkling of what they would achieve with "The Musical Box" and "Supper's Ready." Gabriel calls it a journey song, and that very much sums it up. It starts somewhere and then ends up somewhere else. We start with a folk tune and then we have the suspense going; we know something is coming. There's this sort of tension going on between the melodies. It takes a while to get to it and it turns darker. I like the keyboard solo at that part; it's a weird little touch. And, and I like the melody; it's very sort of British and hymnal.

And I always liked the "Will I wait forever?" section. And then you go into the bombastic ending, where it says, "I want to sit down/I want a drink." It's more focused in the sense that it's going somewhere. You don't go back. You see what I mean? You don't go back in the song; you just move forward. And yet it flows; you have sections that flow into each other. So it's not like you have one section here and then you don't know why the next section happens. It's just good songwriting for the guys being 20 years old. So that's a song that points forward, as much as I think that "White Mountain" does, with respect to the poppy side of it. Conversely "Stagnation" has mystery. We're going somewhere but we don't know where, really, and you'd better listen until the end to find out.

Rand: "Stagnation" is a beautiful song. I guess it's about drinking, being an alcoholic. It's a song that draws you in. And I agree; you don't really know where you're gonna go until you get to the end, you know what I mean? They build it up and they build it up and it's like "Stairway to Heaven." It starts out really mellow and then it climaxes with that "I want a drink, I want a drink!" part. At the time I thought it was about going to a lake and drinking water, but it seems to be more like "Twilight Alehouse," where it's actually about being an alcoholic. And man, at the end, where they're going, "Then let us drink," it's just huge and so built-up. It sounds like a bar-room sing-along with the big mugs in some German pub. Peter's vocal is so stupendous, and he's only like 20 years old. Yeah, I love "Stagnation."

Martin: "Dusk" demonstrates the band's skills at doing drum-less songs, in this case a lush ballad, but hugely arranged nonetheless. Amusingly, Tony considers it somewhat naff, "a bit of a B track," as he calls it.

Tate: Yes, and it's one of the underrated Genesis ballads of all time. I love it. Great acoustic guitar and keyboards throughout with a nice flute solo on the bridge. I picture myself sitting on a hill, looking over at a sunset and just reflecting on life and how I can better myself and how lucky I am to be alive. Yeah, that's really all I have to say about "Dusk." Just a terrific, terrific ballad.

Martin: With a song like this, they really kind of pride themselves on recreating an ideal form of Renaissance music.

Tate: Yeah, especially with Peter Gabriel's flute parts, because they aren't necessarily of the busy and wacky nature of an Ian Anderson. It's just texture, meant to fill some holes in the music and add colour. And yes, "Dusk" I think is a perfect example of that aesthetic.

Rand: "Dusk" is just gorgeous, such a pretty, pretty song. He mentions Jesus in the song, which might be the only time on a Genesis album, until "Jesus He Knows Me." It's that strange "Once had Jesus suffered" line. The song makes absolutely no sense, but it's so lush with those 12-string guitars.

Pontus: "Dusk" is a beautiful song, a beautiful ballad, an English ballad, a folk tune but with a tinge of psychedelia in that "Once had Jesus suffered" part (sings it). It's almost like being in a field in the morning and contemplating with your friends and having a good puff (laughs). Yeah, just experiencing the dawn or sitting in the park in the afternoon and discussing things. It's a song about lost love but it's also where are we going? What's next? It's beautiful. And I also like the delicate percussion, the bells. And also the 12-string guitar playing is quite unique. It puts it in another realm. You know, all three of them—Banks, Rutherford and Phillips—are playing 12-string guitars, so it's a massive sound. You're actually rooted in folk music. You always start there. I think Steve Hackett once said that when we had a song that was guitar-based, it was always acoustic (laughs). So that's interesting.

Jamie: Normally I wouldn't call a four-minute song an interlude, but on this album, I'm doing that since it's so much shorter than the rest of the tracks. It's a pleasant-sounding song with very nice vocal melodies. The band has been known for calling it a weaker moment on the album. But interludes are not supposed to be highlights. They're supposed to help highlight the highlights, right? And it just so happens that most people call the very next song the album's highlight.

Martin: We close with "The Knife," which is pretty universally thought of as the band's first classic.

Ralph: Yes, I guess it's the first... what's that term? Not even legendary track. It's the first staple they created. And then somewhat related, "Stagnation" melodically was something they kept bringing back in medleys, that beautiful, shifting melody that comes in

"Stagnation." But really, if you want to be a hip Genesis fan, "The Knife" is the one people seem to gravitate towards. It's so aggressive and sometimes it's used in a pejorative sense. Like, "Why couldn't they be more like 'The Knife?'" Even though I think they never lost aggression in their whole career; they just transmitted it differently.

One of the things I like about "The Knife" is that it makes me think of things like "Land of Confusion," and to an extent, "Tell Me Why" on *We Can't Dance*, of protest songs, or protest songs hidden within Genesis songs. If I think about two years earlier, with The Beatles recording "Revolution" where they namecheck Chairman Mao, it's similarly using allegory. It's using… I don't know the position or timing of things like Kent State, but obviously the Vietnam war is raging. *Trespass* is recorded only 25 years after the Second World War ended. And before the Second World War, you know, was the First World War and that country has been built… Shakespeare built a career on war, battling, fighting. So I think that's built into you as a British kid. That is the history of that country, royalty and war, conquering and hopefully not being conquered at the same time. So you have that fire over your heads; you have the sense of this kind of 16th century battle.

But also you have this sense that the Vietnam war is raging, and you have protests on campuses and you have students being killed at Kent State. So to me, "The Knife" is evocative of all these different eras. So it feels historical while feeling utterly contemporary. And it's married to, like I said, a very aggressive, dynamic track with sound effects. They pull out all the stops as far as conjuring mayhem and chaos and domination and jackboots and all those types of things. That feels right in 1970, it feels right in Poland in 1941 and it feels right in the moors (laughs). So that's why I love "The Knife." And I don't think it gets talked about for those reasons. I think it gets talked about as, "It's the great statement," which it was. But it was just arguably their first great statement.

Martin: I'm getting the sense that you don't think it lives up to its reputation, except for this other quite interesting and fresh reading you put upon it.

Ralph: Fans can be such… I don't like using the term sheep, but they are susceptible to groupthink and folklore. Having said that, "The Knife" is one of my favourite drum tracks from John Mayhew, who I think is a vastly unrecognised or under recognised player.

I'm certainly respectful of the idea that Gabriel and Rutherford and Banks—it's his birthday today and it's John Mayhew's birthday today, may he rest in peace—but I'm certainly respectful of the fact that they felt they needed a stronger drummer. So they canned his ass. I get that.

What I don't understand is much like Rutsey and Peart—you know, with people going out of their way to be critical of Rutsey— my point is that "The Knife" and what Mayhew did with it from a drumming point of view has always been far more enjoyable to me than what Phil would do with it in a live setting. Phil would make it way too busy, whereas John pounded his way through it; he drove it. Phil, if you listen to how he did it on the Genesis *Live* album, it actually diminished it for me. I know it's subjective, but as a drummer myself, I thought, just lay back, just do what the guy did. Do it better, but do that.

And I always felt Neil way overplayed "In the Mood." Just groove and be Simon Kirke, just for one song. I was at Styx the other night, and Todd Sucherman is another guy, superlative drummer, just an extraordinary player. But man, that guy just ruins what John Panozzo did. You know "Lorelei," he's doing all these stupid licks. It's just like, listen to what John did; it's so tasteful and musical. When you do all your stupid metal clichés, blah, blah, blah, triplets and whatnot, it's just so irritating. John Mayhew wasn't like that. He was a very lyrical and musical player. That's what comes to mind when I play *Trespass*.

Rand: "The Knife" is practically metal, at least by Genesis' standards, and it kicks ass even more so on the *Live* album when Steve Hackett plays it. The first time I heard "The Knife" was on the *Live* album; so that's what made me want to get *Trespass*. Everybody seems to agree that "The Knife" is the big kahuna on the record, worth saving for last.

Lyrically, to me, I hear a war protest song. There are these medieval factions that decide to go to war, and in the beginning, they are devising their plans. It sounds anti-government as well, but it's couched in the metaphor of medieval times. It makes me think of the Catholics versus the Protestants as well. I just think it's a protest song about war, protesting war by singing about war.

They might even be thinking about the Vietnam War. A lot of bands were afraid to just come out and say that the Vietnam War was wrong. Many of them skirted around it. Yes did it with "Yours Is No Disgrace." King Crimson did it with "Epitaph" and Genesis is possibly doing it with "The Knife." I think it's saying that war is futile, that it never solves anything and why can't we have peace and love? And then I think Genesis do the same thing again with "The Battle of Epping Forest."

But I love the charging rhythm of it, the actual beat, and then they change the key and they roll their way back up to the same key again. They go up one and then they go up another. It's the exact same thing that Brian Wilson does in "Good Vibrations," the way they build up back to the key that they started in.

And I like how the very first thing you hear on *Trespass*, on "Looking for Someone," is just Peter alone, really quiet, and now at the very end of the album, it's a massive, over-the-top fanfare. It's the perfect beginning book-ended with the perfect ending. I can't pick that song apart. It's a fantastic song, and the band's first epic.

Tate: Ah yes, "The Knife;" what a way to close the album. This is a great preview of the stuff that they're gonna do on *Foxtrot* and *Nursery Cryme*. I love "The Knife." Mayhew, this might be his best drumming. It shows you how capable of a player John Mayhew was. The opening is like a trot. It passes what I call the mug test, where you're at Oktoberfest swinging your stein back and forth with the music.

Anthony Phillips shows what he's capable of on his electric guitar and he puts in a great solo, topped by Steve Hackett on the live album but still really great here. And I really like the lyrical subject matter of overthrowing a tyrant and the soldiers and then emphasizing that the death suffered in said coup d'etat will be worth the fight, with the freedoms that they're going to enjoy after it's done. And I love the really moody interlude section that leads into a really heavy, funky jam with a great solo from Anthony Phillips.

Still, I somewhat disagree with Ralph. Even though the studio version is great, I think that it's on a whole new level on the Genesis *Live* album with Steve Hackett and Phil Collins. Because if I remember correctly, and if I remember looking from setlists around this time, this is really the only song from *Trespass* that they would play frequently in their sets. Because I'm sure once they released *Nursery Cryme* and *Selling England by the Pound* and *Foxtrot*, they would sensibly move away from it. And then because *Trespass* didn't have Steve and Phil on it, they probably wanted to play the stuff that was more relevant to the current lineup instead of pulling songs from a past lineup. But overall, "The Knife" is a terrific song.

Martin: It's famously called Genesis' "heaviest" song. Do you buy into that?

Tate: Yeah, I can see that. It's at least one of the heaviest songs of the Gabriel era. Because I think there's some pretty heavy stuff in the Phil Collins era also.

Martin: Yeah, 'Down and Out," "Abacab."

Tate: Sure, plus there's some stuff on the self-titled Genesis album like "Mama" which I find pretty heavy in a synth-driven kind of way, plus "Just a Job to Do." But with Phil doing the maniacal laugh in "Mama," that reinforces the heavy nature of it. That laugh alone makes "Mama" pretty great (laughs).

Martin: And this song's got a bit of ELP to it, I suppose, as well, which is oddly and emphatically, not a stated influence on the band, according to the guys.

Tate: Right. Yeah, there's some elements of that as well; I can see that. Tony Banks' organ parts are very Nice- and Keith Emerson-oriented in nature. I can see The Nice writing stuff like that. I'm not sure about ELP. Because I think that this is too… I don't want to say it's too bombastic for ELP, but I see this more as a Nice song than an ELP song. But I totally get where you're coming from with that.

Jamie: With "The Knife," I'm thinking, I know there's 13 months between *Trespass* and *Nursery Cryme*, and I know there's even a lineup change. But when I listen to this song 50-some years later after it's released, I almost feel like there was a mess-up at the record plant. And when the machine cut the album, it cut too far on the vinyl and the first song on the next album accidentally got on the end of this album. Right away, it doesn't sound like anything else on this record. It's almost like a different band. It's faster and rocks harder than any other song and there's a certain heaviness with the distorted guitar and vocals. And the title, "The Knife," is fitting as well, because after hearing the first five tracks, this one really cuts into your senses. Tony's keyboards are very jagged-sounding. It reminds me of the cutting motion you use as you try to cut down boxes to fit into the trash.

Pontus: I agree; "The Knife" is really the outlier on the album. It's them writing something that is much darker, trying to create some contrast. It was nicknamed "The Nice" as a tribute, and you had that sort of Keith Emerson galloping effect. Because you had the single, "America," by The Nice; it's sort of inspired by that. And of course, this is another storytelling song, you know, about protests. I read somewhere that it was inspired by the Kent State University shooting. But I don't know for sure. It's clearly one of the hardest, heaviest tunes they ever did, because there's plenty of guitar. There's not too much electric guitar on this record. There's a bit on "Looking for Someone" but yeah, there's plenty here. And you also have great bass playing. It's very sort of, "Now we're gonna rock out."

Martin: Pontus, is it the fans who nicknamed it "The Nice," or is it the band that called it that?

Pontus: No, it was the band. Peter Gabriel told the story on the DVD of the *Trespass* remaster. He said the band called it "The Nice" and then they changed it to "The Knife." It's a song written by Banks and Gabriel. It's a Gabriel tune where he wanted to make something dark to contrast the other songs. And of course, that's the theme of the album, right? It's the knife. It's funny, because you look at the gatefold and there's a little knife sitting in the tree. So the knife is everywhere. It sets a precedent, with this contrast of being very melodic, but being very sort of disturbing, a bit like King Crimson and almost like Sabbath in a sense. You know, you want to make some mark, and of course, it got a big following. "The Knife," I believe, was played for the last time in 1982 or something like that. So that became the staple of this album.

You know, the title of the album, *Trespass*, shows up in "White Mountain." But to me, the knife could be the trespasser entering a very beautiful world and slashing it and representing danger. Or it could just be the whole idea that they tell on the DVD, where someone at the company said to them, "You'd better make up your mind what you are. Are you a folk band? Are you a blues band? Are you a rock band? What are you? You can't be all of them." And that is also trespassing, trying to invade this sort of established music business.

Martin: Very cool. All right, any closing comments? Anything you forgot?

Tate: Well, I'll just add that the only album that I think even holds a candle to this one in terms of relevance there in 1970 is probably *The Yes Album*. And I love King Crimson and I love *Lizard* and that early part of King Crimson. But you know, a lot of people hate *Lizard* because it was so jazzy and really, really, really out there, so much so that Gordon Haskell and Andy McCulloch didn't even like it. They left.

Jamie: I would say Genesis are more British than King Crimson. There's something about Crimson that is just crazier. I can't picture myself drinking tea to King Crimson. I can drink tea to Genesis. And I will add that a lot of people out there, they come to this album for "The Knife," but it's worth staying for the other five tracks.

Pontus: I generally think that *Trespass* is a very good second album throughout. As you say, the production is great. The playing is all right, and as you described it, it's got powerhouse drumming. Everyone does exceptionally well. Peter Gabriel has these weird stories he will tell and the quality of those stories will progress. And, of course, the next album will feature both Collins and Hackett and everything will be somewhat more organised. But *Trespass* is a beautiful, anarchic sort of album that says, "Here's where we are, this is what we're trying to achieve, and we will be this band that is unpredictable. Mark our words, the songs will go and flow where we want them to."

Trespass

Entangled: Genesis on Record 1969-1976

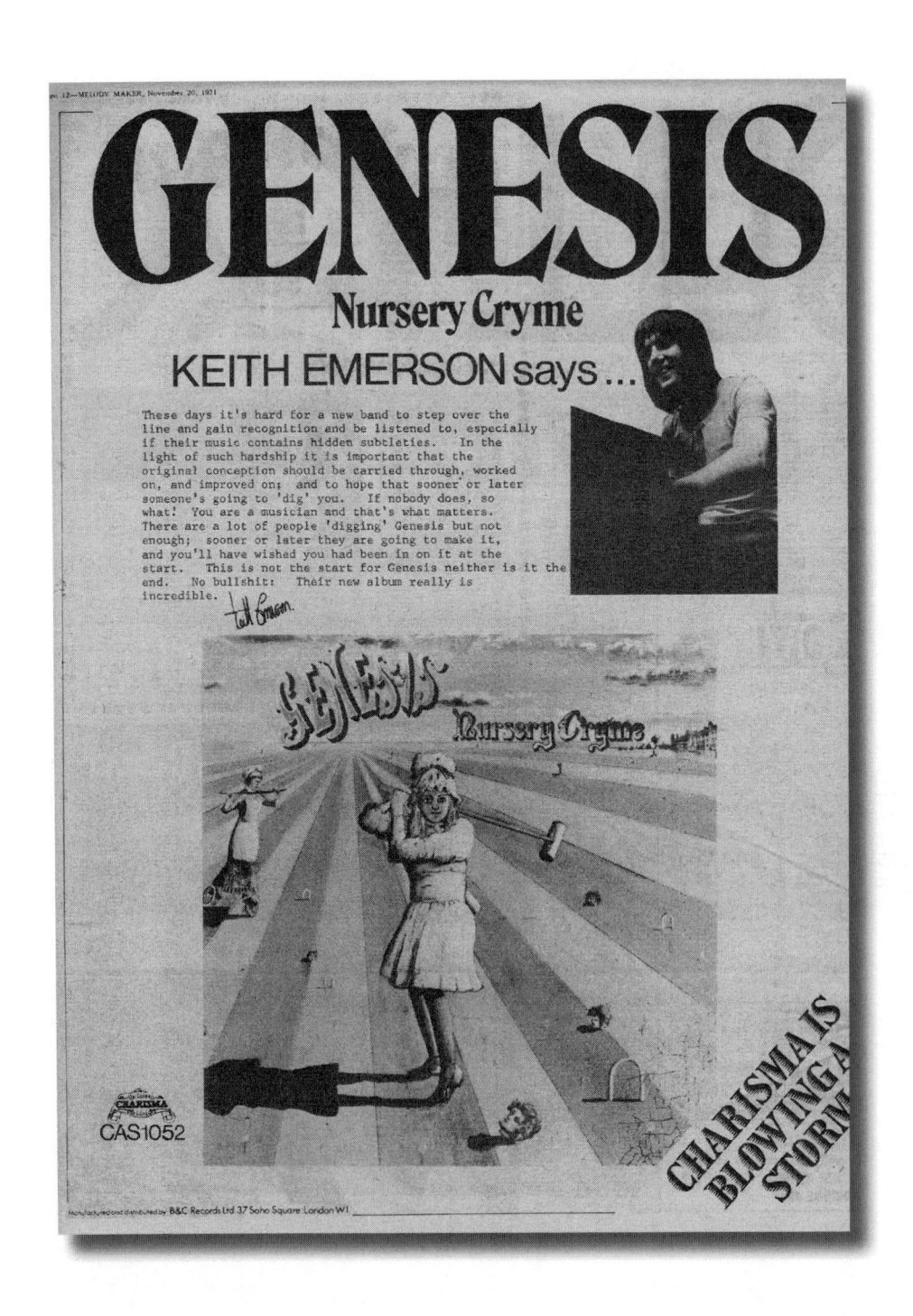

NURSERY CRYME

November 12, 1971
Charisma CAS 1052
Produced by John Anthony
Engineered by David Hentschel
Recorded at Trident Studios, London, UK
Personnel: Peter Gabriel – lead vocals, flute, oboe, bass drum, tambourine; Steve Hackett – electric guitar, 12-string guitar; Tony Banks – Hammond organ, Mellotron, piano, electric piano, 12-string guitar, backing vocals; Mike Rutherford – bass, bass pedals, 12-string guitar, backing vocals; Phil Collins – drums, voices, percussion, lead vocals on "For Absent Friends," co-lead vocals on "Harold the Barrel" and "Harlequin" (uncredited)
All songs written by Genesis

Side 1
1. The Musical Box 10:27
2. For Absent Friends 1:44
3. The Return of the Giant Hogweed 8:10

Side 2
1. Seven Stones 5:08
2. Harold the Barrel 2:58
3. Harlequin 2:53
4. The Fountain of Salmacis 7:54

Entangled: Genesis on Record 1969-1976

A *Nursery Cryme* Timeline

July 1971. The band write and rehearse at Tony Stratton Smith's residence, Luxford House, in East Sussex. Hackett suggests that Tony Banks purchases his own Mellotron, and it becomes central to the new material.

August 2 – September 10, 1971. The band work at Trident Studios, on tracks slated for their third album. Producing is John Anthony, assisted by David Hentschel.

November 12, 1971. Genesis issue their third album, *Nursery Cryme*, which reaches No.39 in the UK charts, albeit not until May of 1974. It charts again in 1984, reaching No.68. The album certifies silver in the UK and gold in France.

November 21, 1971 – March 18, 1972. The band tour the UK, in support of *Nursery Cryme*.

April 8 – April 19, 1972. The band conduct a tour of Italy, followed by UK dates through the summer and a return to Italy in mid-August.

Entangled: Genesis on Record 1969-1976

Martin talks to Rand Kelly, Charlie Nieland and Bill Schuster about *Nursery Cryme*.

Martin Popoff: Okay guys, with record #3, *Nursery Cryme*, Genesis get a new drummer, guitarist and, as it would turn out, an occasional logo. How do they fare?

Rand Kelly: Oh, *Nursery Cryme* is just lightyears ahead of the first one, of course. But it's just a logical step up from *Trespass*. *Trespass*, I think, was the sign of things to come with this album. I mean, Keith Emerson did a review of *Nursery Cryme* in *Melody Maker* and really raved about it. He thought it was good. And that gave them a boost of morale. Peter said that when they read the Keith Emerson review, they knew they had done something pretty special. And this album is a masterpiece; it really is.

It's one of my favourites. This is the beginning, I think, of the true Genesis sound that everybody knows from that era, because in comes Phil Collins and in comes Steve Hackett and they just lift it. I like what Peter Gabriel has said in interviews. He said that when he heard Phil Collins play the drums on the first song, he could just feel it. And then he said something about a band being only as good as its drummer. And Peter's a drummer, so he knows what he's talking about. But he said that Phil Collins just lifted the band to a different level completely. And he said that they knew they had the guy they were looking for. Plus he could sing. Yeah, there's a lot of Phil vocals on this.

Charlie Nieland: Well, all these records are interesting, because they're transitional in a way. And *Nursery Cryme* clearly marks a big transition from *Trespass* in that Anthony Phillips and John Mayhew leave and Hackett and Collins come on board. There's great material on *Trespass* and it's a little more folk-inspired until you get to the last track on *Trespass*, which is "The Knife." That sort of hints forward to what's coming.

The story with *Nursery Cryme* is that after Phillips left, they found Collins first in auditions, and they didn't get Hackett right away. They went out and toured with this stuff. They started playing early versions of "The Musical Box" with Tony Banks playing distorted piano leads for guitar leads and stuff and Rutherford was playing bass pedals more. It stretched them into a new form of arrangement.

And once they auditioned Hackett, they already had a bunch more foundational Genesis things worked out.

So it was an interesting transition, how they ended up with this group, When you read some of the interviews, they were balancing great ambition with this sort of passive aggressive competition that they had with each other, but in this gentlemanly way. You can get this from the interviews that came out with the box set. They're all on YouTube. They do interviews about each album. They talked to all the separate members, circa 2007. This is their chemistry and it really starts to come into its own on this record. And they find a balance; they find cooperation. And the two new members were so good in their own ways, that they kicked them into this forward momentum. *Nursery Cryme* is the sound of them coming into their own, I think.

Bill Schuster: There's a lot of growth here, obviously, after *Trespass*. The big story is the addition of Phil on drums and very many vocals, surprisingly. And of course Steve arrives on guitar, replacing Mick Barnard, who is kind of the forgotten man in between Ant—Anthony Phillips—and Steve. He wasn't in the band very long, but apparently he had a big part in writing "The Musical Box," which is pretty significant. All told, what they come up with is really quite a bit heavier overall than *Trespass*, other than "The Knife." I find that song, in parts, almost early heavy metal. I mean, that's kind of an exaggeration, but on parts of "The Musical Box" and "Hogweed," they do get pretty heavy.

Martin: What do you think of the album cover?

Rand: Yeah, this is by Paul Whitehead. And if you look really close, you'll see that this lady girl, this girl named Cynthia, is playing croquet and all the balls are actually people's heads she's knocked off with the croquet mallet, right? It's pretty goofy but I love it.

Charlie: It's an iconic in its own obscure way. It's so, like, hand-drawn and childlike and really disturbing at the same time. It runs in parallel to what Gabriel was bringing to this record as a writer and a vocalist, mixing these adult and childlike views of the world. As well, they sort of brought this upper crust, British madness thing and that cover really evokes that too. It's kind of Victorian, like some of the music on this record is.

Bill: I absolutely love the album cover. Until recently, it was hanging on my wall behind me here. The CD did a disservice to the album cover. It cuts the head off down below. But, of course, on the record you see the full head, which is a pretty important part of the story related in "The Musical Box." Paul Whitehead's artwork is not technically great. It's actually kind of sloppy, but it's very aesthetically pleasing. It's kind of like the production; it really fits with this album. It shouldn't be too neat and clean and shiny. Because it's supposed to be kind of otherworldly, old-school.

Martin: What do you think of John Anthony's production? He did *Trespass*. He's also done a couple for Van der Graaf Generator.

Rand: Well, crucially, David Hentschel's the engineer, and usually a producer decides what the engineer can and can't do. But the engineer did a great job. David Hentschel is good. And of course I bring this up because you'll find down the line that he's doing the entire production for the Phil Collins Genesis albums, right from *A Trick of the Tail* through to *Duke*.

Bill: The production is not great. Phil, while obviously already a great drummer, even at this early stage, he sounds like he's drumming on wet cardboard boxes and perhaps a bit of Tupperware. I mean, his playing is great, but the sound is not. One thing that I noticed; I have the original, Famous Charisma label vinyl edition of this album that I inherited from my parents here. And then I have the Nick Davis remaster on CD. And I think that the old-school production on the record, despite misgivings, is almost a strength. It actually sounds better on the record to me. I'm not usually a big, "Oh, vinyl is better than CD across the board" kind of guy, but the very nature of this album, its old English horror and fairy tale ambiance type thing, that fits with this production. I don't think cleaner, modern, more professional production would have worked as well with *Nursery Cryme*—the vibe is kind of important.

Martin: Okay, let's dig into the album. We begin with "The Musical Box," which is not only one of the most respected Genesis songs, but it also lives on as the name of the most respected Genesis tribute band.

Rand: Yes it does, and let's begin at the beginning. The first lick there, I always thought that was a harpsichord, but it turns out to be Mike Rutherford and Tony Banks on 12-string acoustic guitars. That's a great song, and historic, obviously. Steve Hackett said that they were recording this thing and he said it's called "The Musical Box," but nothing on that song sounded like a musical box. So when Peter goes, "Play me my song," you hear Steve Hackett playing that guitar line, kind of answering him back. He said he recorded it at slow speed and then played it back faster, so the notes would be really, really high. It was a trick that Les Paul used to do. And that gives it the musical box sound because those little teeny toy boxes have those really high notes. That's what he was looking for.

The lyrics are just bonkers, and they relate to the front cover—the album cover is "The Musical Box." Absolutely. And he tells this story about Cynthia and how this guy wanted to be with her and stuff and he never gets together with her. So he dies and he comes back as a ghost, although it's hard to tell. And he keeps saying, "Why don't you touch me, touch me?" But she can't, because he's a ghost. But you can see him and he wants to have sex with her (laughs). This whole song is about sex. That's what Peter Gabriel said.

And musically, God, when they perform this live on stage, there's no bass guitar. Mike Rutherford is playing a 12-string Rickenbacker electric. And he's got bass pedals on the floor and all the bass you hear on that song come from bass pedals. At least that's the way they did it on stage. I don't know, I don't hear it here either. I don't think there's actual bass guitar on "The Musical Box." It's all pretty much just driven by Mike Rutherford and Tony Banks. Nor is there any Mellotron on "The Musical Box." I was listening really closely. The Mellotron shows up on a track down the road there called "The Return of the Giant Hogweed." There's Mellotron on that.

Charlie: I just want to say first of all that I first heard this material on Genesis *Live* which is an album that came out after *Foxtrot*. So I was very familiar with the Genesis *Live* versions of "The Musical Box" and "The Return of the Giant Hogweed" first, and then I got this album. The live versions are spectacular. But yes, "The Musical Box" is interesting because it plays on that ambiguity I talked about earlier. The song is there as a whole story on the album sleeve. It's about this little girl who lops her friend's head off with a croquet mallet. And then he comes back as a ghost out of her musical box, a fully adult ghost, wanting to touch her. It's very disturbing. You really don't know right away that that's what the story is. The lyrics don't tell a clear narrative. It's impressionistic and ambiguous.

Musically, it's very theatrical. Even the very beginning of the song has this little fanfare from that harp-like guitar that sounds like a curtain rising. Then the curtain rises on this mysterious-sounding harmonic minor mode, and they're using all this Phrygian dominant sort of Eastern-sounding chording that becomes one of their trademarks. And we start to hear Gabriel using his different voices, as he gets into the, "Play me 'Old King Cole'" section. Each line, he approaches with a different vocal persona. Some of the lines are very close and some of them suddenly have reverb on them. I just think that's so evocative.

And the song is just full of elements of surprise. You really get in this song that they take a long time to develop something, although it's deceptive. You think this is going to be a very soft song, and it is for three or four minutes. And then it gets to that explosive power-chording, and it rewards your anticipation with the new full-band arrangement and activity as well as these big transitions that come. It really builds up your expectations of like, what's going to happen? And then this thing happens.

They were saying that they were influenced and inspired by The Who. And you could hear that here when the drums and the guitar kick in and it gets into that fast part. You get sort of Keith Moon-like drumming and big power strums, which is such a contrast from the beginning.

The song is also interesting because it's very linear. It tells a story. The whole first section comes and then it gets to the middle section and Peter Gabriel has one little break where he sings the "Old King Cole" nursery rhyme. And then it all comes kicking back in for more interplay between the keyboards and the guitar. This is where you can hear the difference between Phil Collins and the previous drummer. He really drives it with this incredible verve and these almost jazz-like fills and everything.

And when you get to the end, the whole outro section with the, "She is a lady/She's got time," where he sings in that gentle voice, that's the part of the story… well, I'll get to that in a minute. But it never comes back to the sections in the beginning musically. So this is almost like a through composition—it's episodes. And then it has that final fanfare at the end, punctuating this very dramatic build where he's begging to be touched, saying, "Touch me now, now, now!" It's this drama of repression and desire, and it's accompanied by churchy organ and soaring guitar. They just blast out this neoclassical thing at the end after that fantastic guitar solo. You really hear, all of a sudden, Steve Hackett's ability to rise to the challenge with some power. And as I say, it ends with that hilarious ending sequence, those final chords at the end, kind of like a Tchaikovsky piece. There's a certain whimsy to it, even while it's dark.

Bill: It's a good thing that they actually have the story and the lyrics on the CD. That's one thing about my copy of the record; they were not there. And without these lyrics, I would have had no clue what's going on in this thing. It's a really cool, creepy story once you know what it is. There's this Henry character, who is beheaded by Cynthia Jane. Her young playmate, Henry, he comes back to life, of sort, as a spirit, a fully-aged spirit, two weeks later. He's now lived a life that he doesn't even remember, apparently. He comes out and somehow he becomes a fully functioning and very feeling adult, and frankly a rather horny adult, apparently, because all these urges that he wouldn't have understood as a child somehow come up in this adult spirit version of him. As a result, he sees Cynthia in an entirely new light. Which is rather creepy, really, but very effective for this story, right? I mean, Cynthia's a young girl here, but technically, in his mind, Henry is also still a young boy, even though in his time as a spirit, he's aged well deep into adulthood.

Musically, it shows great use of dynamics. They were masters of this already. They could go from a soft, beautiful passages to something ugly and threatening, exemplified, say, by Tony's harsh organ sounds following up on Peter Gabriel's flute. I love the flute and Gabriel does a fine job on that. The guitar shriek, just the one note, at 4:09, just before Steve starts soloing, that really jumps out— it's almost like a cat screaming. That's pretty cool. I mean, it's a great example of a perfect vegetable stew song—lots of different flavours blending in without overpowering each other. And that's kind of the band in a nutshell too, really.

In any event, most people consider "The Musical Box" to be a top five Genesis song, I imagine. I wouldn't. I'd put it in my top ten maybe, but not top five. But as far as the old-school stuff goes, yeah, it's great. It also has the distinction of being written by many hands. And apparently, initially, it was Ant that did most of the guitar in the songwriting process, and then Mick Barnard came in and did some as well. Steve just added his own little musical box guitar sound at the end of the process. And so it's possibly the only Genesis song that might have as many as seven actual songwriters stirring the pot here, which is pretty neat.

Martin: Good stuff. What are your thoughts on "For Absent Friends?" There's a lot of arranging packed into 1:47, even without drums.

Rand: Yeah, I love it. It's really sad. It's good for listening to when you've lost a loved one. It was written by Steve Hackett completely. And I think Phil did the lyrics, and then somehow, Peter wanted Steve to sing it and Steve didn't want to sing it. And then Peter didn't want to sing it. So they gave it to Phil. So Phil sings the lead vocal. And this is the first time we hear Phil sing a lead vocal. For years, he was able to blend his voice in with Peter's and nobody really knew for sure who was singing what because you almost always assume it's Peter. They have a way of matching their voices, just like John Lennon and Paul McCartney did. It's all about going to the cemetery and meeting the priest and yeah, it's a really great song. Like I say, I like to listen to it when I've lost a loved one. I put that on.

Charlie: Yeah, that was just Hackett and Collins. It presents a different kind of neoclassical approach that's a little more romantic. Banks is very romantic. But you start to hear Hackett's influence. It's a wistful tale of little old people. The modulation into the chorus is pretty. This kind of palate-cleanser happens later on the record too. It's a song rooted in psychedelia and folk. You can draw a line from the stuff that's on *Trespass* to something like this, which is interesting because Hackett and Collins weren't on *Trespass*. In the end, it's a beautiful little piece that works nice as an interstitial thing in between the bigger moments

Bill: Here's Steve and Phil making their mark as new members of the band. It's a simple song, a tale of two widows reminiscing, basically, looking back on their lives. It's so short, you blink and you miss it. This is Phil's first lead vocal and his voice is sweet and innocent as presented here, something that will go away eventually. He sounds so young. It has a whole different dynamic to the Phil that he would become later. The song works nicely as a breather between "The Musical Box" and "The Return of the Giant Hogweed." It's perfectly placed. And that's another thing: this album is very well sequenced. It basically has the big songs at the beginning and end of each side with some shorter songs in between.

Martin: Not that many Genesis songs aren't like this but, you get to "The Return of the Giant Hogweed," and one just marvels at the complication of it all. How do these guys remember these parts?

Rand: Yes, lots going on. It starts out with—and nobody really realised this at the time because it was 1971—but it starts out with Steve Hackett and Tony Banks playing harmony lines, and Steve Hackett's using this tapping technique to do it. This was seven years before anybody had heard of Van Halen. Now, Steve Hackett didn't invent the technique. That goes way back to the classical music days. There are videos on YouTube about the origins of tapping. But the way Steve did it, it just sounds really good. They create this wall of sound. It's like Phil Spector gone prog. Rutherford is probably in there on bass pedals again, which creates a booming effect down low to go with this wall of sound. But it's an onslaught. The whole song is just really heavy and I love it.

Charlie: The title alone is just hilarious. It's a song about an invasive species, and it's very kind of lurid science fiction in the mould of *Day of the Triffids*. It's fun and almost like steampunk sci-fi, you know? It's set in the 19th century, so it's Victorian and yet it has this futuristic vibe. And as Rand has explained, the very beginning of the song is so great with Hackett and Banks weaving that evil counterpoint. And that's where you can hear Hackett bringing his two-hand tapping technique to the band. You can see videos of some Spanish guitar players and some other musicians doing it in the '30s and '40s. But anyway, Hackett brings a lot to this piece and he and Banks create these webs of counterpoint sound. The whole beginning of the song is like being attacked by bees. It's so cool.

And the song itself is so funny. It presents these different points of view telling the story. There's this heavy part which is kind of like a military announcement saying we must stop the giant hogweed and they're announcing the campaign against them. And then it switches over to this lighter part where the fashionable country gentleman is bringing back the hogweed. And it tells the story like a news report in third person. So it switches back between like news report mode and the heavy military mode. It's just really great storytelling on Gabriel's part.

But then it gives way to this beautiful instrumental break, after some verses and choruses between these two sections, with their surreal rhyming and everything. It cuts to this piano arpeggio;

that's just such a great shift. And then the drums start kicking in underneath it, and the guitar starts coming in over this big surf beat. There's this monstrous, bendy guitar solo. You can really hear that distinctiveness of Hackett being able to create these bends that are, I don't know, not bluesy. It has this quality where even if he's playing a blues lick, it still sounds like a piping instrument or something.

And that ushers us into the ending where Gabriel says, "Mighty Hogweed is avenged." And he says the name of the giant hogweed, which is an actual poisonous plant by the way. He says the Latin name of it, "Heracleum Mantegazziani." And then they launch into this, like, gargantuan punk rock ending where they're pounding away at these block chords, playing in this very weird, modulated pattern. I love that part so much. And again, it's best on Genesis *Live*, if you ever want to listen to it. It's so much faster and more powerful at the end. That just blew me away. I've borrowed that feel for songs that I've written before, because it's so cool.

Bill: This one has much in common with "The Musical Box," beginning with great dynamics and sort of horror story lyrics. It's so "big P" prog that they called the instrumental midsection of "The Dance of the Giant Hogweed." I really think it's cool how Steve begins the song tapping in tandem with Tony's keys. And Steve often gets credited—sometimes by his own self (laughs)—for inventing tapping, though I've heard other reports that it was around well before Steve. But he is famous for being one of the earliest innovators using that technique and it's used well here.

Another way "The Musical Box" and "Hogweed" are tied in together, I think the stories are both ambiguous regarding the villains in their respective narratives. Is the villain the murderers or the lecherous ghost in "The Musical Box?" Is it the vengeful Hogweeds or the humans who kidnapped them? I don't know, but I like that ambiguity about it. There's no black-and-white good guy/bad guy going on here. It's open to interpretation who you choose to side with, if anyone.

Martin: What are your thoughts on Peter as a singer and as a personality in this band?

Bill: I think Peter is very charismatic on this album and he does a great job of taking on character roles. But there are times here that with Phil's addition when they sing in tandem, I think Phil almost overpowers Peter and kind of puts him in the shadows, surprisingly. I don't think I'd ever noticed before, now going through this once more, just how much Phil is present vocally on this album.

Martin: Things slow down for side two opener "Seven Stones," but it's no less grand, and definitely churchier. It's funny, but if there could even be such a thing, this record is Victorian rock 'n' roll. I've been known to call The Band "civil war rock," and I've yapped about Creedence Clearwater Revival and even Clutch that way too. Maybe there's a whole genre hidden in plan view here—historical rock.

Bill: Yes, I like that (laughs), and "Seven Stones" fits that description well. I think it's kind of a sleeper track, with clever lyrics by Tony. This is the one time that the muted drum sound or lighter, jazzier performance from Phil, actually works well because I think if he had a harder-hitting drum sound here, it might overpower the song. So the presentation of the percussion fits the vibe. This song doesn't really need to rock.

Lyrically it's pretty cool. One thing about the old Genesis, I always used to think that Peter did virtually all the lyrics and that's just not the case. Everybody took turns writing lyrics for this band, even back in those days, which was kind of a revelation for me. And Tony, I think, has always come up with some of my favourite lyrics. There's three little stories here. Basically, this old man tells three stories and the gist of it across each of them is that everything is chaos, that nothing truly means anything. It's all random chance and that change is of no consequence. "We pick up the reins from nowhere" I used to think was just one of those lyrics that had no real meaning and just sounded cool. But investigating it further, it started to make sense. The lyrics all ascribe to the narrator of the story and his life philosophy.

Rand: "Seven Stones" is my favourite track on the whole album. The lyrics are just so esoteric and can be interpreted in many ways, kind of like Jon Anderson's lyrics. But when I first heard this song, it was like, oh my God, this is just a work of art. It sounds like you're on a ship floating on the ocean. Everything's calm and you're not moving very fast. And it's just come to me lately that it reminds me of Procol Harum's "A Salty Dog."

But there's a lyric in there, "They see a gull." You know, that's clever. And so is "Despair that tires the world brings the old man laughter/The laughter of the world only grieves him/Believe him, the old man's guide is chance." I don't know; that just rolls off the tongue like music. All I know is it's got a crapload of chords and I don't know what they are. I never looked them up because I wanted to use my ear to figure them out. But I'm about ready to give up and go look at the chords. I'd love to play this song. It's just gorgeous. It's probably one of the weirdest Genesis songs because it hasn't got any time changes. And the Mellotron is just to die for on this song, and there's a lot of organ. Tony is out of his mind. But the big selling point for me is that there are so many chord changes. They change chords and keys like you can't believe and yet the timing is the same throughout. It's just this languid, almost detached 4/4—nothing changes. It's an absolute masterpiece as far as I'm concerned.

Charlie: Boy, I love "Seven Stones" too. It wasn't one of those songs that grabbed me when I was a kid, but I eventually came to see it as one of the best developed pieces of music on the record. It's like everybody's contributing to it and it's demonstrating or showing off their impressive arrangement skills. Steve's shifts between these harp-like sounds and sharper, razor-like sounds and Phil's drums are all atmospheric and tumbling around. There's loopy bass lines too, and it's all in dialogue with the vocal melody. And let's just get to that, because the melody is so beautiful and Peter's voice is incredible with all this like jumping of octaves that he does.

There's a tale of three fortunes told, with the tinker, the sailor and the farmer, and each one is told with these little melodic flourishes. It's a really symphonic piece. When it gets to the chorus, that, "Despair that tires the world brings the old man laughter" part, I just love that. Also, the Mellotron is so dramatic in this song. That earlier vocal melody comes back at the end but it's sung all hushed, and it builds into another restatement of that melody, changing key with this delicious Mellotron. It almost sounds like "In the Court of the Crimson King" at the end. It's so heavy and melodic. I don't know; if you just listen to that song, you really hear what Genesis is about at this point. They have the ability to create so many changes that flow gracefully into each other. It's complex and yet it just draws you in.

Martin: Next we get "Harold the Barrel," a sort of perky, piano pop twist, basically an Elton John or Billy Joel song, not that we'd heard much from either of those guys yet career-wise. I actually get City Boy from it as well, or ELO.

Rand: Yeah, it sounds like a Beatles tune from '67 or '68. It's just got this relentless, near constant stabbing piano note—the whole song is like that. I guess you'd call it eighth notes. But the story is bizarre. It's set up like a newscaster reporting the news. You know, Peter goes, "A well-known Bognor restaurant-owner disappeared early this morning/Last seen in a mouse-brown overcoat." It's like he's reporting the news. And then they talk to his mother, who is played by Phil. It's a little play. And it's even structured like that in the lyrics. It tells you who's talking and what's going on. But between Phil and Peter, they're just back and forth with what they call call-and-response. And in the story, Harold goes up on a ledge and the mother says to come on down. If your father was alive, he'd be very upset. The last lines are "You must be joking/Take a running jump."

Martin: The interesting thing there is that we assume it's Harry thinking or maybe even saying out loud, "You must be joking." But if could be the crowd yelling that to him, or his mother hoping that he's joking. And then "Take a running jump;" that could be Harold talking himself into it, but that too can be the crowd egging him on to jump.

Rand: Exactly, and then what is brilliant is that the music, Tony's piano, turns dark but doesn't seem to resolve anything. And then it just fades out, creating a total cliff-hanger. Which is what those final lyrics are as well—we have no idea what happens. It's just absolutely brilliant. I love it.

Charlie: Wow, "Harold the Barrel" is a very needed moment of whimsy on the album, but, of course it's super-dark lyrically. Again, they use the device of a reporter reporting. It talks about our character, Harold the Barrel, who is up on the ledge, thinking about jumping, and the crowd is beneath, with some telling him to jump and some telling him not to. I love the clompy piano. That really drives the song. You don't hear that much piano on this record. I mean, you do in bits, but here the piano is like the central thing. It's like a twisted Bee Gees song, kind of (laughs). The melody in the verses, that, "A well-known Bognor restaurant-owner disappeared early this morning," if you slow it down, it's like "New York Mining Disaster 1941" by the Bee Gees or something. And you know that the Bee Gees were an influence on them.

So it goes on and on with the reporting until you get to the little, beautiful interlude in the middle, where you finally get inside

Harold's head. He's like, "If I was many miles from here/I'd be sailing in an open boat on the sea." I don't know; it's just great musical theatre. And I love the thing at the end, when at "Take a running jump," Harry jumps. Or does he? The music pulls out and the voices hang in the air. And then those piano chords fade out and you're left hanging. To me it's so visual. It sounds like he jumped and then flew and floated away. You never hear him land. I love that, that they did that musically instead of explaining it. It's a great song. Apparently, it's Phil and Peter singing together in the same mic, like in unison, making little harmonies. I mean, there's also backup vocals, but the lead vocal is actually a co-lead vocal. Pretty cool.

Bill: "Harold the Barrel" was one of those where I was thinking that Phil in particular overpowers Peter mostly, but nonetheless they work well together here.

Martin: I get that now, because even though this is a co-lead vocal, I feel like I'm hearing Phil's voice in my head more than Peter's even when it's clearly Peter. It's like the Phil Collins who would dominate the '80s as a solo artist and with all that Genesis success is not only tormenting pure Harry, but he's living rent-free in my head too! (laughs).

Bill: Exactly (laughs). And here's another thing: the lyric sheet is definitely required. Because when I was listening to this, I was thinking it's like a lot of punk songs that have great lyrics, but they can be obscured by the singing style. And that's somewhat the case with this. It's a great lyric, but it's a dark comedy about suicide. And so in essence it's another horror tale, which is a pretty common occurrence on this album. Both of these guys, Peter and Phil, do such a great job playing characters in this song and bouncing off of each other. There's a lot packed in. I mean, is this prog, is it new wave, is it music hall? It's just so rollicking. It reminds me a bit of Emerson, Lake & Palmer joke songs like "The Sherriff." It's that sort of thing, but a bit more successful, perhaps. It goes deeper than the ELP stuff. I did mean to look up Bognor and I never did. Do you know off-hand what Bognor is?

Martin: I checked; it's a seaside town at the south of England, in West Sussex. I guess they could have picked anything and this just sounded provincial. All right, any thoughts on "Harlequin?"

Bill: Thanks for that. Yeah, that was apparently a Mike lyric. It was something that was started with Mike and Ant and Mike finished it off apparently with the idea of what it would be like with him and Ant both playing the 12-strings. So it ended up being Mike and Steve playing the 12-strings instead. It seems Mike is not a fan of his lyric on this song. But I think it's a fine lyric. It doesn't necessarily mean a whole lot to me, but it's evocative. It serves the song well enough. It sounds good and that's all it needs to do here. I'm not looking for anything deep with this song. It's another one of those nice lulls in between "Harold the Barrel" and "The Fountain of Salmacis."

Rand: "Harlequin" is 12-string guitar city. I don't even think there's any keyboard on that song. Sounds like Mike Rutherford, Steve Hackett and Tony Banks are playing their 12-strings and they're just going off, and then Peter and Phil are singing double lead. They actually mesh it together like John and Paul did on "I Want to Hold Your Hand." A lot of people don't realise that "Oh, yeah, I tell you something" line is John and Paul singing at the same time and then they meld it together. Well, that's what they do on "Harlequin." And then sometimes Phil will go "Harlequin" and then Peter will come in behind him and go "Harlequin" and it'll be a different tone—you can tell. But for the most part, it's harmony vocals or what they call dual vocals on the same note. But God it's a beautiful piece. I don't know what it's about. It says, "Order the pieces, put them back, put them back;" I don't know what any of that means. It's just a pretty song; makes you feel good. There's nothing wrong with it.

Charlie: "Harlequin;" this one's quite beautiful. The guitar reminds me of "Blackbird" a little bit. This is a Rutherford song, and it's got really nice two-part harmonies between Phil and Peter. It's a more sophisticated version of something that might have been on *Trespass*.

After the arpeggiating verses, it gets to this chorus where there's strumming with major sevenths and arpeggiated electric piano, echoey piano, and then these beautiful, little fuzzy, bending guitars along with those harmonies. It's calling forward to the dream pop of the '90s, something like Lush. Often I heard little flashes of Genesis in Cocteau Twins, but of course I doubt they listened to them consciously. But sometimes this aspect of Genesis, with the ethereal arpeggiated guitars and echoey touches, the echoey, luminous things around it, I feel like it influenced that strain of music. You can hear Genesis in the DNA of that music, maybe. But again, this is one of these songs that's just a moment of sustained beauty before the deluge of the last song. There's this arpeggiated guitar that kind of repeats and hangs on and fades at the end, which is a perfect set-up for the next song, which begins with a reverse fade.

Martin: How are we supposed to know who's doing 12-string guitars between Steve and Mike?

Charlie: I pretend that I can tell. I don't really know. I mean, because I watch live clips with them and there's sometimes a guitar I thought was Steve, or more like a guitar I thought Mike was playing, and I see that, oh no, Steve's playing that beautiful arpeggio there. But usually on stage, except for things like the intro to "Supper's Ready," usually Steve's playing an electric and then Mike's playing the 12-string. But it's all like a web, you know? They create these beautiful webs of guitar picking that I think are very underrated and not understood for their singular, individualistic, unique beauty. It was a great feature.

Martin: Okay, last one, "The Fountain of Salmacis?" Is it a success?

Rand: Sure, this is another masterpiece on this album. Yeah, and as a bonus, it starts out with a huge Mellotron, as well as an organ part that Tony Banks wrote when he was at Charterhouse school. He had that lick in his head all this time, and he finally decided to pull it out for this song. But the Mellotron, the way it builds up with the volume swells, oh my God, it will just float you right off the bed if you're just laying there listening to it. It's so awesome. I love this tune. And it has all kinds of changes. There's so many time changes in this when there's no singing. The band just went bonkers on this song.

Charlie: I have to say that my friends tend to think "The Musical Box" is the highlight of this record. I love that song, but "The Fountain of Salmacis" is the high point for me of this record. You know you're in for something great here when you hear that sweeping intro, how it fades in and it becomes this deluge of Mellotron and guitar that washes over you. And then it gets quiet again and then washes over again. It just crashes and recedes. And then it kicks in with this this racing heartbeat of a kick drum.

As for Peter, I think this is his best singing on the record. He's jumping moods and octaves and singing in lower voices and whispers and it's this wonderful labyrinth of a melody. It's about this character; it comes from Ovid. Well, actually Ovid did a version of this. Ovid wrote a version of this myth down, about a hunter who finds the goddess in the woods, Hermaphroditus. And she ends up claiming him. And then they're joined, dwelling beneath the lake. And it's this interesting story of androgyny by will of the feminine. You know, Gabriel was very interested in the crossing of genders on this record and in general. So here he creates this story of the feminine claiming the masculine, and I just really like that.

The mood… they have this explosion into the choruses with multiple vocal melodies going on at once. Then it goes back to the verse melody again, and this time with a different backing. This song has a lot of the elements of prog rock kind of coming into place for them, like where they're using melodies in one spot of the song and then recalling it later in a different setting.

And once again, they have a wonderful instrumental break, where they bust into this completely different rhythm. It goes into this galloping rhythm in 6/8, with a kind of polyrhythmic modulation. Plus you hear, again, right in the middle, Steve's two-handed tapping. Then it breaks into this rollicking, percussive bridge piece where the characters are talking. That ends with that "Unearthly calm descended from the sky" bit.

And then after finishing the instrumental break, they give us one last verse. That bridge melody comes in and there's this triumphant finish, where he says, "Both had given everything they had," and everything kicks in at this majestic slow tempo. And that's when we get this beautiful guitar solo from Steve that is just one of the best Steve solos ever, his solo at the end of the song.

And then once again they give you this very theatrical ending where they're playing the last cadence of the guitar solo and they hold the note. Then they get quiet and then fade it back in for one big she-bang. And it's funny, I noticed—because it's on my iPod and was on repeat—that note's in the same key as the beginning of "The Musical Box." So when it flips around, you're like, oh, we're back around again. I don't know if that was intentional, but it's fun.

Bill: I didn't even know how to pronounce The Fountain of Salmacis" until today. I've been saying it wrong for decades. I have long said "Sal-MAY-sis" and apparently it's "Sal-MAW-kiss." So I learned something new today. And yes, that glorious Mellotron opening… if you find a stereotypical old-school progressive rock fan and you play that song, you might need to send them to the bathroom for a couple minutes to tend to their business. That's how excited they'll get over that. That is the quintessential prog sound. And it's awesome that it comes from a Mellotron purchased from Mr. Robert Fripp that was played on *In the Court of the Crimson King*. It doesn't get much more "passing the baton" than that.

Martin: All right, with that image burned into my brain (laughs), any closing remarks, things we didn't cover?

Bill: Well, in terms on the personalities, I'd like to add that I would say Phil Collins is the best musician in the band at this point. I mean, right off the bat, I'm not a drummer, but as a listener, he's the one that's most impressive here. He's already just very creative. Steve finds ways to fit in. He doesn't necessarily have to be the centrepiece of every song and he seems okay with that. Sometimes he just adds colour. I guess he's now part of that whole Genesis perfect stew effect. Later on, he becomes more prominent in the band's career, before he finally leaves, of course. But yeah, at this early stage, it seems like he's a bit in the shadow. Like, he's picking up the reins from Ant and very much following the type of thing that Phillips was doing, and still learning to find his own place in the band.

As for Mike, he's kind of hidden to me at this point. Mike's the John Paul Jones of this band. He does a lot of important things, but they're often in the background. They're often subtle. I don't always know where Mike's at. I mean, when you and I discussed the self-titled 1983 album and the song "It's Gonna Get Better." I had mentioned that I had no idea that that was not Mike playing bass throughout that song. Again, it's a strength of Mike that he is able to be a role player like that at times and not have to be out front. And it's the strength of the band also that I don't always know who's playing what. That's really cool, actually. I have to listen to this stuff a fair amount of times to ascertain, is that guitar? Is that a keyboard? Is Mike on bass pedals? I have no clue sometimes.

Martin: Bill, back for a second about that Mellotron coming from King Crimson, briefly, what is your understanding of the history of the use of Mellotron?

Bill: Well, you've got to give The Beatles credit also. They did their bit, but you might credit George Martin for that. I don't really know if there's much of a history beyond that, that I'm aware of. The big ones are The Beatles, The Moody Blues and then King Crimson; that's kind of the chain there. You had the stuff Ian McDonald did on that first King Crimson album that set the standard after that as far as its use in full-blown progressive rock. And Tony does not disappoint here. It's simple, but so effective. It's such a huge sound and just pure beauty. There's nothing harsh about it at all. It's almost heavenly.

Martin: And back to this album, in the final analysis, where does it rank for you against *Trespass* before it and *Foxtrot* after?

Bill: The difficult middle child; it's actually my favourite of those three. I think on *Foxtrot* they lost a bit of the early innocence. Steve and Phil had become more integrated into bands, so I tend to frame them as becoming better as players on *Foxtrot*. In a way, that album is a more refined version of what they did on *Nursery Cryme*. So yeah, it lost a bit of that innocence for me. *Foxtrot* is probably technically a better album, but I prefer *Nursery Cryme*. And as far as *Trespass* goes, for the most part it's always felt not fully-formed. Ant was a fine guitarist. I'm sure he still is, actually. But I think they needed to move beyond him, even though he was pretty clearly the most important member of the band, to hear the guys themselves tell it, back in the early days. I don't think if he had stayed with the band that they would have progressed as well. So, for me, *Trespass* is a tentative step towards the unbridled, weird creativity on *Nursery Cryme*.

Martin: Interesting. So maybe this is the album that has all the freshness and excitement of the superstar lineup just meeting each other for the first time, just in its formative stages, kind of thing.

Bill: Absolutely; that's a great way of looking at it.

Martin: And with *Nursery Cryme*, with these five guys, have they settled into this identity I keep harping on about, as the most squarely progressive rock band of their day, the band without glaring eccentricities?

Rand: Well, they had their eccentricities, no doubt. I mean, "Supper's Ready" is proof positive of that, as testament to how weird they could get. But at that point they had decided to do like a "Close to the Edge" type of thing. One long piece, except it really wasn't "Close to the Edge." I think it was more like Procol Harum's "In Held 'Twas in I." That was the first band to really do that, because they did that a few years earlier, in '68, I think, and that might have been the inspiration for "Supper's Ready." But again, it's not a full album side because you've got Steve Hackett's "Horizons" before it.

But to your point, they definitely got wackier and wackier as they went along. And they realised that their audience at that time was open to it. There would be changes to come, and I think radio had a lot to do with it, where the prog stuff got kind of weeded out. I mean, people that hear *The Lamb Lies Down on Broadway*, and they're not into prog, they still love "Carpet Crawlers," right? Because it's not offensive. It doesn't do anything weird. You don't get lost listening to it and it's a really nice song. But it's a dumbing-down process, in some specific ways, although any musician will defend themselves and say that no, in fact, we're actually getting smarter, but as songwriters.

But with *Nursery Cryme*, they were all-in. They were just like, hey, we can do pretty much whatever we want, because nobody knows who we are anyway. They hadn't gotten big yet. People don't realise that as good as this stuff is, nobody knew about them. I never heard of them until I got out of the Air Force. I might have seen these albums in the base exchange, but I didn't know anything about them. I didn't know what it was. And in those days, you had to buy an album to find out what it sounded like. You had to spend money. I'm making $1.75 an hour and I've got bills to pay and things like that. So you've got to make your purchases count. I was buying things I already knew.

Martin: Cool, and same question: what is your favourite of these early albums?

Rand: Well, you know, it's funny that you ask that, because after listening to *Nursery Cryme* again yesterday, I thought to myself, my God, this could be my favourite. It depends on… you know, I tell people this and they think it's funny, but it's my favourite album when I'm listening to it. I'll leave it to you to figure out what that means (laughs).

Charlie: Putting aside whether Genesis is the least eccentric prog rock band, I will agree with you that it might be the most British, certainly on the evidence of albums like *Nursery Cryme*. You could say King Crimson is extremely British too, especially given the early

'70s material. The guys in Genesis were so evidently from that British public school system. Which, it took me a while to understand that public school in Britain means private school in America (laughs). I just want to make sure I'm using the right term.

But they were from Charterhouse and I picture them as insular, young British men who were repressed. But in that repression, they were discovering this, like, sensuality that's bursting into these songs (laughs). Like these characters, the females are goddesses or nagging mothers or cruel children. It's like, they're exercising—or exorcising—these pent-up emotions into this very imaginative mythological way. And that is so British. And they're playing with it—Peter's very playful. As we talked about, I'm sure Syd Barrett had an influence on this. And as you hear Gabriel develop, he has that mix of whimsy and surrealism that is deepening on this record. You can really hear it as we get into the side two songs. They're so into their own weirdness and I just love that about it. So yes, it's very British.

It isn't for everyone. I recently played *Nursery Cryme* in the car for my girlfriend. We were driving down to Washington, DC. And somewhere on side two, we got in a traffic jam and she was like, "I can't listen to this anymore" (laughs). "It's too... there's too much." And I'm like, "Really? It just seems normal to me" (laughs). But I've been listening to it for 40 years.

Nursery Cryme

Entangled: Genesis on Record 1969-1976

FOXTROT

September 15, 1972
Charisma CAS 1058
Produced by David Hitchcock of Gruggy Woof
Engineered by John Burns
Recorded at Island Studios, London, UK
Personnel: Peter Gabriel – lead vocals, flute, bass drum, tambourine, oboe; Steve Hackett – electric guitar, 6-string guitar, 12-string guitar; Tony Banks – Hammond organ, Mellotron, electric and acoustic pianos, 12-string guitar, backing vocals; Mike Rutherford – bass guitar, bass pedals, cello, 12-string guitar, backing vocals; Phil Collins – drums, backing vocals, assorted percussion
All songs written by Genesis

Side 1
1. Watcher of the Skies 7:21
2. Time Table 4:47
3. Get 'Em Out by Friday 8:35
4. Can-Utility and the Coastliners 5:45

Entangled: Genesis on Record 1969-1976

Side 2
1. Horizons 1:39
2. Supper's Ready (a. Lover's Leap, b. The Guaranteed Eternal Sanctuary Man, c. Ikhnaton and Itsacon and Their Band of Merry Men, d. How Dare I Be So Beautiful?, e. Willow Farm, f. Apocalypse in 9/8 (Co-Starring the Delicious Talents of Gabble Ratchet), g. As Sure as Eggs Is Eggs (Aching Men's Feet) 22:57

Entangled: Genesis on Record 1969-1976

A *Foxtrot* Timeline

July 29, 1972. Tony Banks marries Mary McBain, however the happy couple resort to a one-day honeymoon so that Tony could get *Foxtrot* made.

August – September 1972. Following writing sessions through the summer, the band work at Island Studios in London, on tracks slated for their fourth album.

August 16, 1972 – February 25, 1973. The band execute mainland European and UK tour dates in support of *Foxtrot*.

September 15, 1972. That band issue their fourth album, entitled *Foxtrot*. The album reaches No.12 in the UK, staying on the charts for seven weeks.

February 1973. "Watcher of the Skies," backed with "Willow Farm," is issued as a single.

February 24, 25, 1973. Genesis play the dates that will appear on their inaugural live album.

March 1, 1973 – April 20, 1973. The band conduct a North American tour in support of *Foxtrot*.

July 20, 1973. Genesis see the release of *Live*, their first live album. The five tracks, with each over eight minutes long, chosen for the album are "Watcher of the Skies" and "Get 'Em Out by Friday" (both from *Foxtrot*), "The Musical Box" and "The Return of the Giant Hogweed" (both from *Nursery Cryme*) and "The Knife" (from *Trespass*). *Live* gets to No.9 in the UK but only manages a No.105 placement on the Billboard 200.

August 1973. The band work at Island Studios in London, with producer John Burns, on tracks slated for their fifth album.

August 24 – 26, 1973. Genesis appears at the Reading Festival.

genesis
see them at the
Oval concert
Sat 30th Sept.
midday-9p.m.
tickets: £1.00 in advance
£1.25 on day
also appearing: E.L.P., Wishbone Ash,
Argent & Focus
new album Foxtrot
CAS 1058
other Charisma goodies...
Dingley Dell.... Lindisfarne CAS 1057
Funny Game, Football.. The Group CS 4

Sundown
MILE END E.3
WEDNESDAY 6th DECEMBER
genesis
CAPABILITY BROWN
ALL TICKETS 50p
THE FAMOUS CHARISMA LABEL
FOXTROT
GENESIS
CAS 1058
Capability Brown
FROM SCRATCH
CAPABILITY BROWN
CAS 1056

Martin talks to Rand Kelly, Luis Nasser, Pete Pardo and Philip-Edward Phillis about *Foxtrot*.

Martin Popoff: So we arrive at *Foxtrot*, a record of which well over half—at least by song title—is top-shelf, classic Genesis. Does this view bear fruit, pointedly as we trawl through fully 23 minutes of "Supper's Ready?"

Pete Pardo: I think it'll be fine! (laughs). I mean, it's one of the greatest progressive rock albums of all time, in my opinion. But really, the whole evolution of Genesis started with the *Trespass* album. And with *Nursery Cryme*, you've got Collins and Hackett coming into the band and I think that rejuvenated these guys. They really became Genesis on this kind of trio of albums. With *Foxtrot*, I think the production is better. You've got Dave Hitchcock producing on *Foxtrot*. The album before it is not a great-sounding album, but the songs are really fantastic. I think *Nursery Cryme* was them really figuring it out and that all kind of came together on *Foxtrot*, for me. And then there's the fact that they were basically playing a bunch of these songs on the *Nursery Cryme* tour anyway, so they were kind of fine-tuning the songs out on the road before they actually went into the studio. So I think this album, it's got some classics, which we'll talk about, but first, it's a good-sounding record. It's one of those albums that's been with me for so long, I'm not even sure I can be objective anymore. It's a staple not only of the Genesis catalogue, but prog rock in general.

Martin: Are they a sort of honorary Canterbury prog band?

Pete: Well, I mean, no, not based on where they came from. And you've mentioned the whole folk thing and the English public school thing. They had that folk vibe, whereas the Canterbury bands came more from a kind of eclectic jazz background. So yeah, the concept is based on where you grew up in the UK as well. And then I'd say Genesis never really dabbled in jazz. They were more from a classical and folk background.

Rand Kelly: I think *Foxtrot* is magnificent. First time I heard it was at the record store where they sold eight-track tapes, at Tower. They had a vinyl store, and then next door they had the eight-track store.

This was 1973 in Sacramento. And I got to know these guys, because I went in there a lot and bought eight-tracks. I had an eight-track player in my house, my parents' house, and I had an eight-track player in my Ford Pinto too. What I would do is I would ask the guy there, "Do you have this album opened?" And they'd go, "Yeah, sure" and open it up right there and I'd go listen to it. You sit in a window and use their headphones. It's 105 degrees outside by the way. The window has no shade on it at all. So I'm sitting there in the window, baking my ass off listening to all of *Foxtrot* (laughs). I get through the whole thing and I'm going, "Nah, I can't get into this." It was a gradual coming-around. When I first heard "Watcher of the Skies" with that long Mellotron intro that Tony plays—by the way, this is a Mellotron, everybody (taps his Mellotron)—I was going, "When does this song start?"

So what happened was, lo and behold, somewhere they put out this album called *Rock Theatre* with a picture of Peter in the Slipperman costume on it, and it was a "best of" kind of thing. And they put a version of "Watcher of the Skies" on there that started out with just that percussive, full-band intro thing, a radio edit single version, which nobody ever played. And I thought well, that's pretty good.

So what happened was, I actually waited a while on the band and went over later on. You'd always go to the vinyl store because you can't get any information on the eight-track. So I go to the vinyl store and I picked up Genesis *Live* from the rack and, oh my God, what a cool-looking cover. I liked the dark blue and everything. There's that stupid thing that the singer had on his head and I read the story on the back and everything and I was going, this is really intriguing. I wonder if I should give these guys a shot again.

So I bought Genesis *Live* and I went, "I'm in!" (laughs). "I'm all-in!" So then I bought *Foxtrot* and I bought *Selling England by the Pound* and I went backwards and bought *Nursery Cryme* and *Trespass*. But we didn't have access to the first one. That started coming out later on, once everybody knew about the band. But it wasn't that cover. It's been repackaged more than any album I can think of. There's 50 different album covers at least for *From Genesis to Revelation* and it wasn't always called that either. The one that I ended up buying later on was the LP on London Records and it was called *In the Beginning* and it had this volcano on the front. Anyway, that's how I came to *Foxtrot*.

Martin: Nice; I always like to hear about the eight-track store! Luis, how about yourself? What do you think of *Foxtrot* first in a general sense?

Luis Nasser: Well, *Foxtrot* is a complicated, complicated album. I mean, people love *Nursery Cryme*, right? It has "The Musical Box," but it's also a little clunky. Whereas this particular record, I think, is where they really perfect their vision all the way through.

Martin: What kind of guitarist is Steve, what does he like to do more of or less of than other guitarists?

Luis: Well, Steve Hackett, first off, he is very good at playing arpeggios. Arpeggios is when you're playing, you know, notes in sequence in a chord instead of just strumming it. But then what he also does is he finds inversions. Inversions is basically, let's say you play an A minor chord. That is going to be an A, a C natural and an E above it. Those are the three basic notes of the chord. But if you play an E, a C and an A, that's an inversion. It's still an A minor, but the highest pitch is now the A, so it gives it a different character. And what Steve Hackett does a lot, first, is his arpeggio work, and then he finds really cool inversions of chords that then facilitate a melody. And they facilitate a particular drone as well. It's just really interesting.

The other thing he does a lot, which people at that time weren't doing, is he finds like angry, little note bursts. I don't know where he plucks these notes from, maybe out of thin air, but they're perfect. They're the exact right notes at the exact right times. Of course, everybody loves him for the long, weepy guitar solos. And that is a cliché of prog, right? In prog, the keyboards are blazing, and the guitars are expected to only play long, weepy guitar solos. Like, "Thou shalt not shred on the guitar." But Steve Hackett can shred; he can shred with the best of them. But sometimes you find that his playing is buried beneath three or four tracks of Tony Banks' keyboards.

Philip-Edward Phillis: Good stuff, yeah, and as Pete says, most people tend to frame *Foxtrot* as the album where everything falls into the right place. You feel that the musicianship is much more in place, pointedly because of how they gelled on the very successful tour that came right after *Nursery Cryme*. So yes, *Foxtrot* is justifiably termed as one of the classics of what back home in France we would call orthodox prog. Where I come from, we're pretty strict about the term prog, and see it as the combination of like, the classical form and jazz musicianship all in some kind of rock framework, with rock instruments.

What kind of prog album, then, is this? I would say like most of the albums of the early Steve Hackett era, it's very British. It's very much related to a particular British tradition that harks back to the Renaissance with John Dowland's music and madrigals, and even Shakespeare, to the present at the time—well, to their present—in the '70s with *Monty Python's Flying Circus* and a culture that is literary, cinematic, musical—everything.

And that's largely thanks to Peter Gabriel and his over-the-top personality, his insane creativity. The guy was very knowledgeable. You could tell that he read a lot of literature and poetry. He was also probably well versed in the universe of the so-called Ealing Studios, which was something like a smaller scale response in England to Hollywood, with films that were actually very funny and satirical, but maintaining a certain seriousness that we associate with British culture and a British kind of attitude. And all of that is very much present in *Foxtrot*.

Additional to that, you get whimsy, because Peter Gabriel is known for writing lyrics that are absolutely, at times, silly but at other times contain literary references that go from, I don't know, Shakespeare to Keats. And he's also perfected the art of punning, which you get on "Supper's Ready." Lots of insane punning.

Martin: What did you think of that album cover? What does it say to you?

Philip: Yeah, well, if you've studied a little bit of art history, you will possibly recognise the style of Giorgio de Chirico, the surrealist painter, who was always under the shadow of Dali, at least in the minds of most people. Paul Whitehead's painting has that kind of three-dimensionality that Chirico has as well in his paintings.

And when you look at this cover, first of all you have to look for all the Easter eggs. I mean, the cover and the inner sleeve, the whole thing, is replete with Easter eggs that go back to *Nursery Cryme*, with the game of croquet, which is now kind of in the background. And then if you read the lyrics, you can start to break down the cover and understand all of its references. Because on its own, it's quite bizarre.

You have the name *Foxtrot* so you see a fox, but since Gabriel is so topsy-turvy, so subversive and upside-down in his humour, he has dressed the fox in a red dress, which he himself then would wear on tour.

There are references to "Supper's Ready" with the four horsemen of the apocalypse, who are all wearing masks, some of which Gabriel would wear later. One of them is wearing a kind of mask that I think is a reference to Stanley Kubrick's *A Clockwork Orange* with the gang of droogs. And for a funny Easter egg, one of the horses actually has an erection. So there's a bit of taboo humour for you, at least on the back cover. And yeah, there are political references to England being in crisis at the time.

Rand: The original LP of that in America was not a gatefold. All you could see was the front cover and the back cover. And once I found the import and found out it opened up with that really nice gatefold, man, that was beautiful. I can picture it in my mind right now. It's like you're in a spaceship and there's this rainbow thing off to the side. All the lyrics are printed and everything. Oh, that was a religion for me. I got so into that album. I used to just lay on my bed and just read the lyrics for hours.

That's actually my favourite Genesis album cover of all time. You've got the fox figure wearing the red dress standing on an ice floe. There's a submarine and a whale in the water. And then on the back, you can see parts of *Nursery Cryme* where they're playing croquet. It's by Paul Whitehead, who provides great conceptual continuity, as Frank Zappa would say, by adding elements from the last album into this one. So when people are looking at it in the store, and it's sitting next to the *Nursery Cryme*, they can look at them and compare. Also, with these two albums, that's the only time that they used that logo, which I always thought looked cool and very early '70s They never used it again. They changed it for *Selling England by the Pound* and then *The Lamb Lies Down on Broadway* uses what they call the Egyptian font, which I like a lot as well.

Martin: What are your thoughts on the production, on this particular sound picture?

Rand: Yeah, they weren't happy with this production. Once people started talking about the band more regularly and they were doing interviews and stuff, poor David Hitchcock got thrown under the bus, a little bit, especially by Phil Collins. Phil seems to have a perfectionist quality about him that nobody else in the band really has, although Tony Banks is kind of like that. But Collins just said, well, the productions, they didn't sound very good. He would just say things like that: "Those early albums didn't really sound very good." They were happier with the albums that David Hentschel was producing because he had given them the crystal-clear quality that they were looking for. But I don't think *Foxtrot* sounds bad. Of course I've got remasters of it and stuff.

Pete: David Hitchcock had been around the band quite a bit and he'd work with other bands like Mellow Candle and Caravan, also East of Eden. There's a murkiness to *Nursery Cryme* that's not present on *Foxtrot*. It's a little brighter-sounding. I think also, the band is starting to utilise lots of different keyboards and guitars. In the mix, you hear the 12-string acoustics, you hear the six-string electric guitars, you hear the flutes. There's Hammond, there's Mellotron, there's piano, all this wonderful stuff, bass pedals, and it all really comes crystal-clear in the mix. Peter Gabriel's vocals are also recorded really well on this album, which is a challenge, because he's playing different parts and characters. It really shows off Peter as a storyteller. So I think David Hitchcock was the right guy for this time, even if it's going to be just the one album for him. But I think he managed to capture and translate this particularly artsy era of Genesis quite well.

Philip: *Foxtrot* is pretty much my favourite Genesis production, so I'd say David Hitchcock did great. It's heavy. You get a good sense of the bass and drums at the forefront. Everything is perfectly mixed together and I feel like there's a sense of tension. It's also cinematic; it feels very much like a soundtrack album. It's absolutely gorgeous, I think.

Martin: Okay, *Foxtrot* opens with a Genesis classic, "Watcher of the Skies," and I feel like it's so popular because once you hear it a few times, it's hard to get out of your head. Bottom line, it's memorable and hooky; at least the verse structure is. And its hooky from both a vocal melody standpoint as well as rhythmically.

Rand: I love it. I learned how to play—sort of—the intro and the outro. For a keyboard player who's never had a lesson, that's a really hard thing to play. Tony Banks came up with ideas that I would have never thought as a musician to even do. I mean, this is how innovative that is. But once they start doing that stuttery riff, it's almost like Morse code, isn't it? And it's in 6/4. I heard that and I was hooked.

It's my favourite song on the whole album. But I didn't like it at first. First time I heard it, I couldn't get into it because of the Mellotron chords. I remember thinking what the hell is this? Where's the band? Where's the beat? Why isn't something happening? But now it's like, oh my God, I wish I would have thought of that. Like I say, I learned how to play most of the beginning of that and those chords are not easy. Tony Banks is an absolute genius.

But yeah, it's a Mellotron and an organ kind of put together, I guess. The Mellotron has an organ sound in it; I know because I own one. You can set it up to play the strings and the organ at the same time, and that's what Tony did. Phil Collins and Mike Rutherford are so tight on the *Live* album version of this song, and that's the opening number. You've got to be really good to whack those kinds of notes out and not miss, because when you have all those different spaces in there, nobody can play in the wrong place. Otherwise, the audience would go, "Oh God, what did they do?" They're a machine on that song.

Luis: "Watcher of the Skies" is a ridiculous opener (laughs), at least as far as I was concerned, because it's the first time I heard Mellotron being used in that way. You know, you're using the tapes, as long as they will go. That's the thing here. We're gonna hold the chord until right before it restarts. right? Plus that whole intro has that 6/4 meter; it's not a 4/4 thing—it's 6/4.

And then on top of that, you get the maturity of what became the Genesis master class of songwriting. That is the thing with Genesis above all else. Everybody can play their instruments very well. But man, could they write. So you have that pedal point in the bass and the guitar, that F sharp (sings it). You have that going, and then you have all these chords moving on top of it. And then on top of that comes a vocal melody that presents a rhythmic counterpoint to that ostinato in the F sharps and all that.

It sucks you right in, in a way that other Genesis songs hadn't done for me up until that point. So when I first heard that song, I was instantly hooked. It's just a classic, right? It's not only a classic; it's a prog reference. In much the same way that Pete Townshend showed the world how to use a sequencer with *Who's Next*, Genesis is showing people how to use Mellotron in the context of prog rock. Amazing; such a great song. So overall, I will say this. From my own perspective, *Foxtrot* doesn't really have any weak tracks, but it's quite obvious front-loaded and back-loaded, because it begins with "Watcher of the Skies" and then it ends with "Supper's Ready."

Pete: If you talk about "Watcher of the Skies" from a live perspective, you've got Peter wearing the bat costume, right? That's one thing. But back to the record, those opening Mellotron chords are just so ominous and haunting. If you go read kind of the lore of the recording of this album, originally the producer, David Hitchcock, didn't even want to include that. And now you just can't imagine "Watcher of the Skies" without that drone.

The band bought the Mellotron from King Crimson, and they were highly influenced by King Crimson and I would argue that some of the best Mellotron sounds of this time period are on this album. They obviously learned their lesson from Crimson very well, because those first two or three King Crimson albums use Mellotron spectacularly. You've got this wonderful use of Hammond organ as well in this track. Tony Banks is just a master of the Hammond organ and piano and Mellotron early on, so there's all of that. And then he went wholesale into synths later on and became well-versed in that as well.

You get the weird lyrics, which are partly inspired from the Watcher character in Marvel Comics, the all-seeing guy that kind of transcends time and space and whatnot. Arthur C. Clarke's *Childhood's End* was also an inspiration. You've got big, fat bass lines and then angular guitar licks from Steve Hackett. That riff's got this kind of military-type thing going on, which is really interesting. And then there's Phil's nimble, skittery drumming all over the place.

I love the dramatic ending. I mean, the song itself is just so dramatic. Like so many prog classics, this song has this way of incorporating both drama and quirkiness, which is a hallmark of many of the British bands. And again, at the end, you've got Collins playing these rolling drum licks and there are these yearning cries from Hackett's guitar—it's just so awesome. "Watcher of the Skies" starts out dramatic and ends dramatic, and then there's all this cool stuff in between. So there's a structure and a terrific flow to it. Just a masterpiece of a song.

Philip: Well, "Watcher of the Skies" opens out of the gate with a polyrhythm. I don't know; it goes from 6/8 to 5/8. I mean, I'm a musician myself, but it's hard to break down. Whatever it is, it screams prog rock.

Martin: It's interesting. I was going to push back on your use of the term polyrhythm, but now that I think about it, as that verse kicks off, there's a different rhythm to the music in totality against Peter's vocal phrasing: those two elements together create a polyrhythm.

Philip: Yes, that's a good way of putting it. And the opening is a very difficult rhythm to execute. It was even difficult for them, apparently. And some Genesis scholars say that on the Genesis *Live* album that came right after this, that they were more in-the-pocket, so to speak. Which for me, it's never been an issue. I think there's a ton of groove on the studio version. Phil Collins was a genius at smoothing out difficult drum parts, translating them for easy listening by non-drummers. He could make, I don't know, smarty pants drumming sound groovy and even accessible. And that's very present here.

And I have to sing the praises of Steve Hackett, who in my opinion is under-rated as a guitar hero. He rarely plays particularly demanding guitar parts. What is demanding in him is his sound, the way he attacks the strings. For lack of a better word, it's his emotion, the feel he has when he hits certain notes. But he basically plays very nice melodies. Another thing, his arpeggiating passages are hard to play because he does those with finger-picking and not with a plectrum.

Martin: Things settle down for "Time Table." It's another one that adds to the idea that Genesis play a type of historic or timeless music, embracing traditions back through classical music and Renaissance music and the music and milieu even of medieval times.

Philip: Yes, agreed. In fact most of the early catalogue, all the way up to the end of the Steve Hackett era, supports that kind of reading. As Luis says, this album is bookended with "Watcher of the Skies" and "Supper's Ready" and we tend to ignore some of the more minor tunes due to the fact that they are mostly shorter. But shorter songs like "Time Table" can be more cohesive. It's lyrical and even has a bit of a pop hook to it. At the same time it has a classical music sensibility. You can tell that there's classical training within the band, certainly with Banks and to a lesser extent Hackett. But I just love the synergy between everyone, how no one overpowers anyone else. We see complaints later of Tony dominating the band, or with *Lamb*, where people complain about lyrics and vocals taking centre stage and the music coming secondary. But here there's perfect synergy.

Rand: And yet "Time Table" is considered not very popular with Genesis fans. I like it a lot. I don't think there's anything wrong with it. Again, it's one of those songs that doesn't change as far as the rhythm goes. It's very subtle. You don't even really need a drummer on that song. It's mostly piano-driven, and yet Peter Gabriel is so good on it. It's another song of theirs that questions war and why we're killing each other when we don't have to. Musically, I think it's very Baroque and there are actual vocal harmonies on it, done by Peter and Phil, I believe. It's fugue-like, with Tony playing two different kinds of lines on the piano. There's a lot of piano in that song. They're trying to sound classical on that song, just using traditional acoustic instruments, or at least leaving out the Mellotron. And Phil's drumming is very laid-back. I also found it interesting that they never say "time table" in the song.

Luis: It's not that I don't love "Time Table." It's just that what really stands out to me are those three songs, "Watcher of the Skies," "Get 'Em Out by Friday" and "Supper's Ready." Those are the super-powerful statements and the other songs are perfect inbetweeners.

Martin: I don't feel like Phil's anywhere near that iconic sound and style, yet, that would become his trademark. Not on this softer song or even any of the more active tracks.

Luis: Yes, but when you hear him play on that live album, he's starting to do that. He's starting to flow more, even when he's playing these songs. He was the new guy still. I think he always viewed it like that, when thinking about this era. Plus he came from a different social background; he wasn't that preppy. So it took him a while to feel comfortable enough to assert his musicality. But Phil Collins is just such a brilliant drummer and also, let's not forget his singing. It blends really well with Peter's. He's doing all these really high harmonies and he's nailing them. So that's a secret weapon that you almost never get from behind the kit. He was like the Michael Anthony of Genesis.

Pete: After "Watcher of the Skies," you can't plough ahead with something similar. So why not throw in a quirky, modest, British pop song? It's a lovely little tune, with a nice piano melody from Tony Banks. You've also got this charming little vocal from Peter that kind of floats over the top. Mike comes in with the bass and you've got these lush guitar textures from Hackett, while Collins keeps the drumming simple. It's just a pleasant British pop tune, but with a chorus that has some power and drama.

Also, when I listen back to "Time Table" all these years later, I can see where they would go on albums like *Duke* and the self-titled. Even though the band would change radically between those two albums arrangement-wise, there's a strong narrative of writing well-crafted pop like "Time Table." This song is a photograph or glimpse of where they would go.

Martin: Things pick up again for "Get 'Em Out by Friday." One the cool things about this is that Phil's doing an early version of the Purdy shuffle here, a.k.a. the Toto "Rosanna" beat. And there's almost like a regular version, a soft rock version and a double-time version.

Rand: Actually yeah, that's really cool. The first time I heard this song was the live version on Genesis *Live*. Peter does a way different version of that as far as when he says, "It's my sad duty to inform you of a four-foot restriction on humanoid height." On the studio album he sings "height" kind of low and sombre, in this character. But on the live album, he's much creepier and kind of howls it out. (laughs). And I remember thinking, wow, this cat is weird.

But yeah, strange tune. Lots of flute playing on it; there's harmony flute with Tony Banks' Mellotron set up like a flute, and so you have these two lines going together. The bass playing on this is just next level. Mike Rutherford is one of the greatest bass players I've ever heard. If anybody doubts how good this guy is, listen to "Get 'Em Out by Friday." This could have been a King Crimson song, because they go into these sections that were kind of being done by Crimson on the first album and *In the Wake of Poseidon* and actually *Lizard* too.

Martin: What do you like about Mike's bass playing?

Rand: Well, he plays these melodic lines, kind of like Chris Squire or John Entwistle. He's not afraid to explore the instrument. A lot of people, American bass players, for instance, used to be afraid to play high notes. They'd say, "Oh, the drummer will get lost if I play those high notes." People used to tell me that and I'd say, "Well, the instrument's designed to play. It's okay to play high frets." You heard Paul McCartney, John Entwistle and Chris Squire, and now all of a sudden Mike Rutherford, and he's just taking it to a different level, especially on *Lamb*. The bass playing on *Lamb* and *Selling England by the Pound* is just phenomenal. But it starts with "Watcher of the Skies" and really opens up on "Get 'Em Out by Friday" and also "Can-Utility and the Coastliners." He's so different from everybody else.

Martin: What's the story told in "Get 'Em Out by Friday?"

Rand: Well, it's about this lady, Mary and she gets a visit from this guy called the winkler, who says that we're going to buy this property up. But don't worry, we're going to set you guys up in a different place and you'll be fine. And then they come up with more and more reasons to screw them over. And then they tell them that they can't have a roof that's higher than four feet. And then he tells her husband what she did. And he goes, Oh Mary, what have you done, kind of thing. And, "We agreed to leave" and stuff like that. It just sounds like people who didn't stand up for their rights and put their foot down and say, hell no, we won't go. I think that's the message or moral of the story. It's kind of serious but comical at the same time. But if I was going to turn someone on to Genesis, I certainly wouldn't play "Get 'Em Out by Friday" as the first song they were going to hear.

Luis: I'm quite partial to "Get 'Em Out by Friday." It's an interesting, well-assembled tune that gets overlooked. It's basically in 6/8, at least at the beginning. It's in A sharp major. Or if you want to call it, you know, F sharp minor, which is basically the same thing. But to me, it sounds like A sharp major. And it has this really good bass line. And this may be just a coincidence, but the main rhythmic pattern of the bass happens to be exactly the same rhythmic pattern as the keyboards in The Who's "Love Reign O'er Me." (sings it) The bass plays that rhythm. And I know that Pete Townshend was very much into King Crimson, and Pink Floyd. He liked the prog rock as much as he would like to pretend, like all those guys did later, that they were not into prog at all. I think we both know that's just bullshit. They were totally into it, because they knew it was interesting to be doing new things in the rock format

But here's where we get into the difficulty of talking about Genesis songs. Because I can't tell you, well, it's a song in this key. Because they change keys all the time. Any given Genesis song is going to have no less than 11, 13 chords, right? But at the same time, it's an ear worm. And that's what's remarkable about them, and why I think of them as master song-crafters. They were able to come up with stuff that takes you through this crazy journey harmonically. They really do borrow that from classical music, the classical writers. Sometimes you'll see, oh, this is, whatever, in A flat, but then they modulate regularly; they change keys. And the further along you go from Mozart, the more people take these liberties. And these guys—we tend to forget this—these dudes are like, 22, 24, when they're coming up with this stuff. I can't say enough good things about how smart the songwriting is and how advanced they were.

But "Get 'Em Out by Friday," I would encourage anybody who is a musician to do this exercise. If you have a guitar or piano nearby, just try to follow along. And I'm not saying play everything, but just the basic chords, right? Like the campfire version of the song. Strum the chords to see what's happening. You're gonna find that the movement of the chords is really unexpected. There's a lot more to it than you ever imagined. And secondly, the way they connect a chord with the next one is always changing and is very, very smart. So again, something like "Time Table" is evidence that on *Foxtrot* they really caught lightning in a bottle, maybe for the first time. It has that vibe all through it.

Pete: We go from "Time Table," this atmospheric pop track, to 'Get "Em Out by Friday," which is quirky and fast-moving, with lyrics inspired by problems that Peter was having with his landlord at the time. This is paired with what was going on in the news about issues in this one neighbourhood near where they lived, where people were complaining about the landlords and the price of rent, and the utilities and all that sort of stuff. So "Get 'Em Out by Friday" is about dealing with that, you know, when the rent is due and how much you're paying, and why is it going up? All that sort of thing. And if you can't pay it, you gotta get out by Friday. Peter Gabriel really becomes the master storyteller here. He's using different voices for different characters. He's portraying the crazy, cranky landlord. He's portraying the guy who can barely come up with the money.

Musically, you've got these kind of weaving Hammond organ passages. You've got the busy bass from Michael and then Collins' really cool drum grooves. Steve Hackett does this really noisy, kind of overdriven solo in the middle of it all. And then that just stops in typical Genesis fashion—nothing ever lasts too long—and all of a sudden, you've got this quieter section with Peter's flute. Again, there's that deft use of light and shade. When Rutherford and Collins kind of pop back in, it's got this complex groove where the full band comes back and takes you to the end of the song. Again, it's the peaks and valleys thing, the light and shade, never settling into a groove for too long. Which leads you to wonder, if you were part of the recording process, were some of these parts shorter pieces that were then stitched together?

Philip: Yeah, again, odd to say, but when I listen to this, I can see the influence Genesis had on heavy metal artists, or certainly progressive metal artist, even Iron Maiden. I hear galloping rhythm, the fast-paced, staccato rhythm and then the amazing musicianship on top of that. But I like that right out of the gate you get that galloping aggression. It feels to me like a vision of the future and like I say, even though it's not particularly heavy, I see this as part of the DNA of some of the more adventurous heavy metal from years later.

Martin: Next is "Can-Utility and the Coastliners," which musically and even lyrically is more traditional than its disorienting title. I think that title does this song a disservice.

Rand: Yeah, that has something to do with some king. But somebody sure was reading a lot of literature to come up with these fanciful ideas. That title sounds like the name of a '50s band. I remember thinking, what the heck is that? But when I listened to it, all I thought was, holy crap, this song is really cool. But yeah, it's inspired by King Canute, from the 1000s, King of England and Denmark. It's not from the Bible. The song describes what happened on the beach, scattered pages of a book by the sea and all that. If you don't know the story, it probably doesn't make sense. But musically, that song has a lot going for it. They get into this long jam, where they just stay in the key of D minor. For like, quite long, actually. Maybe they just thought, well, this is fun; let's just do this. Or they ran out of ideas and thought, let's just stay in D minor. We'll just jam and everybody can take a solo or something.

Pete: As far as the lyrics go, apparently it's based on King Canute. I don't know who the hell King Canute is. But apparently it's all about the coming storms and tides and how the king is just doing everything he can to save his community from the devastation of all these tides and stuff coming in. Really nice song, wonderful use of 12-string acoustic guitars here from Rutherford and Hackett and I think Banks as well. And that goes back to what we talked about earlier, Martin, about this whole folk thing. Genesis really had a firm grasp on layering a lot of their songs early on with these types of elements.

So you've got all these really lush 12-string guitars, and then the Mellotron comes in at like the two-minute mark, just absolutely splendid. It's dramatic but dreamy and textured at the same time. Again, the influence of King Crimson looms large. Collins is tight and in-the-pocket, and then you've got this amazing organ solo from Tony Banks, which is a thing of beauty. And then once that's done, you've got Hackett coming in with this typical, looping, oddball electric guitar solo. And then here comes the vocals again, because there's always these lengthy instrumental passages, even if the parts segue into each other nicely. It's not like one guy sits and solos for two minutes. You've got this blending of different players playing these little pieces, which I think is really cool. And then there's a big crescendo at the end of the song. After Gabriel comes back, you've got Hackett's guitar and Banks' Hammond closing things out with this big crescendo.

Philip: A lot of time goes by and you get used to listening only to "Watcher of the Skies" and "Supper's Ready," especially with the recent Steve Hackett Genesis Revisited touring, where he revisits more or less those two tunes. But "Can-Utility" is another example of a tune with lovely pop hooks and great musicianship, but it's not tiring. It's not exhausting. You think of bands like Gentle Giant who have short tunes, but love dissonance and jazz influences. This is not that. "Can-Utility" is friendly to the ears, not only because it's shorter, but because it's actually accessible, despite it being what today we call prog.

Martin: All right, over to side two and we have "Horizons," which is the type of thing Steve is going to be known for on his solo albums one day. It's positioned just before "Supper's Ready" but it wasn't written with that in mind.

Pete: Yeah, "Horizons" is beautiful. That's basically Hackett inspired by Bach and creating a classical guitar, acoustic guitar piece. It's just lovely. It's interesting; early on he got more credit for his acoustic and classical work than he did for his electric work. Nowadays, people look at him and think what an amazing electric guitar player he is, in addition. It's cool how this is just kind of thrown in there. I don't even think he expected it to make the album. But he brought it to the table and the band said it would work as an intro to the big epic. It's warm and inviting and yet haunting, or at least sort of foreboding and historical, and it leads to "Supper's Ready" just absolutely perfectly.

Philip: Yeah, he's basically riffing on Johann Sebastian Bach, essentially, creating an interlude. It's Steve showing off his classical training. It's a nice little break before you get to the massive epic.

Martin: Okay, so the rest of the side—long in itself for a side of vinyl at 23 minutes—is "Supper's Ready." Take us through this one.

Rand: Well, it's a trip, just with all the subtitles. It starts with "Lover's Leap" and then it goes into this piece, that piece and then another piece! Part e., "Willow Farm," is completely different from anything else on the album. And then they work themselves into "Apocalypse in 9/8," which is probably my favourite part of the whole piece. That's incredible. That "666 is no longer alone," that'll give you shivers up your spine (laughs). What a great way to end an album. I mean, I have no problem with *Foxtrot*. It's an amazing record, and "Supper's Ready" is a big part of its success.

Martin: As a keyboardist and synth guy yourself, what are your favourite bits?

Rand: Oh, "Apocalypse in 9/8" for sure. Tony Banks, he's the Hammond organ god on that song. He gets a tone out of it there that almost sounds like a flute. You know, there's ways to do Hammond organs. I own one. Actually, I have a portable one that works really good. It's a Hammond but Tony's using different kinds of Hammond than most of the bands. A lot of the rock bands, the blues bands used a B3. But Tony has an L series. And it's got actual presets where you can push these little tabs down. They've got little white tabs on them and you can push these things down and get different combinations. Well, he gets a sort of high-pitched flute sound on "Apocalypse in 9/8."

And the thing is, you don't know where he's gonna go with it. It just builds and builds and builds and gets so intense. Like I say, my favourite part is when Peter goes, "666 is no longer alone/He's getting out the marrow in your backbone." I get chills to this day just hearing that. I can hear it in my brain right now. The hairs on my arms are standing up—it never fails. But the best line in the whole song for me is, "There's an angel standing in the sun/And he's crying with a loud voice/'This is the supper of the mighty one.'" I feel like my whole body floating off the bed when I hear that.

But the path to get there actually starts with that separate opening piece, "Horizons." A lot of people forget this. They always say "side-long epic" bit it's not. You've got "Horizons" with Steve Hackett playing guitar, which sets you up for "Lover's Leap." It's so gentle and so mellow and then so is "Lover's Leap."

To put it very factually, "Supper's Ready" is like seven or eight songs that are hooked together. It's like the second side of *Abbey Road*. Starting with, "You never give me your money." So anyways, "Lover's Leap," beautiful song, not sure what it's about but it's talking about turning off the TV and being with your girlfriend and everything like that and seeing what's going on outside.

And then all of a sudden you're in this battle, and that whole "Itsacon" idea, it's not real, as in "it's a con." But in general, Peter's essentially riffing on the Book of Revelation. But it feels like another song where the underlying message is condemnation of war. It's heavy, it's light, there's battling, there's "Bang, bang, bang" and then they put down Winston Churchill.

It's a really weird song. If you were going to pluck a single from "Supper's Ready," "Willow Farm" would be the only thing you could release because it's an actual full song. Everything else on "Supper's Ready" is not an actual full song. It's like John Lennon complaining about *Abbey Road*. He said those songs aren't finished. We just hooked them together to make one big song. And that's basically what Genesis did with "Supper's Ready." But yeah, "Willow Farm" is an actual full song.

Martin: And what can you tell me about "Willow Farm?"

Rand: I love the Mellotron in the background on there, and also what Steve Hackett plays is really nice. There's a lot of discipline attached to that song. For example, there's no guitar solo. It's organ and Mellotron that really propel that song. And then when they work their way down into "Apocalypse in 9/8," it's roller coaster heaven from there.

Martin: What can you recall about the closing "As Sure as Eggs Is Eggs (Aching Men's Feet)" section?

Rand: Well, I've only seen pictures of this because there's no actual video—nobody filmed it. After the "Apocalypse in 9/8" song and all that, Peter would come out of the ceiling on these suspended cables. He was barefoot and he looked like Jesus coming out of the clouds, and then he would land on the stage singing that last bit, around that "I've been so far from here/Far from your loving arms" section. It's very biblical but there's no mention of Jesus. But Peter sings that part and then these big flash pots go off. It's very visual. I should clarify that there's video of this song, but none of him descending from the ceiling. He's always just already standing on the stage. They don't show him coming in. What I think is that the rig might have screwed up and never worked and they just said, "Well screw that; we're not doing that anymore."

One last thing I wanted to say about "Apocalypse in 9/8." Mike Rutherford. doesn't play bass guitar on that. He's playing bass pedals, bass organ pedals. And just one note, E. But what's weird is that it's in 9/8, of course, so it's timed 1,2,3,4,5,6,7,8,9, like that. But on the bass pedals, he's doing 1,2,3,1,2,1, repeating that, 1,2,3,1,2,1. He does that through the entire song. And to do that on stage?! Man, that takes discipline. With your foot?! Are you kidding me?! And at that point, he's probably holding a 12-string guitar and sitting in a chair. But yeah, mapping that 1,2,3,1,2,1 to nine beats... that's absolutely brilliant.

Luis: I know a lot of the prog people are not gonna like me much for saying this, but I feel like it's my duty to be honest. A lot of prog fans like to say that they're very open-minded, and that they're forward-thinking. The reality couldn't be further from the truth. Prog rock fans are incredibly conservative. And they like what they like. It's like the Genesis song from *Selling England by the Pound*, "I Know What I Like (In Your Wardrobe)." They know what they like. You can't really push them very far away.

So "Supper's Ready" is an astonishing accomplishment to me, but it's been kind of ruined by the fact that it's become the "Free Bird" of prog, the song that everybody talks about and the song that everybody wants you to play. It's the song that everybody who's a fan grabs a guitar and attempts to play at the after-hours party of any prog festival. It's become overplayed. So I try to avoid people who are so into it because I still want to be able to hear it and enjoy it.

But "Apocalypse" is a nice section. That is a very interesting thing. You're a drummer, Martin; this is a good example of one of the things that these guys can do very well. Everything is structured in such a way that the complexity is not apparent, right? But when you hit "Apocalypse in 9/8," you better have blinders on if you're trying to play your part for that. You cannot listen to the other guys. Which is very counterintuitive, because the whole point of music is that we're listening to each other and having a conversation, right?

No, in this particular case, it has been composed and you will do this thing and this thing alone. And the commandment is "Thou shalt not fuck it up." Because if you do, then the whole thing falls apart, right? So if you play that, you have to be in the zone, and you just play your part. To me, that is the format that eventually led to bands like Meshuggah—just take that and play this thing and this thing only. But with them, now we're gonna do it for the whole song and not just a little section. So to me, they even foreshadow Meshuggah, in a way, with that little bit.

And I love the lyrics as well. I'm not gonna sit here and tell you that I really understand them. I think Peter Gabriel was being a bit too playful. He was mixing in maybe too many references. But again, these guys were in their early 20s. So absolutely I give my respect to them—they just kicked ass.

It takes us through all these all these sequences, right? If you were to summarise it, it's two lovers who go on an extended trip. And the tongue-in-cheek thing is that this trip clearly involves a lot of heavy drugs. I guess you could summarise it like that. You might say, well, but why is that interesting? Listen to what they did. Listen to how interesting they made that trip. And the other thing—and I think we should be clear about this—this is not a song you can play while you're high, right? You absolutely cannot. So to me, Genesis are the ultimate prog nerds and are the beginning of that and I love them for it.

Pete: Yeah, this is one of the great prog epics of all time, 23 minutes of bliss. Whether you like this or you like "2112" or you like "Close to the Edge," any other prog epic, it's definitely got to be up there when you rank or debate songs like this. Seven parts to the song. Again, you've got more of those gorgeous 12-string guitars leading in. You've got Tony's really cool electric piano and then the Hammond. And that all kind of leads into these different parts. It's another perfect example of a band writing all these separate little pieces, and then in the studio, kind of weaving them all together. In the end, it totally makes sense.

But each part has a different flavour. So you've got that opening section and that leads into "The Guaranteed Eternal Sanctuary Man," which is one of my favourites of the whole thing. I mean, that Hammond organ just sounds so haunting. You've got Hackett's cool, little volume swells on the guitar and then Gabriel comes in and he's doing all these little cool parts. You've got some flute, then more organ, and then the band of merry men moves into battle, right? Which is really cool—"Bang, bang, bang." More organ, the military drum beats... you get this great solo from Hackett, it's just looping and stabbing and just so weird-sounding but it totally sounds like it belongs here.

And man, his tone is so good. He's got this kind of weird, fuzzy, distorted tone but it's not too, too much. It's just enough that it cuts right through the mix. And then you've got this thing that he does with Banks. You've got Banks playing the organ, and Steve's doing this really early tapping stuff. Like years before Eddie Van Halen. Nobody ever talked about it back in the day, but now all these years later it's like, that's kind of where that all started from. And Steve probably didn't think twice about it. It was just another way to get a cool sound on a guitar, and he was the king at that.

And then you've got "How Dare I Be So Beautiful?" leading into "Willow Farm," you know, butterflies, foxes, musical boxes, all this kind of weird, witty, lyrical stuff going on. He talks about Winston Churchill, you know, entering the story here. It's all very British and quirky, and that's what makes it unique. You had a lot of British bands at the time doing this progressive rock thing, but Genesis always sounded the most British. Yes never really had a British sound and nor did Gentle Giant. And I know you always like to say that King Crimson was a Krautrock band and I can hear that too.

You've got flutes and acoustic guitars and then the big "Apocalypse in 9/8," where it gets really serious. You've got Collins and Rutherford driving the beat and that wonderful, ascending organ solo from Banks, which goes higher and higher and on and on and on. And flute comes in, with Mellotron in the background, and then you know, Gabriel comes back in with the "666" and the whole story of good triumphing over evil, the whole "Take us to Jerusalem" thing.

Now, all of a sudden, it's quite religious and whatnot. But it's such a wonderful crescendo. And then Hackett's little solo at the end kind of takes you out. By the time you're done, you just kind of take a breath, like, wow, that was quite the ride, right? And can I do it all over again? So yeah, it's just a masterpiece of a song. But again, what they must have done in the studio to put this all together from pieces, I can only imagine. I sometimes stop to think what it would have been like to be a fly on the wall to see a track like this, or "Close to the Edge" by Yes, put together in the studio? Because it couldn't have been easy. It must have been a lot of work between the arranging and the production to kind of weave all these little sections together. But it all makes sense. It just becomes like an admirable seamless listen.

Philip: I recall at first thinking, what the hell is this title "Supper's Ready?" I was not yet familiar with the universe of Gabriel, who tends to hark back to certain British traditions like Gilbert and Sullivan. I actually recently taught an English class and I did something on Gilbert and Sullivan. And I discovered for myself that there's a lot of this kind of topsy-turvy, subversive humour that tends to look a bit silly, but actually, it's quite serious. As well, it's a great example of Peter Gabriel doing what many British thinkers, writers and artists do, which is to take the piss, as the Brits say, but also to find an artistic and literary core in what he does. You've got to marvel at the theatricality of Gabriel.

As for the music, it's a journey. I want to listen to it from beginning to end, with all of its various passages, because it sticks perfectly together. You've got "Lovers Leap" and "Ikhnaton and Itsacon and Their Band of Merry Men" etc., but you don't feel that there are gaps between each passage. Like Pete says, everything flows seamlessly from one to the next.

You know, I talk about British traditions, but specifically this is actually based more on the traditions of Gabriel Garcia Marquez and Borges, the two most important literary figures in what we call magical realism, which is a form of surrealism where the idea of reality is invaded by elements that are… not science fiction, but just unrealistic and totally break from any kind of logic. It also leans a bit toward Samuel Beckett and the theatre of the absurd and all that. I find all of that in here. As for the story, it's two lovers who go through a great adventure and learn about good and evil. In the process, they encounter many bizarre situations and figures. They even encounter bloody war, and ultimately, they come out of that and find a new Jerusalem. You just have to appreciate the sheer absurdity and also the genius of this absurdity.

Martin: Sweet. And so in summary, as we leave the album as a whole, what are your closing impressions?

Philip: Well, despite the complexity both philosophically and musically, I find that Genesis' songwriting style ultimately was quite user-friendly. Yes, for instance, or Gentle Giant or King Crimson, tend to be difficult for average listeners. But you already find a lot of the pop Genesis in their prog phase; it's built-in, even going back to *From Genesis to Revelation*, really. And that blends well with all the classical music references, which are also comfortable and familiar, to European listeners, certainly, with the references to Renaissance-era Britian, John Dowland, whatever. Put that into rock form and Genesis could—and do—become hugely popular. I mean, they actually got into the UK Top Ten with *Selling England by the Pound*, all the way to No.3, so there you go.

Luis: Remarking on this side of the band's British-ness, I'd say that Jethro Tull kind of competes on their level, also through that approach to self-deprecating humour that British people love so much. But Jethro Tull is not viewed with the same reverence as Genesis because they never really use those grandiose keyboards.
    I mean, Banks, to me, if I had to nitpick—and I've always said this—the great shame of *Foxtrot* is how under-mixed Steve Hackett is. And I never really realised that until I got a chance to see Steve Hackett play all of *Foxtrot* live and I heard his guitar work in the proper context. There are a lot of interesting things that he's doing that Tony Banks is just not letting you hear. And that's a shame because the guitar is just so creative and so vital across *Foxtrot*, and in "Supper's Ready" in particular, but it's under-represented in the mix. Once you get the chance to see Steve Hackett play these songs live, it's not that the guitars thunder and drown out everything. No, it's just that the ecosystem is better represented, or at least the ecosystem the way Hackett would have preferred it originally.

Pete: For a final thought, I'd like to circle back to the folk aspect of the band. I'm a big horror movie fan, and I love folk horror, which deals a lot with mythology and religion. And there's a lot of that going on in some of these early Genesis lyrics. It may not make sense to a lot of people, but I think it makes more sense when you think about the type of music that they're playing. Peter's definitely a storyteller and his lightly horrific sort of folk tales marry up perfectly with the kind of acoustic and electric neo-folk that Genesis are proposing.

So most of this stuff is very fantastic, other than a song like "Get 'Em Out by Friday," which is based on real shit happening. The rest of it is fantasy mixed up with science fiction and religion and other weird themes. For the common person reading these lyrics, you're probably like, what the hell are they talking about here? But to people who want something more obscure and opaque, more abstract and maybe more thought-provoking, I mean, Genesis deliver that. And then they put it on top of music that is really, when you break it down, pretty sympathetic and easy on the ear.

Rand: Except there's nothing on *Foxtrot* that's commercial in the traditional sense—nothing. That's the thing. It's so inviting and melodic and yet strange at the same time. Remember, the term progressive rock hadn't even been invented yet. Back in those days, Martin, it was just music and you liked it or you didn't. I'd go into the store and go from A to Z and whatever suits my fancy I'm walking out with it. You had no way of knowing what you were getting. We'd get together and listen to these records and go, "Oh, wow, that band, they sound awesome." You know, they're doing this. And then you'd put on Alice Cooper and you're looking at Alice Cooper doing *this*. And then Uriah Heep was doing *this*. That's how it went. There were no categories yet.

Entangled: Genesis on Record 1969-1976

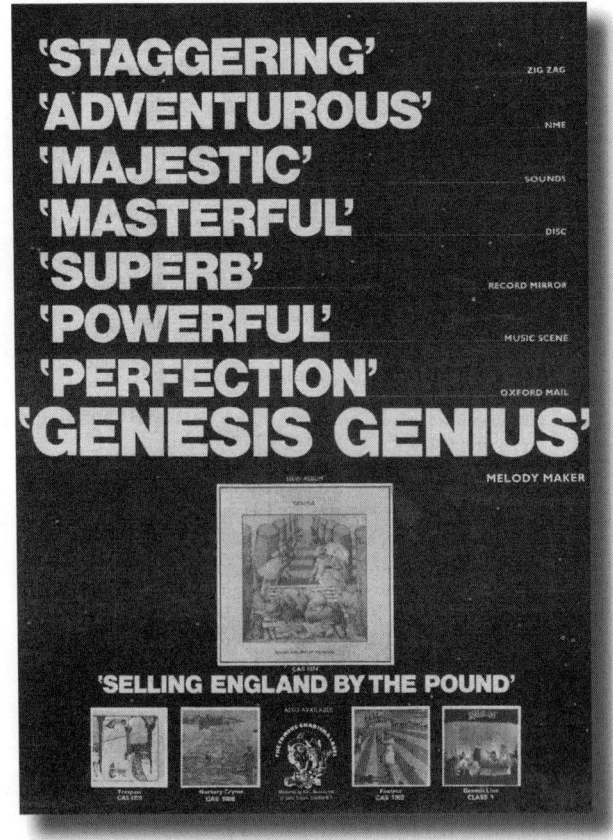

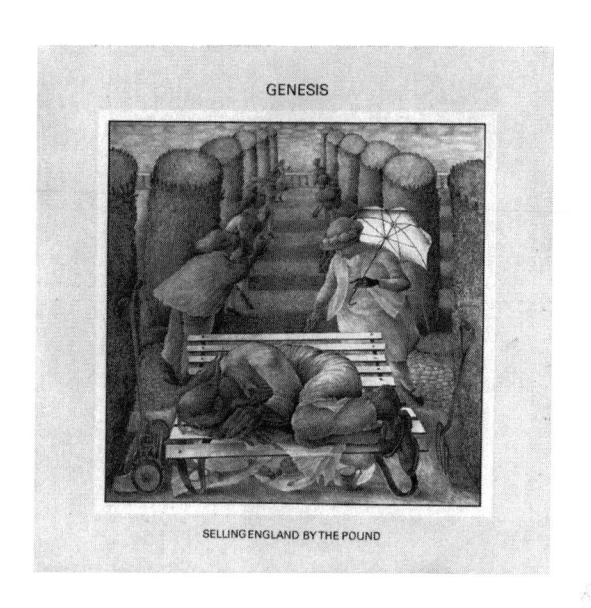

SELLING ENGLAND BY THE POUND

September 28, 1973
Charisma CAS 1074
Produced by John Burns and Genesis
Engineered by John Burns; assisted by Rhett Davis
Recorded at Island Studios, London, UK
Personnel: Peter Gabriel – vocals, flute, oboe, percussion; Steve Hackett – electric guitar, nylon guitar; Tony Banks – Hammond organ, Mellotron, Hohner Pianet, ARP Pro Soloist, piano, 12-string guitar; Mike Rutherford – 12-string guitar, bass, electric sitar, cello; Phil Collins – drums, percussion, lead vocals on "More Fool Me," backing vocals
All songs written by Genesis

Side 1
1. Dancing with the Moonlit Knight 8:02
2. I Know What I Like (In Your Wardrobe) 4:03
3. Firth of Fifth 9:36
4. More Fool Me 3:10

Entangled: Genesis on Record 1969-1976

Side 2
1. The Battle of Epping Forest 11:43
2. After the Ordeal 4:07
3. The Cinema Show 11:06
4. Aisle of Plenty 1:33

Entangled: Genesis on Record 1969-1976

126

A *Selling England by the Pound* Timeline

September 9 – October 28, 1973. The band conduct European (and mostly UK) tour dates supporting *Selling England by the Pound*.

September 28, 1973. Genesis and Charisma see the release of the band's fifth album, *Selling England by the Pound*. It reaches No.70 on the Billboard charts and No.3 in the UK and eventually certifies gold in both territories, as well as gold in France and platinum in Canada.

November 7 – December 19, 1973. The band play shows in Canada and the US in support of their fifth album. Included is a six-night stand at the Roxy in Los Angeles and an appearance on *The Midnight Special*.

January 13 – March 1, 1974. The band play the UK and mainland Europe.

February 1974. "I Know What I Like (In Your Wardrobe)," backed with "Twilight Alehouse," is issued as a single.

March 3 – May 6, 1974. The band return for a second tour leg of North America.

Entangled: Genesis on Record 1969-1976

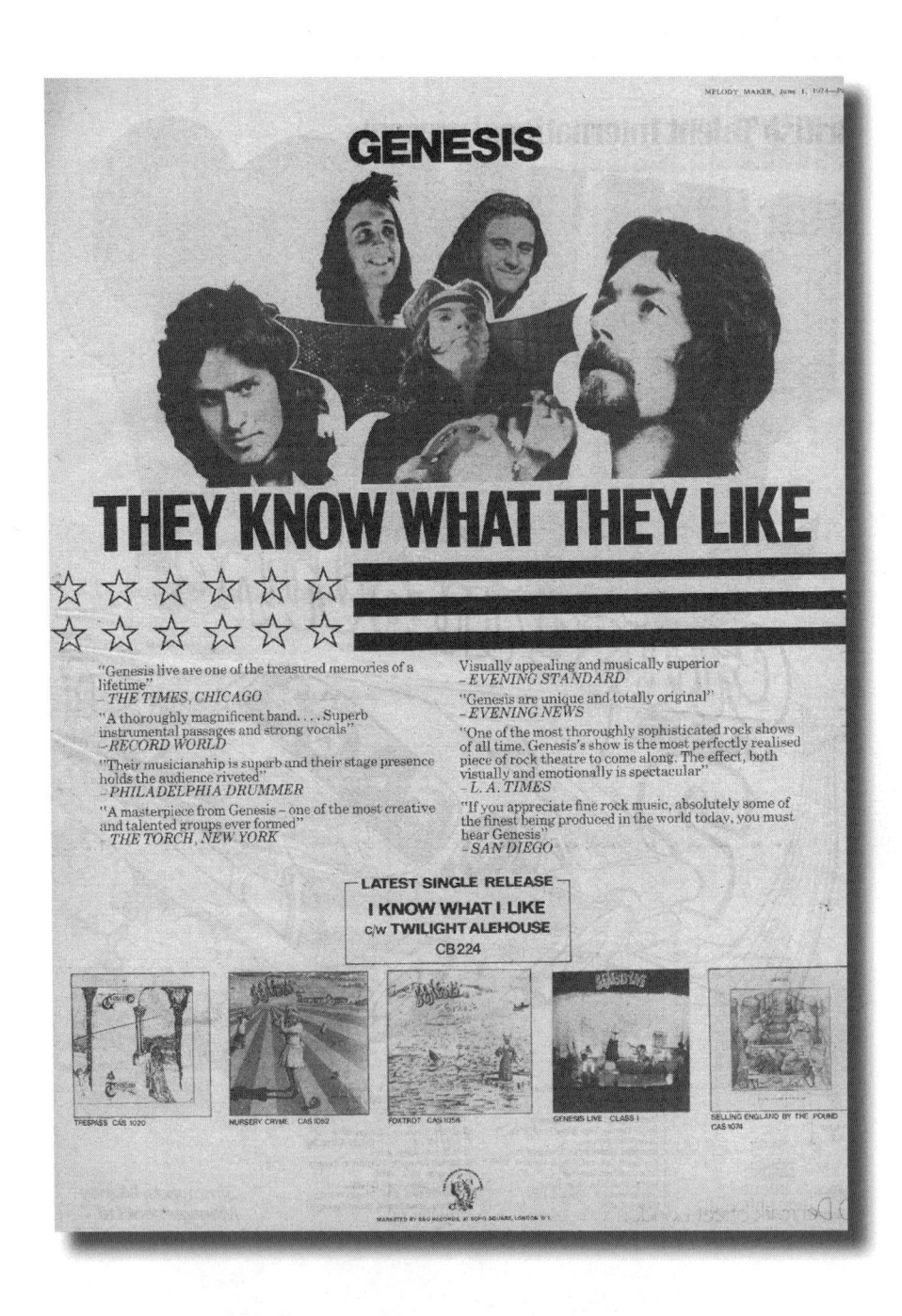

The rest of the band considered Anthony Phillips critical to the lineup, but after two albums, his stage fright got the better of him and he quit, initially leaving Genesis pondering its future. (courtesy of Alan Hewitt)

The debut album, *From Genesis to Revelation*, made little impact. But due to the band's later success, it was regularly re-released, sometimes with very unusual cover designs such as this UK version from 1974.

January 24, 1971, at the Lyceum in London. One of the earliest gigs to feature Phillips' replacement Steve Hackett. *(Colin McLeod)*

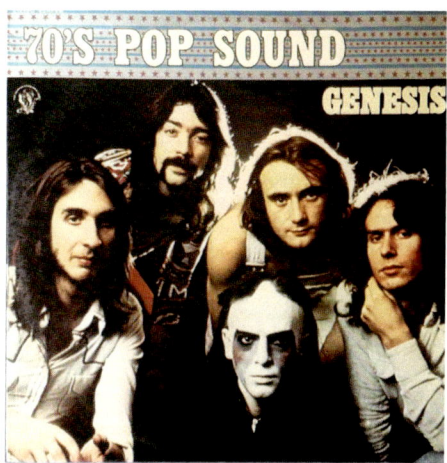

"I Know What I Like (In Your Wardrobe)," October 15, 1973, at the Dome, Brighton, UK. Gabriel's performances became increasingly theatrical. *(Richard Haines)*

Charisma in Spain released this compilation in 1973, comprised of tracks from *Trespass*, *Nursery Cryme* and *Foxtrot*.

Mike Rutherford at Headley Grange, July 1974, during the making of *The Lamb Lies Down on Broadway*. (Richard Haines)

Peter Gabriel at Headley Grange, July 1974, during the making of *The Lamb Lies Down on Broadway*. (Richard Haines)

Phil Collins at the same rehearsal sessions as previous, preparing to construct what would become the band's only double album.
(Richard Haines)

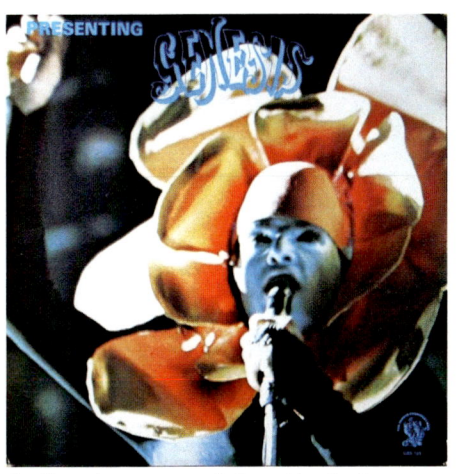

Another obscure compilation of tracks from *Trespass*, *Nursery Cryme* and *Foxtrot*, this time from Canada.

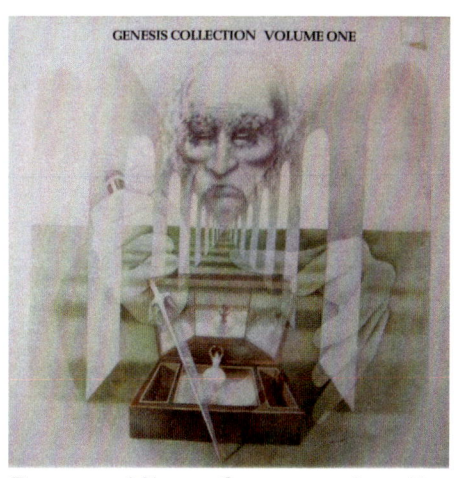

Trespass and *Nursery Cryme* were reissued in the UK in a box set with a poster in 1975, just prior to Gabriel's departure.

GENESIS

And then there were four. *(Atco Records promo photo)*

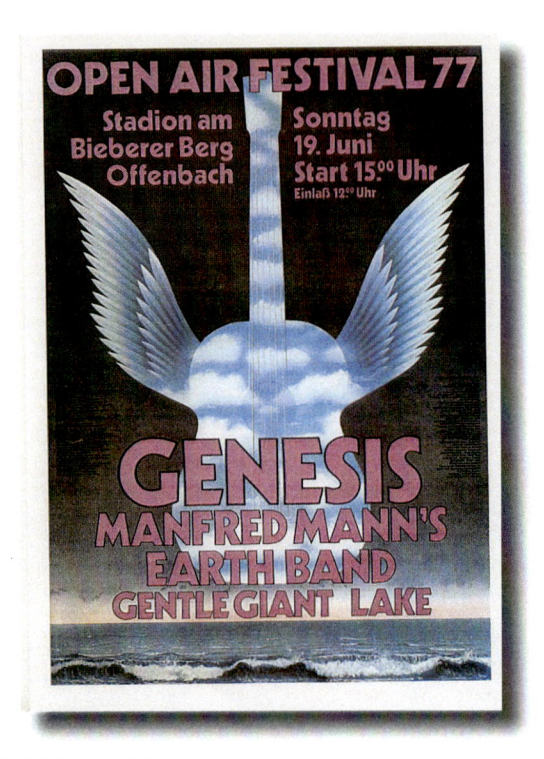

STEVE HACKETT · TONY BANKS · CHESTER THOMPSON · MIKE RUTHERFORD · PHIL COLLINS

GENESIS

After one tour with Bill Bruford, ex-Zappa drummer Chester Thompson was added to the touring lineup, as captured on the live album *Seconds Out*. (Atco Records promo photo)

Martin talks to Phil Aston, David Gallagher and Philip-Edward Phillis about *Selling England by the Pound.*

Martin Popoff: All right, fifth album in five years, first with producer John Burns... what are your general impressions, first off, of *Selling England by the Pound*?

Phil Aston: Yes, it's 1973 and if I may, let me begin with a personal perspective. If you just dial it back and think about how Genesis fits into this term, progressive rock, at the time this came out, I was 14, 15 years of age. So I was coming out of Slade, T. Rex, getting my apprenticeship in Sabbath and Purple, you know, moving around, and there was this other music that was called progressive rock. But even before heavy metal was termed as a label, bands like Deep Purple and Rory Gallagher, with Taste, were seen as progressive.

But the difference with Genesis is that this form of progressive music was not driven by guitars. I always felt there was Yes in the middle of the dial, and then on the one side of the dial was like Van der Graaf Generator, Gentle Giant, King Crimson, the real kind of prog, and on the other side of the dial, as far as you could take it, was Pink Floyd, who were releasing *Dark Side of the Moon* at the same time as this album.

And really, if you take a few steps back, *Dark Side of the Moon* is actually full of pop songs. They're not prog; they're commercial, they've got choruses and very nice melodic hooks. So I always saw *Dark Side of the Moon* as more pop. I know that now it's seen as very different from that, but it's very much pop when you compare it with *Close to the Edge* or Van der Graaf Generator, who are also far off towards the left-hand side. And Genesis, I felt, were always right at the other side of the dial next to Pink Floyd, and maybe Barclay James Harvest and The Moody Blues. But this album, I think it still sounds fantastic.

Martin: And with *Selling England by the Pound*, do they maintain this reputation as exceedingly British? Maybe the most British of the prog bands?

Phil: I think so. They are still quite pastoral. It always comes down to the keyboards. It's always Mellotron, Hammond, probably a sprinkling of flute, you know, soft instrumental passages, not necessarily aggressive time changes, but just something that gives the music room to breathe. There isn't a feeling of like, well, we've come 'round now in this melodic circle and we're working on that chord sequence and so now we'll go somewhere else. Genesis more so just drift from section to section (laughs). And I think this is the first Genesis album that had this sound. It's the entry point, for a lot of people, for Genesis. A lot of the albums that came before this, I feel were accessible, but it was more of a closed club. It was more difficult. *Selling England by the Pound* opened it up, I think, because of the way it sounds.

Martin: They're never going to scare you, kind of thing, right? They're not loud and the melodies are pretty.

Phil: That's right. Yeah, the loudest parts are literally Tony Banks coming up with a more synth-based solo. That's as aggressive as it's gonna get. And you know that pretty soon he's going to pull back again. But Phil Collins is about to move into more of a jazz rock feel with things like *A Trick of the Tail*. But here they're just coming together. This is why *Selling England by the Pound* is seen as the definitive Genesis album in many circles, isn't it?

Martin: Although to push back, we're somewhat established at this point.

David Gallagher: Yes, and to give a rather glib answer, we've obviously got a couple of quote unquote "real" Genesis albums behind us, with *Foxtrot* and *Nursery Cryme*.

Martin: And how do you rate *Trespass*?

David: Reasonably highly. I don't think there's a clanger amongst the classic Gabriels. And the fact that I refer to them as the classic Gabriels probably tips my hat in what direction I'm leaning in terms of the question. It's varying degrees of what I'm in the mood for that day. I wouldn't put *The Lamb* on for a quick and easy listen, for example. But I think *Trespass* is an excellent record with a couple of peaks and a couple of valleys but generally speaking overall, it's a wonderful record. I don't think they've got an album from start to finish that's perfect. I don't think they've got a total stone-cold brilliant start-to-finish record. Which isn't to say the albums themselves can't be brilliant. But I don't think each constituent part, taken apart—which they're supposed to be; it's an album—is always perfect.

Martin: Speaking of pastoral, it doesn't get more horticultural than this album cover, although there's obviously a statement about societal shortfalls in and amongst the hedges.

Phil: Yes, at the time, we were just joining Europe, in the UK, back then. We were having power cuts, we had an oil shortage, there was a lot going on. The political scene in the UK at the time was pretty dire. But for us as teenagers, that went straight over our heads. I think part of what they were getting at with that title is that the tax for musicians who started to become successful was a pain, literally like 90 pence to the pound here in the UK. So I guess that was partially a dig at what it was like being in the UK at the time.

Martin: So this was when the UK joined the European Economic Community, the forerunner of the European Union?

Phil: Yes, a lot that discussion was going around at that time, and the UK joined on its third application in 1973. And around 1972, '73, we were having like a three-day week, because of the conflicts in the Middle East and lots of things going on like the miner strikes. There was a lot of political upheaval. I mean, there's nothing to kind of suggest that in the titles of the songs. I know "The Battle of Epping Forest" is based on a couple of gangs having a fight, wasn't it? But Gabriel was observational with respect to day-to-day life. He wasn't reading books about hobbits or wizards.

But I like this cover. It pulls you in. There's the lawnmower, which is part of the second track. And that picture, it's a feeling of... you can hear the bees in the background and the lawnmower in the distance and the guy's obviously had a drink and he's lying down on a bench and having a bit of a rest. The artwork fits the name of the band, it fits the name of the album, it fits the songs. It looks as if it was well thought through. How many times do we have albums where the cover is disjointed and just used as a sales technique? Conversely, this is a perfect marriage of lyrics and music and painting. And in fact, put it all together, if someone asked me, "Where should I start? I want to get into Genesis," this is a good place to start.

David: Knowing one rather glib thing about that cover, it's about selling out to America. And then okay, we'll do something incredibly English (laughs). And it'll be a kind of pun, as indeed Peter does quite consistently through this record. Okay, we'll sell out, so we're selling England and we'll sell England by the "pound." I like the artwork. I like the addition of the lawnmower, to reference "I Know What I Like (In Your Wardrobe)." They commissioned the artwork and the mower had to be added on later. But it's a striking cover, and quite different from *Foxtrot*, from *Nursery Cryme* and most definitely from *The Lamb Lies Down on Broadway*. There's a Lewis Carroll sense to that painting. With slight variation, it could adorn an edition of *Alice in Wonderland* or something of that style. It's perfect for prog, really, especially something as British as a Genesis album.

Philip-Edward Phillis: First off, that cover's a big departure from Paul Whitehead's painting for *Foxtrot* which, as we've discussed, goes back to Giorgio de Chirico. This is a painting by Betty Swanwick called *The Dream*. It has more painterly qualities. It appears that this very bizarre-looking, almost grotesque figure on the cover is the character from the second song, from "I Know What I Like," a character called Jacob who is some kind of reclusive introvert or something. And there's a reference in the song to someone with a lawnmower, and he's sleeping on a bench next to a lawnmower. But there's a discernible streak of Englishness in that cover. It feels like something you would see on the wall while you are having tea and cakes.

Martin: What are your thought on the production? It feels very analogue, although there's some hair on the bass.

Philip: It's definitely a more lush and soft production. We use all these terms to talk about production, which are weird and make no sense. But between us, I guess it does make some sense. I think it's a more pop production, like I say, softer. Maybe that's also a reason why when Genesis would reunite, a couple of times through the noughties, they would also play some tunes from here, which have even more pop hooks than *Foxtrot*. They'd even play "Firth of Fifth," which is a prog rock staple but still relatively hooky. But yes, this is not a heavy production job at all, and in that respect, quite a contrast to *Lamb*, which is also by John Burns.

David: It's a miracle that *Selling England by the Pound* sounds so good because these two sides are far too long for an LP length. Theoretically this should sound absolutely awful, given the restraints of LP technology, going 25 minutes on one side and 29 on the other. Which is ridiculous; that should not happen. More recent pressings and whatnot sound much better, but that's maybe because the studio tapes always existed in good quality even if the original LP may have suffered, certainly on side two. But yeah, it does sound great. You're able to hear the constituent parts. It's well-separated as well. For 1973, how many records can we name that, oh, there's great music here but it sounds like crap? Whereas everything here has a very sympathetic production. If the music is pastoral, then it has a nice soft production. And then the few parts where it really needs to rock out, it does. It's got an aggressive production style that is sympathetic to that. So nobody here is on top of them in terms of a producer presence or label presence establishing their style above what the band needs, and most importantly, what the song needs in each case.

Martin: All right, into side one of the original vinyl, and we have a dizzying, eight-minute labyrinth of prog moods, parts and sounds called "Dancing with the Moonlit Knight." Are you guys on board with what the band are doing here in 1973?

Phil: Yes, definitely. "Dancing with the Moonlit Knight" is a perfect example of pastoral prog, and it's egregiously English, immediately, with that introductory vocal from Peter. It sounds like you're out there in the middle of an English picnic with the sun going down in the distance. This music is driven by keyboards, plus Mellotron and even flute, which differentiates it from Yes, which we think about as being about keyboards and guitars equally, and even Chris Squire's bass.

"Dancing with the Moonlit Knight" is probably my favourite track off this album. It's exciting, it's dynamic, it's got a great story, great passages in it and yet it's accessible. You know, Genesis fans are older now, more experienced listeners, but you have to remember that these were guys in their 20s making music for teenagers, essentially, but it was music that was definitely challenging them. It isn't "Metal Guru" by T. Rex and it's not "Smoke on the Water." There's a lot in it. There's a lot to get your head around. I think in the end, this kind of music has become more valuable or more appreciated as the audience has gotten older. And it's funny; the band members themselves look back and they talk about the fact that they might have been messing around with a bit of Mellotron and guitar, but they didn't know they'd still be playing it 40, 50 years later. They had no idea that there would be this level of value attached to it. So yes, "Dancing with the Moonlit Knight" is like that; it still stands up as a monumental piece of progressive rock.

David: The acapella opening on this song, "Can you tell me where my country lies?," establishes this rough theme of some of the albums—not all of the albums, regardless of what some people say—of not wanting to sell out to Americanism, and to retain Englishness. It's quite a popular theme at the time that, in retrospect, can look a bit parochial, especially when we know that everybody involved here is going to sell out to Americanism and then some, in their various careers as solo artists and with Genesis itself. They're going to have no issue with embracing American styles and going to play stadiums in the US non-stop. And even then, at worst, it can look like Englander syndrome, where it's why not? Shouldn't you be internationalist?

And frankly, as I alluded to, Peter Gabriel's lyrics are full of witty puns, but in terms of chronicling England, he's no Ray Davies. He comes at it from a point of view that tells me you're a public schoolboy and you've not really experienced much of what England actually is. There's a sense of trying to come up with a mission statement for an album that perhaps you're not quite qualified to deliver. Whereas Ray Davies, coming from Muswell Hill, very much was; he knew a lot more of England by default.

However, the music comes in with those minstrel acoustic strokes, a medieval minstrel style, to kick off the record. Again, going back to *From Genesis to Revelation*, there's a few folky aspects being put down here. But then the chorus on "Moonlit Knight" is unexpectedly massive, sounding like "Lay Down" by Strawbs, but supercharged, if you will. Hackett's guitar work here is just as ferocious as Phil Collins' drums. Obviously, we can't imagine what that debut album would have been like with Hackett and Phil in the band, because they wouldn't have been recorded correctly anyway. So there's no point in doing so. But what they're able to do on this record is, again, supercharge this kind of music where if you want to change the tempo, if we want to change the time signature, we've got two brilliant musicians who are able to.

Hackett and Collins are two masters of their own instruments, whereas I don't think you can really say the same about Mike Rutherford. Tony, you can say that about, on piano. I think he's often a slight victim of wanting to explore new technology and the technology is not quite being established enough for him to know how to explore it sometimes. But regardless, we're not in medieval England here for the rest of the track. And Tony shows how far the Mellotron has come in the interim between these records by synthesizing the full chorus of voices. So there's no need for a cheap choir to be hired for overdubs when it's added here, organically. Tony is wonderful at coming up with that kind of stuff.

Puns about wimpy bars and green shield stamps are lost now, not just on overseas audience who might not have got those kinds of references anyway, but they're now lost to time, barring one who wants to do some exploring into these lyrics. But that's kind of the point perhaps, that this particular England was lost and perhaps didn't exist anyway. But it was always something for the home fans. And there's some lovely 12-string guitar from Steve to take us out, almost harp-like, just gorgeous stuff. "Dancing with the Moonlit Knight" is a sublime opening to the record. It's wonderful.

Philip: Straight out of the gate, we have Peter Gabriel impersonating the character of Britannia, thinking about England and the pound at the time, when apparently there was something of a financial crisis in the UK and lots of issues with inflation, as though somehow not a day has passed since then, today with England. And he's going back to the tradition of the madrigal again, Renaissance-period England, singing about where my country lies and how Father Thames has drowned.

I'd probably have to do some reading to fully make sense of what he is saying and why he's saying it and what his intentions are. But with this song, you already get the feeling that there's a concept here and that concept is England. Britishness. This is the most British album of their career. Yeah, there is a concept of Britishness running through this, either with references to England at the time or with the fact that he's using all the means of the poets and even *Monty Python* and Gilbert and Sullivan and puns and taking the piss and all these sort of things that Gabriel has always been a genius at doing.

And that happens on "Dancing with the Moonlit Knight," which is actually quite a heavy song, at least in the instrumental section, where the guitar is really saturated, which was not very common for prog bands. Plus Steve Hackett employs his tapping technique on this tune, further building his case that he's one of the more important proto-tappers, before we get to Eddie Van Halen.

Martin: Good stuff, and how about "I Know What I Like (In Your Wardrobe)?" Which is half as long and twice as sensible of structure.

Phil: Yes, the next song is very different. "I Know What I Like (In Your Wardrobe);" that title is so English and so quirky. I don't think anyone else could have done it. You know, Peter Gabriel was already dancing around dressed as a daffodil or whatever, the year before. It's such a beautiful chorus and a great song in general. It was released as a single, and the B-side was "Twilight Ale House," which is non-LP. It could have easily broken through, and if it did, I wonder if it would have taken them in a slightly different direction. If it had been a hit, the label might have said, "We need more of those!" Instead, they were basically given carte blanche to kind of write their own music, really.

David: Yes, this was the first hit single, charting at No.21. It was the only Peter Gabriel-era single that would be much of a hit at all. I did a little search to see what was above them in the charts. It was such classics as—and I mean that non-sarcastically in some cases—Mott the Hoople's "Golden Age of Rock 'n' Roll." That was above them that week—great. Queen's "Seven Seas of Rhye"—fantastic. Little Jimmy Osmond's "I'm Gonna Knock on Your Door." No, thank you, not today. Bill Haley's re-recording of "Rock Around the Clock." Why? And for the top three, which shows how bizarre the music scene was at this point in 1973 in the UK, we had "Everyday" by Slade, "The Cat Crept In" by Mud and then at No.1, "Seasons in the Sun" by Terry Jacks.

So that rather bizarre list of songs I read out there kind of puts into context that Genesis were real outliers in terms of approaching the charts at all here. For them to have this one song that kinda creeps towards the chart shows how out-of-step they were. Mott were great, but they had a commercial side. Same with Slade, same with Mud and for goodness sake, same with Little Jimmy Osmond. So this is a sample of songs that are all above them, putting them at No.21. And it's the only Gabriel-era Genesis song that ever charted.

The next Genesis track to even remotely chart would be "Follow You Follow Me," which, frankly, I think is the beginning of the end. Because that's such a cloying, tedious song. But regardless, the actual song itself, which I will always struggle to remember, "I Know What

I Like (In Your Wardrobe)," I wonder if the protagonist, Jacob, is happy to be cutting grass here while staying at home and everyone surrounding him is suggesting that he get a real job. I really wonder if he's something of a counterpoint to where Peter Gabriel would come up with Rael from *The Lamb*, who is also a young man kind of at a crossroads in life, but has a very different choice and most importantly a very different background. Rael doesn't have the chance to say, okay, I'll just lay in the hammock today and then mow the lawn later.

So this is very much a suburban youth probably a lot closer to home for the likes of these guys who come from privilege. They all were public school boys. So Peter Gabriel's writing from something closer to his point of view, where you can imagine that his parents—and I'm not saying this definitively—but his parents or Tony's parents or Mike's parents would say, "Okay, pop music, but are you really not going to get a real job?" Come on, at some point probably they had variations on that. So that's basically what the theme of the song is, that Jacob is being told you can't just mow lawns all your life. You need to get a real job. But he says I'm happy being who I am. While everyone around him is suggesting that you can't be Peter Pan. You need to leave Neverland one day. And indeed, Tony Banks has always looked like a barrister, so you might as well become one, I suppose. He never looked like the epitome of a rock star.

Famously, or at least among Genesis fans, this song was rejected for *Foxtrot* when Hackett brought it up, for being too Beatles-like. God forbid, why should you try and replicate the biggest selling act of all time? (laughs). And it's a real example of the band expanding on an idea, taking a small step up and blowing it up like a big band, rather than their usual style, later adopted by the likes of Marillion, of jamming for ages and ages and then just putting constituent parts together into songs and trying to use Tony's talents, especially, to stitch them together. This is an example of, okay, Steve's got something here, there's a glimmer, there's a gleam, let's see what we can do to expand upon it, which is where that comes from.

And indeed, there are parts here, like sitar parts from Mike, that do invoke The Beatles. But there's a funkiness to the track that really explodes with that chorus. And I'm quite convinced it's the catchiness of that chorus that pushed it as high as No.21 in the charts in the first place. It's not really a prog song. I mean, in isolation it's a poppy song. And hey, there's some flute on it, as there is on the rest of the records at this part of their career. And why not? Tull were massive at this point. Speaking of Marillion, Fish would later cover "I Know What I Like" on his *Songs from the Mirror* record from 1993. But yes, I think this is a good example of how Genesis could be more commercial without being quote unquote "sellouts" as they worried about, as per the title of this album, and as per later on criticism of them. This is a good example of selling out without selling out.

Philip: Yeah, "I Know What I Like" is the first big pop tune by Genesis. Peter's lead vocal is mixed perfectly with Phil Collins' backing vocals and it's got great hooks and also great musicianship. After the spoken word intro, we get an electric sitar, of all things. You would expect that that would scar the tune as demanding on the ear, that it would require many listening sessions to assimilate. But it's actually a very catchy tune, thanks to the songwriting, which does indeed evoke The Beatles and I actually love it for that. I'm a bit of a snob when it comes to all the pop stuff in Genesis and other prog bands, but this is totally up my alley. And those lyrics, again, are whimsical and silly.

Martin: I've asked this before, but does this band have, like, at least one foot in the idea of Canterbury prog?

Philip: Sure, somewhat. They're not considered exactly part of the Canterbury scene like Renaissance, for example. But again, you can hear overt Englishness in Steve Hackett's playing. As we discussed before, my number one reference is John Dowland, the Renaissance composer. He wrote stuff that later would be brought to the surface by Sting. He did a Baroque album with many reprises of Dowland's material. But Hackett also goes back to that for sure as well. And that possibly goes hand-in-hand with the Canterbury school.

Martin: Next is "Firth of Fifth" and it's hard to think of a song more indicative of the Genesis of this era.

Phil: Yeah, "Firth of Fifth" is one of my favourite tracks on it. The latter part of that track is where you've got Steve Hackett really developing. You get that volume pedal-led guitar playing, which became a huge part of the Genesis sound. Although because he never really came up above the parapet to really stretch out, that might be why that when he left, they didn't replace him. I think they felt that between themselves, they could probably recreate that. If you look at Steve Hackett now and all the tapping and aggressive, almost metallic guitar playing he does now, he wasn't doing that then. They just worked together, although I think he was the outsider still, with them all coming from public schools, etc. But there's a feel with this album that it's Tony Banks who is really driving the musical arrangements.

But that's got to be some of Steve Hackett's finest guitar playing on there, in that style that he had, and still has, that's unique to him. He's on that track, but like I say, there's no doubting that this period of Genesis is still very much the Banks, Rutherford and Gabriel show—it's their band. Steve is part of the classic lineup, but he doesn't lead, if you know what I mean.

Martin: And at the lyric end, again, I feel like when Genesis get into the fantasy realm, it feels like we're out in nature with the faerie folk.

Phil: It does, but it's interesting that over the other side of the fence, Led Zeppelin were talking about rampaging Vikings and also hobbits. Whereas Genesis actually never sang about *Lord of the Rings*-type stuff. You're right, it's a similar environment, but there's something more observant about what Peter Gabriel was doing, and often quite urban or societal. And then we get even further away when we get to *Lamb*.

David: Perhaps it takes a Scot to remotely care about it, but the title is a pun on the Firth of Forth, which is an estuary that connects Fife and Lothian. The Forth Bridge goes over that, so the Firth of Forth becomes "The Firth of Fifth." So again, we're having puns, or the approximation of a pun, and again for no reason. It's not a bad pun, I suppose.

It's a piano showcase for Tony, of course, but it also has one of Steve Hackett's most iconic guitar solos. The intro piano piece is stunning, part composition and then part improvisation. So we're based in the classical, and that's the part, of course, that's more composition-oriented. And Tony, you can definitely hear he loves Rachmaninoff; there's a lot of that in there. But then it goes into the second part of the piano production, where he's improvising, expanding upon what he's done. He's taken the improvisational nature of progressive music as it's become at this point in time and applying it to something classical, because classical music, like jazz or like prog, can be an exercise in improvisation. So he's adding to that more rigid classical form.

The live versions are often sans the piano introduction because they had to have just standard synths out there, which didn't have the ability for pure piano sound at the time. Those takes often suffer in comparison to the wonderful studio version. There's a great version from, I want to say Montreal '73, where the piano version is played. So it's quite a rarity for that full piano introduction to be played.

The relatively straightforward rock verse/chorus structure for a few minutes betrays that they were trying to stay sober and balanced. Okay, that was the experimentation part. Now we're going into a very standard rock and pop style. But my goodness, no; it then builds up again with the kind of unsure flute of Peter Gabriel, over Tony's MIDI'd and slightly playful piano. Again, there's a dichotomy in Tony's playing at this point in his career where he's able to, with each individual hand, project two individual moods at the same time. It's quite an animated aspect of his playing.

This builds up to a lovely interplay between Phil's drums and Tony's really intense synthesizer, where he seamlessly jumps from piano almost mid-note; it's a wonderful transition. And then of course, you get the reprise of the opening piano melody, this time with the full band. And when Steve Hackett plays his guitar solo, it shows why Steve Hackett still sells out shows to this day, because he was just that good at this point in time. For a lot of Hackett fans, we don't really understand why he isn't regarded up there with the true greats. He is in the progressive sphere, but very seldom do you see him on short lists of just general great guitar players.

Martin: And you know why, Davey? I swear to God, it's because he does two things instead of just one. He's loud, howling Steve Hackett and he's a beautiful, Spanish guitar-playing Steve Hackett, right? It's like a visual artist. Their instructors at art school will tell them to come up with your style and don't deviate from that style.

David: Yeah, which, I can't imagine anything more antithetical to art than to, you know, keep painting *The Mona Lisa*, please. Why? But yeah, when he does play that passage, he's up there with any quote unquote "guitar god" that you care to name. It's bluesy, it's haunting and it's beautiful with those sustains that just hold until the music reaches the heavens. It's melodic, intense, gorgeous. You can throw any hyperbole in there and it all seems to fit somehow. It's an all-encompassing kind of solo, and painfully so in-place. I've heard some solos as good as it, but I can't think of any that do this kind of solo particularly better. Roy Buchanan comes close on a couple of tracks. I think he's quite a similar player when he's doing this more bluesy style, if you want to compare him to Steve Hackett.

The resolution of it, to go back into the verse/chorus structure, shows how far they've come as a unit, and how far they've come as composers, again, led by Tony Banks, who I do think needs to be given more credit for that aspect of these kinds of songs. He was often the one saying, "No, we can't just go from that to that; we need to have something in the middle." He's the seamstress, if you will, of the band (laughs). He's the one that's making sure that the stitches are all taken care of, that everything will stand the test and won't rip the first time you put on. It just makes it more palpable for the ear, essentially.

Philip: "Firth of Fifth" was, for a very long time, my favourite Genesis song of all time. As a teenager, I absolutely was in love with the instrumental section. which was surprising because I was always into all the shredding stuff at the time, listening more to prog metal. But this one just absolutely captivated my imagination, because of that instrumental section. It's all thanks to the melodies of Steve Hackett on the guitar. You could call it a guitar solo, but it's not what we typically call a guitar solo, because it's more a long, winding kind of melody, in E minor, I think, which is not difficult even to learn if you're a novice guitar player.

But what is cool about it is the bending technique of Hackett. He doesn't do the kind of bending that's associated with B.B. King or the more conventional thing that's kind of diagonal and fast. He has the style of Eric Clapton, which is more vertical and more aggressive. And that's what provides that kind of haunting, trebly but lush sound to the melody he plays. I absolutely love the synergy between Rutherford and Collins, who are in-the-pocket. They really create the framework for Hackett and Banks to really shine on this one.

Martin: You know, early on, Genesis had a group credit, with this one in particular reading "All Titles Done by All," in two places, on the back and right on the label. But is there a type of song we tend to get from Mike versus, say, Tony?

Philip: Yeah, I think so. Apparently the lyrics of "Watcher of the Skies" were not by Gabriel, but by Rutherford and Banks. But they tend to address similar themes. Musically, I think you can tell the difference. "I Know What I Like" is probably more of a Peter Gabriel song. And going back to *Foxtrot*, "Time Table" is more of a Banks song, with more piano to it.

As for "Firth of Fifth," it's also more of a Banks tune. I must say that it stands up to something like "The Knife" in terms of heaviness and some level of aggression. There's this buzzy bass tone and the instrumental section, thanks to Phil Collins' drums, is very intense. He doesn't just play a certain tempo—he's all over the place. You can hear the influence of Collins on someone like Mike Portnoy, all these drummers who are maximalists. Collins is quite extroverted on "Firth of Fifth;" he unleashes a lot of power, although it has ups and downs and softer and louder passages.

Martin: Closing out this already long side is a drum-less ballad called "More Fool Me."

Phil: Yes, and it's the only song on the album featuring Phil on lead vocals, It's not the most memorable track, if I'm being totally honest. Now in the CD age or streaming age, it's presented more like an interlude that is sandwiched between two epics. It's like popping out for a tea break before "The Battle of Epping Forest," which is absolutely massive. It's a bit like "After the Ordeal" and "Aisle of Plenty" on side two.

David: Thinking about "More Fool Me," I'm much more of a fan of Peter Gabriel as a vocalist, communicator and an artist than I am of Phil. And as easy as it is to make fun of Phil Collins, it's also fun (laughs). And by that I mean the later Phil Collins. At this point he's still quite manageable. But I do give him his props. He's got a lovely voice. And I admire his willingness to do this, which is only his sophomore lead vocal on a record, for goodness sake. But to push that falsetto, it does strain. They're not doing a retake to say, "Ooh, I can hear the cracks in your voice at the top." That seems to be very much the point of it, to show that aching, that yearning that is cracking right at the top. There's a vulnerability there.

And it's quite odd to me that a couple of years later they embarked upon such an epic search for a new vocalist, knowing that Phil Collins can do this kind of thing. And how similar his timbre is to Peter Gabriel already. It always baffled me. I can see the point if Phil had always just been the drummer and sat there in the background.

But knowing that he's already done lead vocals on your stuff and has knocked it out of the park, it has always baffled me. The song itself is nice enough, but the journey of side one has been so wonderful that I don't think the destination quite matches. I don't particularly love this song, but the journey has been so wonderful that I'll forgive them.

Philip: It's poppy, accessible, catchy, just acoustic guitars and vocals, although lots of both. Big harmonies on this one. I tend to skip over these songs to pay more attention to the full-band epics, but "More Fool Me" demonstrates how, once upon a time, pop was actually quite complex and played with a lot of musicianship.

Martin: Well, you get your wish, because here comes "The Battle of Epping Forest."

Philip: Yeah, but, here's the thing, "The Battle of Epping Forest" gets lots of complaints, with people saying that Gabriel takes up too much space with his vocals and with the many characters he's trying to impersonate. We talked at some point about concept albums and how some albums have just one song on it that is conceptual. *All* of these songs are concepts, but this one is the most detailed and precise. It goes back to stories in the newspapers at the time of rival gangs battling it out on the outskirts of London. And Peter turns it slightly absurd and *Monty Python*-esque, although we also get some insightful commentary on the state of England at the same time. I think the lyrics are absolutely hilarious. Later in the story, they seem to be taking the piss with the church, with the idea of a priest who is somehow being tempted or something; I'm not entirely sure.

Personally, I don't have a problem with the fact that Gabriel takes a lot of space on this song. Sure, it doesn't leave enough room for the music to breathe, or for an instrumental section that's as long as, let's say, on "Firth of Fifth." But I can enjoy it by celebrating Gabriel's voice as another instrument and there's lots of entertaining ear candy as well, provided by him, under the umbrella of vocalizing. He does all these silly voices, one character over here and, all of a sudden, one over there. You actually have to pay attention to it to figure out what's going on, and that makes it fun. That represents another aspect to the band and this song that is inherently British, the whole idea of going down a rabbit hole and having strange experiences which are usually allegorical of something.

David: "The Battle of Epping Forest" is a battle, so of course we need to start with marching drums and military flutes. Some consider this a bit of a masterpiece and I don't. But I can see why they would. It's lyrically dense, with characters depicting working class gangs fighting each other, and Gabriel coming up with lots of over-the-top characterizations for them and lots of witty individual lines and ideas.

In some respect, I do wonder if this is where *The Lamb* is born. Because there's 12 minutes here, and it's actually 12 minutes where there's no air in the room at all. Peter has to sing super-fast to get in the story he's concocted in 12 minutes. Dare I suggest if your story is struggling to be condensed into 12 minutes, you should probably have allowed either more time for it, or you shouldn't be writing it. And I think that's the lesson learned for *The Lamb*, that Peter's ambitions probably extended past even some of these epic-length tracks. It perhaps was the ultimate reason why the band and Peter had to go their separate ways shortly after.

Because I can see *The Lamb*'s ambition in "Epping Forest," with the density. I'm not sure the story and the ideas justify 12 minutes here, which the idea of *The Lamb* does do, for me, over two full pieces of vinyl. And that's the clincher here. Maybe there's a version of this that's a seven-minute masterpiece. Maybe there's a version of this that's a 34-minute album with various musical ideas all unto themselves that's a masterpiece.

But what we have in the middle here is not quite right. It's the opposite of Goldilocks; the one in the middle ain't quiet right. It needs either more judicious editing or more distinctive sections. That's another egregious thing in this for me. For 12 minutes, I don't think there's enough dynamics in it. Which was seen on this album already. There are dynamics all over the place, up and down, slow and fast, quiet and loud. I don't know why this track has to stick quite rigidly to its structure, apart from Peter's got such an epic story to tell that needs to be told, apparently. He's nearly rapping over it, not in the rap music fashion, but more in terms of just having to spit a story out as fast as possible. It smacks of authorial excess, really.

Willy, for an example, is one of the gang leaders and in this song alone, to keep up with it, you need to remember that when he says Bill, Billy and William, he's referring to Willy. So just one character has four names throughout the song. If that doesn't tell you you've probably got too much going on, I don't know what does. Yeah, I don't think this is the classic some make it out to be. I think it may be—and this is always a hyperbolic statement to make—the most overrated song of the classic era.

Phil: Agreed. It's obviously a huge, epic track, but it isn't one of my favourites off the album. Still, the more you listen to it, it's intricate and there's a lot going on. It's easy to be amazed, looking back through the lens of time, to imagine that these guys are just sitting in a room and rehearsing this. They're young guys and really, they haven't got much looking behind them or ahead of them to know where to pull this from. So they're creating something that has never dated, really. It's still as much of an interesting and intricate experiment to listen to now as it was then. In the end it's complex and not particularly accessible, but it's absolutely seen as one of the cornerstones of this album.

Martin: Next we have an instrumental, "After the Ordeal."

David: Which was well-named, given my opinion of "Epping Forest." Famously, Gabriel and Banks wanted to cut this whole track. But Peter said, "I want to cut some of Tony's stuff from 'The Cinema Show'" and then in comes Steve Hackett as well, saying, "If you're cutting his thing, you have to cut this and..." So everybody's saying no cuts after all, is the ultimate response. Everybody's asking for cuts and the resolution is no cuts. So we get this song kept, and it ends up making side two far too long, for LP length. I would like to know, actually, if the LPs did suffer as a result.

Martin: It's really not too bad. And it's not that I was tone-deaf to this kind of thing, because the AC/DC live album and Dokken's *Back for the Attack* definitely did suffer. Maybe if it's less heavy metal, tight grooves can be more sympathetic.

David: I'm sure some audiophiles on Steve Hoffman Music Forums have broken it all down, with the different pressings. But yeah, it's a lovely little breather, really, between two epics. You do need that. You can't go from "Epping Forest" to "Cinema Show." But even this could have been shorter, But hey, when it's four minutes and "Epping Forest" is 12, I think I'll give Mr. Hackett a break on that.

Martin: Next, I'm suspect of the arrangement on "The Cinema Show," and actually a lot of the busier passages on this album, but without reservation, these are my favourite chord changes, specifically in that earlier slower section, which they give up on entirely at the halfway point.

Phil: Yes, absolutely, such a wonderful sense of melody. Of course, it's stayed within the set for Genesis for years to come. And of course, Steve Hackett dips in and out of it as well, as he does with "Firth of Fifth." But he's bound to, because it features such a huge part of his playing. But "The Cinema Show," again has got a wonderful English sunset or countryside kind of feel to it. It feels effortless. But the main guys, again, are Rutherford and Tony Banks. They are the driving parts of this, really, especially Tony with all that synth.

David: So everything I said about "Epping Forest" being overrated, inflated and deflating, you can kinda reverse, because I am not feeling that way in the slightest when it comes to "The Cinema Show." It is indeed a masterpiece. It starts with that stunning 12-string courtesy of Mike, which is breathtaking stuff. Peter's and Phil's harmonies are gorgeous. I always thought they should have utilised those two singing in harmony a lot more throughout the catalogue. I wonder if that may have happened if there hadn't been a big split at some point, if egos allowed for it.

And again, unlike "Epping Forest," this has the distinct parts with each being compelling, unique and enticing, leading organically into the next part. The 12-string may envelop the first eight minutes or so but it doesn't drown out the other elements that are there. Tony's section with the four-minute-long ARP Pro Soloist demonstration, which was a brand new bit of tech at the time, he does a solo that shows well that particular synth, which to modern ears probably sounds incredibly dated. But what Tony is doing with it still sounds wonderful to my ears. His playing itself—if you can get past the fact that that synth sounds very early '70s—is quite remarkable. He's not given credit as he should be for his love of experimentation and where he takes it.

That's part of adopting new technologies in music: some of it won't date well and some of it will date proudly. If it was done on Mellotron, it might have dated better to a prog ear. But we can distinctly hear what Tony is playing here in a more piano-like fashion, on a dated synth, with the APR Pro Soloist, because he's pushing it to its limits. If he was playing it on a Mellotron, with the sustain that Mellotron has, it wouldn't be the same at all. All told, it's just a remarkable composition that's properly summed up by the title of the song. There's a cinema show. It's very visual. It conjures up images in the mind's eye throughout the song and it takes you on a journey. People say that about "Epping Forest," but it's "The Cinema Show" that does that for me.

Philip: "The Cinema Show" is very much a top five track for fans of this era. It very much has all the hallmarks of prog rock. It has a long instrumental section that just grows and grows and climaxes and has a fantastic kind of staccato, again, almost heavy metal rhythm in the background that's sort of like galloping. This gives a lot of room to Banks and Hackett to each demonstrate all their musical prowess, I think.

And I think the sequencing here is just perfect. You have a strong opener followed by a pop moment to break with the intensity and soothe any wearing patience "Epping Forest" might have caused for the listener. Then you get "The Cinema Show," which is a second great epic full of emotion. I love those arpeggios by Steve Hackett. That's probably the most challenging part of his signature style, those long finger-picking arpeggios, which are very hard to play cleanly and clearly. He makes them sound like a cascading waterfall. That, for me, is what makes Steve Hackett Steve Hackett. Not his solos or his sound; it's those arpeggios. And then sequencing-wise, we get another light moment to take us out. So in effect, this record doesn't end with a huge epic the way *Foxtrot* does.

Phil: Yes, because we have a named track, "Aisle of Plenty," which becomes the perfect way of bringing the album to a close.

David: Which again, we have a pun for the title: "Aisle of Plenty"—I love plenty. You're getting a bit done with the puns at this point. If you're reading along with the lyrics of the songs, you're all punned out. Essentially, it's a bookend for the record, isn't it? It's not much of a piece in itself. It resolves "The Cinema Show" as a refrain, and then picks up with "The Moonlit Knight" from the opening. Tony's chordal Mellotron returns and is stunning here and Peter's vocals are quite low in the mix, even though he's singing so loud, which again, makes it sound like he's in the next room but shouting. And unlike bad production, where if that happens, we think he's too far away or too low in the mix, here it's been done intentionally to give that sense of desperation. He's having to scream almost to be heard. It creates darkness at the end of the record. There's a struggle at the end of this album and it isn't resolved, thanks to the fade-out. There's no climax; it fades out on that kind of mad scream, as we leave Peter in the booth.

Martin: Excellent—love it. Now that we're done, does anybody want to take a shot at where *Selling England by the Pound* ranks among these pretty similar four early Genesis albums?

Philip: Well, for me, it ranks probably at number one. I always sway between this one and *Foxtrot*. This one feels most complete. It doesn't have a 20-minute epic on it that takes way too much space, both on the CD and in our minds. It's more spread-out. It's both well thought-out and much better thought *of*. I think the members of the band are becoming more mature but also possibly progressing too fast, which is going to lead to burnout and fatigue and a change of direction.

David: One thing I'd like to add is that with the guys in Genesis at this point, there's a relatability with the fans, even though Peter's coming in there dressed as a fox on occasion. But there's a sense that, okay, he knows that it's a performance. Still, maybe I'll avoid the lead singer. But the drummer, he's just wearing, you know, a shirt and a turtleneck—I'll go and talk to him. Oh look, the bass player's just wearing a V-neck and he's got a regular beard; he seems a regular sort of guy.

There's nobody coming out here in capes. There's nobody as aloof as Robert Fripp in the band. Nobody is detached from the audience as Robert Fripp. There is nobody as intentionally above the audience as Emerson, Lake & Palmer made themselves at this point in time. Obviously, this is all relative. But for the major prog bands, the guys in Genesis, at least before the big multi-platinum pop era, were certainly the closest to relatable. They're the ones who could most seamlessly be part of the same audience they're serving, again, with the notable exception of Peter. If Peter was wearing the fox head and the audience were dressed as a flower, there may be a few issues going into the pub afterwards.

But that's always been the strange dichotomy of prog, that Rick Wakeman is a very relatable person, a very funny person, as you know, having interviewed him. He's a humane, down-to-earth guy who loves a good curry. But he came out there in a cape and had

Camelot on ice and the like. So there's no relatability there. There's an eccentricity, a pretentiousness. And that doesn't quite exist to the same extent with Genesis; there's a little less of a barrier.

Still, I think there's a healthy barrier, as there should be with any kind of music. Because if there isn't any barrier and they're just one of us, then it's not impressive enough for you to really care. Which is fine in something like a punk gig, where it's all attitude and they're one of us. But when you're intentionally going for something a bit more mind-altering—and you were probably on a lot of mind-altering things to go to these kind of gigs—then you want a little bit of reverence for who you're seeing. And that's what Genesis seem to ask of you—just a little bit of reverence, but not too much.

Entangled: Genesis on Record 1969-1976

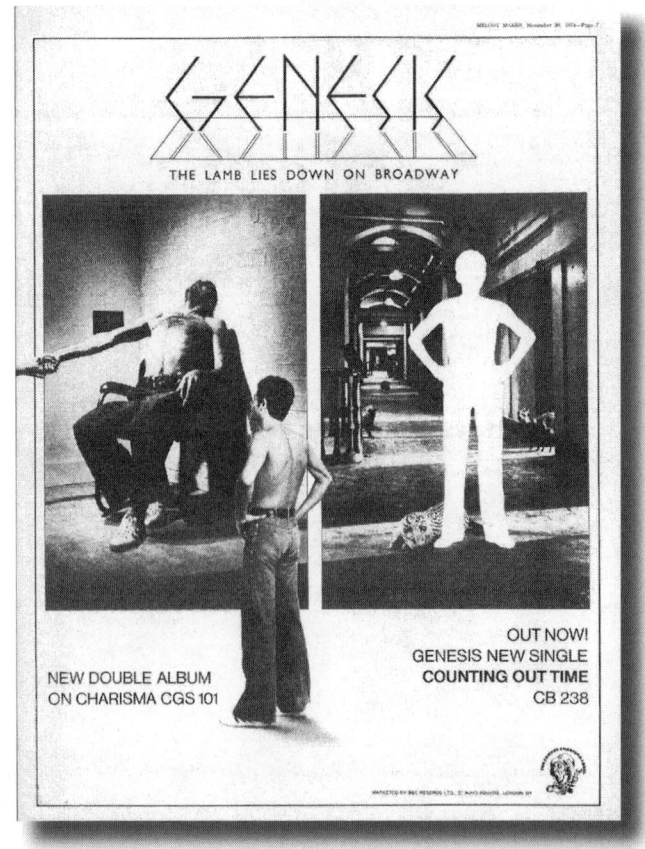

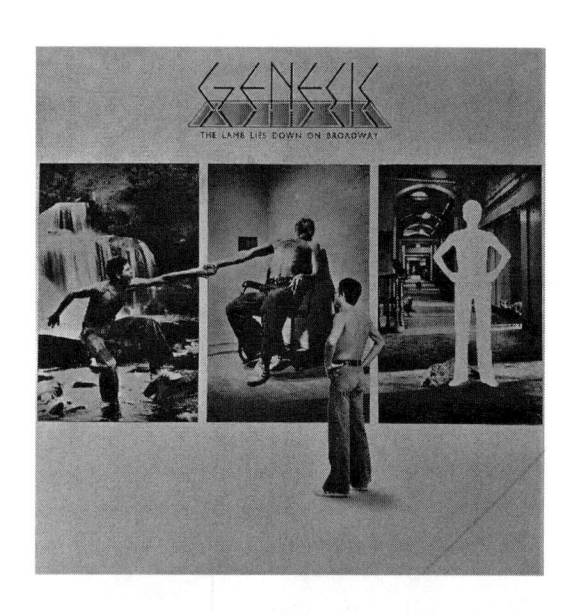

THE LAMB LIES DOWN ON BROADWAY

November 22, 1974
Charisma CGS 101
Produced by John Burns and Genesis
Engineered by David Hutchins
Recorded with the Island Studios Mobile at Glaspant Manor, Carmarthenshire, Wales, UK
Personnel: Peter Gabriel – lead vocals, flute, varied instruments, "experiments with foreign sounds;" Steve Hackett – acoustic and electric guitars; Tony Banks – Hammond T-102 organ, RMI 368 Electra Piano and Harpsichord, Mellotron M-400, ARP Pro Soloist synthesizer, Elka Rhapsody string synthesizer, acoustic piano; Mike Rutherford –bass guitar, 12-string guitar; Phil Collins – drums, percussion, vibraphone, backing vocals, second lead vocal on "Counting out Time," "The Supernatural Anaesthetist" and "The Colony of Slippermen"
Additional musicians: Brian Eno – "Enossification" on "In the Cage" and "The Grand Parade of Lifeless Packaging"
All songs written by Genesis

Entangled: Genesis on Record 1969-1976

Side 1
1. The Lamb Lies Down on Broadway 4:55
2. Fly on a Windshield 2:47
3. Broadway Melody of 1974 1:58
4. Cuckoo Cocoon 2:14
5. In the Cage 8:15
6. The Grand Parade of Lifeless Packaging 2:45

Side 2
1. Back in N.Y.C. 5:49
2. Hairless Heart 2:25
3. Counting Out Time 3:45
4. The Carpet Crawlers 5:16
5. The Chamber of 32 Doors 5:40

Side 3
1. Lilywhite Lilith 2:40
2. The Waiting Room 5:28
3. Anyway 3:18
4. The Supernatural Anaesthetist 2:50
5. The Lamia 6:57
6. Silent Sorrow in Empty Boats 3:06

Side 4
1. The Colony of Slippermen (a. The Arrival, b. A Visit to the Doktor, c. The Raven) 8:14
2. Ravine 2:05
3. The Light Dies Down on Broadway 3:32
4. Riding the Scree 3:56
5. In the Rapids 2:24
6. It 4:58

Entangled: Genesis on Record 1969-1976

A *The Lamb Lies Down on Broadway* Timeline

August – October 1974. The band make use of the Island Studios Mobile, setting up at Glaspant Manor in Carmarthenshire, Wales, to record tracks for their forthcoming sixth album.

October 29 – November 12, 1974. A scheduled UK tour with this timeframe is cancelled when Steve Hackett injures his hand crushing a wine glass.

November 15, 1974. The band issue "Counting Out Time," backed with "Riding the Scree," as an advance single.

November 20, 1974 – February 4, 1975. The band conduct a North American tour in support of their new album, which gets performed in its entirety.

November 22, 1974. Genesis issue a two-LP concept album called *The Lamb Lies Down on Broadway*. It reaches No.41 on the Billboard charts and No.10 in the UK and certifies gold in both territories.

November 25, 26, 1974. During the band's two-night stand at the Music Hall in Cleveland, Peter tells the guys he's leaving the band.

February 19 – April 12, 1975. The band conduct an extensive campaign in mainland Europe.

April 14 – May 2, 1975. The band tour the UK. The Empire Pool, London show is recorded and partially broadcast by the BBC.

April 18, 1975. Genesis issue "The Carpet Crawlers," backed with "The Waiting Room (Evil Jam)," as a single.

May 8 – May 22, 1975. The band return to mainland Europe for a final tour leg in support of *The Lamb Lies Down on Broadway*.

August 1975. News is leaked that Peter is leaving Genesis, and he writes a statement entitled "Out, Angels Out" to explain himself.

September 27, 1975. Phil Collins marries Andrea Bertorelli. He legally adopts Andrea's daughter and together they have son, Simon, the following year.

Entangled: Genesis on Record 1969-1976

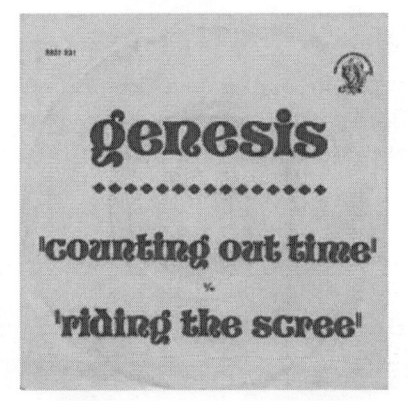

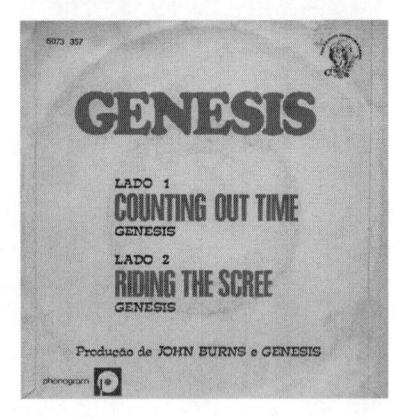

Martin talks to Phil Aston, Luis Nasser, Charlie Nieland and Philip-Edward Phillis about *The Lamb Lies Down on Broadway.*

Martin Popoff: All right, with *The Lamb Lies Down on Broadway*, we arrive at some sort of apex or turning point in the career of Genesis. It's a beloved but sometimes infuriating album, and the opaque, obscure story doesn't do it any favours. Before we look at individual songs, set the scene for us in a general sense.

Phil Aston: This is progressive rock, isn't it? For one thing, it's four sides; 2) it's a concept album; and 3) it's dripping in Mellotron and everything you'd expect arrangement-wise. So how it fits in the scheme of things is that it's the most ambitious thing Genesis ever did. All the lyrics are by Peter Gabriel. I know the band weren't happy with that. But he has written the story and the story is interesting. Because as I mentioned earlier about Led Zeppelin singing songs about hobbits and Vikings conquering the land, this was a story about a teenage guy and his rites of passage. There's probably more songs about sex in this album than there are in Led Zep *IV*.

But yeah, when you actually look at it, it's got everything. This character, called Rael, is kind of grown up, he's trying to fit in, he ends up going off with these strange creatures and kind of sleeps with them, and then he ends up being castrated by a doctor. It's got everything in it, but it's very off-the-wall.

Now, I know some critics have said that sides one and two are really well put-together but that it kind of drifts on side three and then pulls together for side four. But I always loved side three, to be honest. But all told, it's very different to *Selling England by the Pound* because it's a concept album. Some of the songs are literally little segues and you get the feeling that Gabriel was thinking bigger when he did this. He was thinking of maybe theatre or film, how it was all going to be put together in a giant production.

I'll also add—and I know some people may disagree—but I think this is an album again where Steve Hackett is not at the forefront. He's in defence if he was a football team. Tony Banks is in the forefront and Hackett is kind of support, a supporting artist. I know there are some tracks where he does come forward, but, to my mind, a lot of the instrumental sections are driven by high-powered synth solos from Mr. Banks.

Luis Nasser: Let me begin by saying that I've had an interesting story with this album. When I first heard it, I heard it as a bootleg. I grew up here in Mexico City and I was pretty broke most of the time and couldn't really afford records. So I would just buy these bootleg Memorex cassettes. So I didn't even know what the cover looked like and I didn't know anything about the story. All I had was the music, and from what I could understand from the lyrics, that together was enough for me to know that I was embarking on a dark quest. That was my main feeling as a kid when I first heard it. Now, this is a record that makes sense to me, growing up in a part of Mexico City that had gangs and was very violent, even if Peter's story was fantasy-based. But it spoke of an inner alienation that people like me and everybody around me were going through as teenagers, right? So it made sense to me from that perspective.

The story included on the album, when I finally read it, confused me at first. But only because I had made up my own story for all these years. And then when I heard the actual story, it turned out that I kind of liked my own better. I was committed to that one. To me, there are parallels with *Quadrophenia*, which also extended the story beyond the lyrics and into the packaging, although that album has none of the fantasy elements you get here. But it still paints a picture of a world that is alien, at least to me, right? What the hell do I know about British kids?

And with *Lamb*, we see how a young man from Britian, Peter, envisions gritty street life in New York. But yes, there's an admission very early on that this is going to be more like a Dante's *Inferno* kind of thing, not really a tale of the streets, but more like a fever dream or nightmare. And I like how the music doesn't really support that; it sends different messages. It has an edge and a raw power to it that I thought was lacking in the other records. Even when you hear "The Knife" played by Steve Hackett with Phil Collins, it's an entirely different thing and you get that added aggression here as well. *Lamb* shows you what Genesis could have been if they had not been too self-conscious about actually rocking out more. And the music, along with these lyrics, makes this the darkest album they ever made.

Martin: Nice. Philip, again, just in a general sense, where does *The Lamb Lies Down on Broadway* sit with you?

Philip-Edward Phillis: I'm afraid that for me, this was a Genesis album where the concept and Gabriel's obsessive-compulsive need to sort of act out many different characters and situations and voices tends to take up much more space to the point of overpowering the music, the musicianship and the rest of the band. Still, in many ways it's a masterpiece. I don't agree with the consensus that's it's the first or second greatest prog rock album of all time, along with *Close to the Edge*. I've heard this from many, as you say, wise music swamis, on YouTube and whatnot. Even though I'm a prog fan and like challenging, demanding, epic music, at 93 minutes and with this story, this album is too much for me.

I take issue with the format of it, the idea that you have so many tunes that are more or less four or five minutes, interspersed with three seven- or eight-minute songs. And it's a confusing album, where they're not certain if the direction they want to go in is still one of adventurous prog rock, or, as Gabriel has said, he was seeing on the horizon the arrival of punk and of an anti-prog tendency where music fans would want something not so pompous as traditional prog.

Plus Peter was infatuated with New York and US culture after touring there, and so you get references to JFK, Martin Luther King, Lenny Bruce and of course New York. And the character in this concept is a half-Puerto Rican who is apparently lost in Manhattan around Broadway, and then goes on an insane adventure. And sure, there are songs I absolutely adore, like "In the Cage," "Back in N.Y.C.," "The Lamia" and "The Colony of Slippermen," but I can't listen to this album from beginning to end as one big concept double album because it's not cohesive enough. It doesn't hold my attention well enough because it seems to lack in musical direction.

Charlie Nieland: Some people think it's the apex of Genesis, their high point, and other people, like my brother who loves Genesis, he's like, I can't listen to that record aside from a few songs. So I understand Philip's concerns with it. For me, as a quick aside, I discovered Genesis in early '76. I was 14 years old and that's when I really started getting into prog. We had moved to Milwaukee from Chicago in '74, when I was 12. My neighbour had records and that's how I immediately got into Yes and ELP and Bowie. But I didn't hear Genesis right away. Then in early '76, *A Trick of the Tail* came out and they were touring. And I remember, there was an ad on the FM radio, where they quickly cycled through a bunch of different songs. And one of them was the chorus of "The Lamb Lies Down on Broadway" and it sounded really cool. It's like, that's Genesis?! That sounds good. So I ran out and bought it and *The Lamb Lies Down on Broadway* became my first Genesis record.

Let's just talk about the idea of double albums. There was a bunch of bands doing them at the time; even the Rolling Stones did it with *Exile on Main St*, plus Elton John with *Goodbye Yellow Brick Road*. Right there you see two different approaches to a two-record album. Sometimes it's just like, we have so many songs—let's just release it all. Then you had Yes with *Tales from Topographic Oceans*, which I'm going to just admit that I'm a huge fan of that. That was another record my neighbour had. I was listening to *Fragile* and *Yessongs*, but then I listened to *Tales* and it was like, oh, cool, big kid music. I wasn't thinking, what is this? What mistake did they make here? It just seemed like more of a journey.

And I think *Tales* and *Lamb* are the same kind of album, two-record albums that were intentional, where they wanted to create more of a long-form experience. *Tales* was more diffuse. *Lamb*, on the other hand, embodied this interesting tension. Gabriel wanted to do something less fantasy-oriented, based on an everyday setting—in this case it was New York City—and this character, Rael. But at the same time, there's a really metaphysical story. So he creates this tension between this tale and the urban setting. And it works like a musical, rather than something so obviously abstract like *Tales from Topographic Oceans*.

Martin: And how does Peter fare as a singer?

Charlie: Man, his voice is like a landscape, with all these textures and deep valleys. It feels like he found all his characters in his voice rather than making up voices to be characters. It's not just B-movie voice acting. It's like he drew these versions of himself from his own physical instrument, which makes it so authentic and attention-grabbing. He can sound like some little old man one minute and a goddess another. And that's true to this day, through his solo stuff.

Martin: What more can you tell me about the narrative?

Luis: There's speculation about whether or not band politics is somehow wrapped up in this story. There's a whole thing where Peter Gabriel was writing the lyrics on his own and the band was working on music. It's influenced by a movie by Alejandro Jodorowsky called

El Topo, or *The Mole*. Look, I'm not going to recommend that movie, because it's very weird. But it features a lot of the things that you see in *Lamb*, you know, people in cages, these naked women, and a narrator going through this kind of rite of passage. But *Lamb* also has this William Blake influence, specifically "The Parable of the Wise and Foolish Virgins," where you're basically trying to figure out what is the right way to go through life so you may ascend to Heaven. A pilgrim's journey through Hell, is how I view this record.

I know it bothered Phil Collins that he never really understood the lyrics; he found it difficult to relate to the material. He knew that if he was asked interview questions about it, he couldn't explain anything. Because that's not who he is. And to my mind, it's the only Genesis album where the music takes a backseat to the story. People complain about the story, that it has holes, but I would argue that it has less holes than *Tommy*, and *Tommy* is viewed as a classic. The power of *Tommy* is similar to the power of *The Lamb Lies Down on Broadway*—they both ask big questions. But the narrative here is weak; it's not a novel. Maybe it doesn't even have great lyrics (laughs). But it's a curious work of musical theatre.

On the music end, it's very front-loaded. I think album one, side one and side two are a lot stronger than sides three and four, where you start to be distracted by the filler pieces between the songs. I think we also get on this album Peter's best moments as a singer. Tony Banks felt that the record is a little off. I don't think he liked the idea that it was story-driven, and that they had to write music to suit a story. He was thinking more in terms of singles, and then albums that are just collections of songs, as opposed to songs that are thematically connected.

Philip: Like Luis says, the concept overpowers a lot of the music. And Luis mentions Chilean filmmaker Alejandro Jodorowsky. Gabriel was actually in touch with him after seeing *El Topo* and he actually wanted to try to make a film with him inspired by *The Lamb Lies Down on Broadway*. And it would be a perfect fit, because *Lamb* is a work of, I suppose, psychedelic literature, surrealism or magical realism, with these meandering encounters and style of storytelling that goes in weird directions with no kind of sense or logic.

Martin: Can you say a little bit more about the narrative?

Philip: Sure; from the get-go, it's quite absurd, or, again, as Marquez would put it, it's magic realism. You have this character, a seemingly unpopular character for a British concept album, a half-Puerto Rican street artist who's called Rael. That's an anagram of real, if that means anything. He's suddenly trapped in some kind of cloud that's called a wall of death. From there it turns into this *Alice in Wonderland*-type story with many bizarre allegorical encounters. God knows what Gabriel's trying to say with these allegories; it's always left open to interpretation.

At the end of this insane journey, he's looking for his brother who's apparently in this river. The second-to-last song is called "In the Rapids." He finds his brother and he looks at him only to discover that his brother's face is his. That's a concept that is very much in tune with the cinema of the '70s, for example, *Performance* by Nicolas Roeg, where Mick Jagger's face is someone else's. There's often drugs involved with these transformations. But it's not something we expected to see on a prog rock album.

Phil: Gabriel really wanted to set this in the States. He came up with the name Rael, and then he found out that The Who had used that name on one of their earlier albums, *The Who Sell Out*. He was a bit upset about it, but then he just carried on anyway.

Martin: For the cover art, Genesis go to famed UK design house Hipgnosis. Is the collaboration a success?

Phil: I'd say so. It's mysterious and we are to presume that's our hero on the front cover. It's intriguing how the story is laid out in the gatefold. It's dense text and the story ends and then starts again and then cuts off. It's as if it we're being sent around again, in a circle.

Charlie: The album cover is such a departure from Genesis' previous records. Like you say, they contracted Hipgnosis instead of going with Paul Whitehead or other illustrators. I love it. It looks like stills from a movie. It makes you wonder what's going on. It evokes certain aspects of the story visually, like the hallways and the water. He's sort of cut out there looking back at himself, which we find is a major theme in the record, with Rael trying to rescue his brother from this place.

Philip: I'd somewhat disagree and say that this is not a particularly successful Hipgnosis cover, given their high standards. I find that the use of black-and-white photography is not suited when we're used to Paul Whitehead paintings that have a certain sense of Britishness about them. The gatefold has a few pictures that are darker and more ominous and even more three-dimensional with almost painterly qualities. So I actually prefer what's going on in the gatefold. And as Phil noted, in the gatefold, they are giving you the story, more or less, and then it just begins again. And you think, is this an error? Do I have some kind of rare copy of this album? Or is this on purpose? With Gabriel, you can anticipate that he's just toying with us, because he has that sort of artistic mind.

Martin: How would you characterise the production, the sound picture, on the record?

Philip: I'd say it's dry and boxy, less warm and majestic than the previous records, again, as if they are anticipating future musical trends when prog rock would be less in fashion. The drums sound pushed to the background. I prefer the greater depth that you get on *Selling England by the Pound*.

Martin: I understand that. There's a certain crowding to the mid-range on here, but that gives it its own kind of tough, visceral sound. It makes it more rhythmic, which is helped by the stonking bass tone as well.

Phil: And we have to factor in the lengths of these albums. You think about the first Montrose album from 1973; it was 32 minutes. *Selling England by the Pound*, same year, is 54 minutes. So they were pushing the envelope in terms of what you could get out of vinyl. You can imagine somebody saying, "Well, you're gonna have to edit that down; that isn't going to fit." But they didn't. *Lamb* is 95 minutes long, isn't it? It's a long album, which would have affected the bass response for some vinyl pressings. And I know that there's been lots of talk in Genesis groups about the various CD versions and remasters and how some have been almost ruined by the way they've been put together.

Luis: Yes, the production is a point of contention. I like it because it sounds angry. I like it because it matches the intent of the music. But I am also not a hi-fi kind of guy. I don't have a very expensive stereo with super-duper speakers. I listen to this on a cheap stereo or in a Walkman or in my car.

I would agree that there's a very aggressive bass tone from Mike Rutherford, which I really enjoy. He's using a Rickenbacker bass and he has it dialled in just right. He has enough of that warmth and compression and gain where the bass is right at the breakup point but it's not fuzzy. All of those added harmonics that he's getting from the compression and just that little bit of distortion gives the bass a lot of clarity in the mix. So I like that. I love the sound of the drums too and the keyboards in Genesis are always interesting-sounding. I like that Steve is prominent in the mix. You hear more actual rock guitar, but in a prog rock context, of course.

Martin: All right, well, we don't have to touch down on every track, but let's deal with the key songs for sure. What are your thoughts on the opening track, which I imagine is the most famed, given it's the title track and the most memorable and remembered, in terms of pretty much everything!

Philip: Yes, love it. It's got that ominous piano introduction and then becomes epic, panoramic. But it's a different kind of epic to something like "Watcher of the Skies," less majestic, more straightforward, with less over-the-top musicianship. That's a tendency with prog bands anyway, to tone it down, become more accessible and try to write proper songs and not just meander for an eternity. This is a good example of that.

Charlie: What a great song. It's very visual. It evokes the sound of the city humming with tension and traffic and the glowing lights. It's full of these sorts of suspensions that you get from the quivering Philip Glass-like keys and the guitars. And Peter really digs deep, using different voices on different lines. He has this kind of guttural, sassy voice for the first lines and then he sings gentle on other lines. And when he gets to the, "Rael, imperial aerosol kid," it's very deep, in a head voice, like he's the leader of a British choir. So he's playing with all these voices.

And Phil and Mike are driving it with super-tough drums and a sort of octave-jumping bass line. Phil's drumming on this record is spectacular; he's really starting to really come into his own. He's doing Brand X at the time—or he was about to—and his drumming is just full of funk and fiery asides. He helps create that tension along with the sort of hovering keyboard line and Mike's bass.

Martin: It's quite the bass sound. I mean, he's pretty much the lead instrument on what's basically the showcase song across the entirety of the album.

Charlie: Yeah, snarling bass, and it provides great contrast. It creates a landscape for Peter's character to dart across, you know, back and forth with his radical changes. I was wondering if you heard *Diamond Dogs* by Bowie in that; that's also a record that evokes this bleak, urban landscape, and like Gabriel, Bowie is using his voice in different ways. I like to think it was an influence. It's a really great ensemble piece.

Luis: "The Lamb Lies Down on Broadway" begins with this brilliant piano arpeggio, and it just sort of comes out of the fog, right? It is a perfect opener for a story. The song presents you with this idea of the lamb, The Death of Innocence. And also how New York has affected a young Peter Gabriel's sensibilities. New York is a city that has had an impact on the careers of many, many British musicians. This song is not easy to play. I'm not a pianist, but I know a lot of people who struggle with it. To be that articulate and get that degree of clarity as you go through all the chord changes, that's a workout. So it's technically very challenging, at least for keyboardists.

And then when it kicks in and you get that heavy bass, it's prog at its best. It automatically puts you in the middle of the action. It's kind of like how *Quadrophenia* starts with the ocean waves and the whispery thing, "I am the sea" and all that. And then you get Keith Moon and Pete Townshend and John Entwistle and Roger almost shouting, "I went back to the doctor." You're in the middle of the action. And that's what "The Lamb" does. It basically puts you in the middle of this conflict that Rael is going through.

Martin: "Fly on a Windshield" is just as fresh and different as the opener, as far as I'm concerned. The drum-less first half is uncommonly dark and then when the whole band is steaming away; it's actually pretty heavy.

Luis: Absolutely; it's slow and pounding and they're kind of just chugging along in E. But on top of that, on the bass, the chords are moving through this incredible sequence. It's E five, B minor seven over E, B seven sus four, C. It's then finally resolved to A minor and B sus four, but then they go back to the pedal point in E. C sharp diminished, E minor at nine. I mean, it's always the same with me. Whenever I start to listen to Genesis, I start to break it down. Because these guys really know how to use chords in an interesting way.

And what it represents, this is when this black wall is moving through Manhattan, right? And Rael's feeling imminent doom, like this wall is gonna hit him and he's just like a fly about to hit a windshield. And the music evokes this feeling that everything that's gonna happen is inevitable, that there's really no escape from this wall. He has to go through hell; he has to go through this process. It's hypnotic. It's almost like this character has no free will—he has to go through this. And you can take it literally or you can imagine that it's something that he's dreaming.

You're presented with difficult choices. What would you do in that situation? At the beginning, you resign yourself to fate—you're a fly on a windshield. But deeper than that is the idea that in order to grow, you have to let go of things that you thought you knew. And that is what this guy is going through across this record. It's a lot of introspection and questioning of previously held notions.

Philip: With "Fly on a Windshield," this is where you really hear the drums sounding more contained, compressed and a bit drier. I read one Genesis book where the writer thought Peter sounded like David Bowie on this one. Maybe that's a tendency of Gabriel's, to be like a magpie and adopt voices of others. He was a great interpreter after all. He didn't have the vocal range of Phil Collins, but he was a great interpreter with his theatrical prowess. And, sure, he sounds a bit like Bowie here. He's toned down his head voice and is not using these techniques for louder singing.

Charlie: The first song and "Fly on a Windshield" and "Broadway Melody of 1974;" what a great three-song setup to the story. We situate the character in New York City on the first track and with "Fly on a Windshield," we come right into Rael's perception of this cloud coming, and nobody sees it but him and he gets frozen. It's like a nightmare scenario where you can't move.

Musically, we have this beautiful, exotic, oriental 12-string and the quiet Mellotron. And then with the final words, "Waiting for the windshield on the freeway," it drops into this incredible rad transition, like the wall of death he's talking about. We get Steve Hackett with these pirouette-like leads plus these droning bass pedals underneath and the Mellotron playing these tension-creating chords while the bass line stays the same. Hello? That's a formula Genesis use to great effect throughout their whole career. Phil plays these beautiful heavy drums, while there's this swirling, Asian-feel dialogue going on up top, and this is all happening three months before Zeppelin does "Kashmir," right? Right at the end it modulates up, there's some killer drum fills and then we're seamlessly into the next song.

Martin: "Broadway Melody of 1974" represents a third song in a row where we get some pretty hard and heavy rhythms. In fact, Mike's bass sort of takes the place or plays the role of power chords, although I imagine Steve is part of that sound somehow as well.

Luis: That's another really interesting piece of music. It's just this very basic figure in 4/4, but with a triple feel. How can I put it? It's deceptively simple. This is a trope of this band. You get fooled into this very basic 6/8 waltz kind of a thing. But then, suddenly, they're sliding between that and 13/8 and it never feels odd or contrived. The groove is never really broken. And so "Broadway Melody of 1974" is one of these very polymetric songs that begins in 6/8, then it's 13/8, then it's 4/4 and back to 13/8 and it just keeps changing through all these sections but it's actually very pretty.

Martin: All I'm hearing is 4/4, although I understand why you might say "triplet feel." Then again, maybe the keys and Peter's vocals break the 4/4. I do love this sort of nattering vocal.

Luis: Yes, the vocal melody is interesting, non-standard. It has a lot of jump, as does the phrasing, which I guess is more what you're getting at. For my tastes, Peter Gabriel's singing voice is most powerful and at its very best at the places in "Carpet Crawlers" and here where it's kind of low. All the high parts are taken by Phil, the harmonies. So Peter's mostly singing in this low voice. Because when he sings high, he sounds like Roger Waters. It's at the point of breaking, which gives it an edge but less power. But I love the combination of these two songs. They really capture what Genesis was like at their best as a songwriting entity.

Charlie: It's a list song. It's a list of all these creepy characters. I picture a chorus line, like a Broadway chorus line, as they all march by. Something about Peter's delivery calls forward to post-punk.

And the prominence of the bass and drums, that's a motif you hear throughout the record. And then it ends with this beautiful harp-like guitar from Steve that sweeps us into the next scene.

Phil: "Broadway Melody of 1974" is a tiny song, 2:11, that helps bolt the story together. We get a New York reference right in the title. I imagine Gabriel deliberately set it over in America to move away from the English pastoral kind of viewpoint they'd already traded in so much. I think it's got a timeless element to it, although it goes off into sci-fi in certain places, which makes it a bit more surreal.

Martin: "Cuckoo Cocoon" sounds more like traditional Genesis, although at 2:14, it shows remarkable restraint.

Charlie: Yes, "Cuckoo Cocoon" is a little scene-setter; it sets us up for "In the Cage" which is just a towering track.

Philip: It's poppy, a bit more accessible and playful than what came before. Both "Lilywhite Lilith" and "Cuckoo Cocoon," these tunes, I don't want to sound snobby, but they're simpler, more stripped-down and hooky.

Martin: Although even without drums, it's a fairly elaborate arrangement. And I'm detecting an increased level of skill at creating hooks, evidenced by the strength of this song's chorus. All right, this leads to "In the Cage."

Philip: Yes, fair point. Now, "In the Cage" takes us back to old Genesis, back to "The Knife" and to *Trespass* and their kind of faster, more galloping, more musical songs. But it's not like that for the entire album, of course; there are many highs and lows for me.

Phil: "In the Cage" is obviously one of the great tracks, driven by unexpected or very enthusiastic keyboard and synthesizer solos and breaks plus, of course, Mellotron. Brian Eno is part of the mix, isn't he? He's credited with Enossification on this track and on "The Grand Parade of Lifeless Packaging."

Charlie: "In the Cage" became part of their set for decades. It's got that heartbeat bass in the beginning, and then it bursts open into this really beautiful and urgent 6/4 verse structure. Gabriel, once again, uses a variety of voices to tell the story, and there's organ and there's evil guitar from Steve that sounds like gnashing teeth. Remember that Brian Eno provides some sound engineering and treatments to this record. He was in the neighbouring studio, and you can hear the Eno touch on the guitars. It's these kind of swirling Roxy Music guitars, sent through synth filters and stuff, dialoguing left and right in the mix.

So there's all this tension, but then after three minutes, they break into this great fusion section with an ARP synth solo that is a total Bach moment—Banks has his own song within a song there. Again, this is something that would go on for like four or five minutes in "The Cinema Show" on the previous album. But here they do it all in about two-and-a-half minutes. It builds up to this held-out high note and Gabriel comes in with, "Outside the cage, I see my brother John" and the keyboard goes off like a siren and they all kick in with this power chord. It's such a great arrangement, so dramatic, very much signature Genesis stuff. All the transitions are so seamless. There's no wonder why this song was one of their go-to songs for so long.

Martin: Closing side one of the original vinyl is "The Grand Parade of Lifeless Packaging," which is appropriately framed upon a march structure, although a fairly progged-out march structure as opposed to something The Kinks or The Who might do.

Charlie: Yeah, "Grand Parade" is great. It's almost children's music. It's like a march that becomes surreal. This is one of those songs where you might be hearing a Syd Barrett influence. And like you say, there's plenty of great arrangement stuff in that song.

Philip: As a title, "The Grand Parade of Lifeless Packaging" is absolutely hilarious. Is he criticizing consumerism? How he manages to fit all these little commentaries and viewpoints into what is otherwise a meandering, over-the-top adventurous story is beyond me. It's remarkable with this man. But I think you can also sense that there's something ominous coming on the horizon, which would be the breakup narrative.

Martin: This is one of two tracks where Brian Eno gets a credit. How do you think he figures into the equation?

Luis: This is not going to endear me to Genesis fans, but I think that Tony Banks is a control freak. I think he likes to be able to really say exactly what's going to happen and bringing in Brian Eno took away that kind of autonomy from him. I think that Brian Eno did some cool things on this record and Peter Gabriel was really into it. Peter Gabriel, at that point in time, was beginning to get interested in working with other people. His head was full of possibilities as he contemplated things that could be done musically that didn't have to fit into the context of Genesis. It's just too bad that there isn't a movie that goes along with this album, because I could picture Eno being really involved with the soundtrack album. Some of his more ambient stuff, I find those pieces by themselves are a little tough to sit through. But if they were part of a movie, if they were part of a larger narrative, that would make perfect sense. On the album, it's about the lyrics and most people don't really latch onto the lyrics, or wouldn't in the context of a film. A movie helps you focus your attention, and some cool Eno music would make a lot more sense because they'd create moods that would become part of the narrative.

Martin: Over to side two, we get "Back in N.Y.C." another strong, defined song that demonstrated Genesis' advancing skills in focussing their efforts on sensible songcraft.

Phil: Sure, I'll buy that framing. It's gritty and it's aggressive and you're right, there's a different feel to Genesis here. We're almost moving out of prog into a hard rock zone, with good, beefy production on the drums and bass and guitars. Collectively, this is the ultimate prog album in some ways, but individually, here's why I think it's different. If you play the songs individually, it doesn't feel like a progressive rock album. "Back in N.Y.C." in particular is a rock track. It's only because it's part of the story that we call it progressive rock.

Luis: "Back in N.Y.C.," I'd say, is one of the most covered Genesis songs by other prog enthusiasts. I know Kevin Gilbert did a cover with Mike Keneally and I know District 97 has covered it live extensively. I like that song. It has a cadence that that is uniquely a Genesis thing. And it has a very heavy 7/8 beat, which I'd say Rush perfected later on. They really took that and just ran with it. There's a powerful, driving, rocking edge to this song that is very much missing on other Genesis albums, which were more pastoral. "Back in N.Y.C." has an attitude that says we're gonna rock and we don't give a shit about the past. I love that about it, and also that Peter is singing at the breaking point of his voice, which adds to the energy of it. But it also goes through a lot of chords and key changes. But the main thing about it is that it maintains an edge throughout.

Charlie: "Back in N.Y.C." is one of the best songs on the record, as far as I'm concerned. I hear a hint of Krautrock in that song, with the Kraftwerk-y keyboards and Peter's complete dive into the character over the top of the music. He's fully in attack mode with his vocals. And it's like *A Clockwork Orange* meets "Baba O'Reilly" with the anthemic keyboards and anthemic chord changes and then Peter sounding so raw and nasty over the top of it. You find here that Rael is scary. He's not nice. He's full of vengeance, but also vulnerability. That's the contrast. It's this contrast between his vulnerability and his screaming rage and it really comes to the fore in this song.

Philip: "Back in N.Y.C" has a steady and hypnotic but complex rhythm and a pop sensibility that make for a catchy, hooky combination. I love the way Peter Gabriel sings on that one. He goes into his higher register and there's this saturation on his voice. He's really good at that. I don't know; even though he was not exactly this kind of professional singer with great range, all those things we say often about Phil Collins, I love what he does. And yeah, I just love the kind of stripped-down, meat-and-potatoes kind of hard rock rhythm here, even if it's set to an oddball time signature.

Martin: I guess "Hairless Heart" is what we call an interstitial piece of music.

Charlie: Yes, it's a short instrumental and I wish it was longer. It begins as a sort of neo-classical hymn with a beautiful melody from Steve, gently played on volume pedal guitar. It them kicks into this Pink Floyd-esque full-band statement of the same melody with bass pedals and these dense keyboards, with Phil playing a beautiful, slow groove. It's so ethereal and dreamy and yet heavy at the same time. it's only two minutes long but it's so good.

Martin: "Counting Out Time" is more unexpected, sort of Beatle-esque.

Philip: Yes, pop and playful and almost silly. It's Peter as an almost whimsical, *Monty Python*-esque figure, although maybe he's trying to write a serious pop song that just happens to be under four minutes long? Then again, the silliness comes from the music too. But yes, it's very accessible and friendly for most listeners.

Phil: "Counting Out Time" is when our hero, Rael, is kind of becoming more sexually active. It's this intimate song, but on its own, it sounds quite quirky and nursery rhyme-ish in places, which, again, is part of the Genesis sound. It sounds odd in conjunction with the story. But yes, "Counting Out Time" is a coming-of-age story, with mention of erogenous zones and whatnot. It's quite tongue-in-cheek with double entendres and all that. One interesting dimension to this is that it feels like the soloists were paying attention to what the lyrics are and playing something sympathetic to them, rather than thinking, here comes my solo spot and playing or composing something nice to fill that time without any heed to what the lyrics were. Even though the band probably battled and had a few disagreements about what the story was about, there's a feel that all the instrumental sections feed off the lyrical content, which I think is why it works.

Luis: "Counting Out Time" is a song on here that I particularly love, and I don't know that it's beloved by too many Genesis fans. Full disclaimer for your readers and for you because you're my friend and I respect the hell out of you, but I love this record and I love Genesis, but I am not a conventional prog fan. I'm a metal guy, even though most of the music that I play is prog, or jazz. My favourite Genesis tracks are probably not everybody else's.

But here's the bottom line. I love "Counting Out Time." Although it appears deep in the album, to me, it's kind of like a flashback song. It's a call-back to before Rael was this badass, spray paint-wielding street dog. It basically retells the story of a young kid who was completely inexperienced, and he has this idea that he's going to successfully romance and turn on a woman, right? And he decides to go get himself a book to teach him how, which, again, showcases just how nerdy Peter Gabriel and those guys fundamentally are. And I don't say that as an insult, because, I mean, nerds are my people. But it's actually very funny. And of course, predictably, the method fails. It doesn't really matter how much he digs into the erogenous zones, he doesn't really know how to do it. He's following this formula, like, so many seconds here, so many seconds there. It's the whole counting out time idea, which is hilarious.

To me, this song plays the role of "Pinball Wizard" on *Tommy*, how Tommy is this deaf, dumb and blind kid who has been abused, and had all these problems. It's actually really heavy. And now, all of a sudden, he just happens to be this pinball champion so we have levity. "Counting Out Time" provides similar levity, even though it's in the key of A flat major (laughs). What's also interesting in that it's mostly 4/4, but then the only real hook in the song comes with a 13/8 bar. So, again, it showcases just how wicked Genesis were at weaving in these crazy time changes into the music. They just float by and you don't even notice them.

Okay, the other thing I really like about this song—and I'm sure I'm not the only one who's ever realised this—but Hackett's guitar solo is actually played through a guitar synth that makes all these jokey, bouncy sounds, which to me is the perfect way to highlight Rael's failure at getting this lady of his esteem off, right? Anywhere near an orgasm is completely out of the question. It just works really well, and like I say, it brings a little bit of levity to *Lamb*. But musically, it's not a joke song at all. I know that Emerson, Lake & Palmer liked to use joke songs on their records, like "Benny the Bouncer," and to me, those songs are meant to be jokes, where they really are not very well put-together or anything; they're just filler. "Counting Out Time" I don't think is filler. It's a solid piece of music and one of my favourites on the record.

Martin: Next we have "The Carpet Crawlers," a famed Genesis song, and in fact the second single from the album.

Phil: Yes, and the first one where you really feel like you're drifting into this world of Genesis. This actually worked on stage. Lyrically, without knowing the story, it's out there, but as a song it's beautiful. Is it a ballad? Is it a prog song that happens to be quite laid-back? Whatever it is, it sets the tone that the story is moving into a different realm now, toward the mythological. It's a highlight, and probably the song that if you were trying to get your friends into this album, you'd play "The Carpet Crawlers." You'd also play the opening track and you'd play "In the Cage," because of the instrumental prowess on it. And you'd play "Back in N.Y.C."

Philip: "The Carpet Crawlers" is mellow and brooding, but not too brooding, more like wistful. Peter is really digging into his lower register here. Yes, it's a famous song because it's accessible and catchy.

Luis: In my view, "The Carpet Crawlers" is a perfect example of everything that makes Genesis a band that is unique in terms of songcraft. First of all, there isn't a single banging chord, right? The entire song is a sequence of arpeggios, which, again, is playing all the notes of a chord in sequence, one after the other, as opposed to just all of them together. But the harmony and the counterpoint are really a masterclass. The tempo is slow, like 70 BPM. The organ is playing cascading, descending 32nd notes. So they go from a high note to a low note. Meanwhile, the guitar is playing ascending arpeggios. So you have this kind of disorienting situation where the keyboard is going down at the same exact time the guitar is going up. It creates a kind of a swirl; it's very hypnotic.

And then you go through all the chord changes. You start on E major seven, then an A augmented fourth, F sharp with an added fourth, C sharp with an added two, C sharp minor; I can go on, right? It's just like, wow. And it just keeps doing this through the whole intro. And then when the verse begins, now the organ changes from descending 32nd notes to descending triplet 16ths. But the guitar is still doing the ascending 32nds. So what happens, which is really interesting, is the harmony settles down into a very basic, you know, D major, E minor, D major, E minor thing. So that kind of gives your ears a rest. But not entirely, because now there's a new sense of confusion in the rhythm. That's an interesting thing that they do in that song. And then once your ear is accustomed to the D and the E minor, well, then they hit you up with an F sharp minor, an A, G, D, E minor. Again, they go nuts.

Now, another brilliant thing about the song is we were saying before that the lyrics came before the music. Okay, so it's up to the band to figure out a way to write music for these words. And the words are really interesting. The narrator of *Lamb* is this Puerto Rican kid called Rael. As Phil mentioned, Pete Townshend already used that name for a character, on *The Who Sell Out*, on "Armenia City in the Sky," all that stuff. So he was really distraught, but he decided not to change the name and that's fine.

Now, the narrator suddenly finds himself in this hellish, surreal environment and he's wanting to get out from it. But what is interesting is that he is not alone. He's surrounded by all these people. And the first thing the song tells you is, "There is lambswool under my naked feet" and "The wool is soft and warm/Gives off some kind of heat." So you have that symbol of the lamb, representing purity. That's what he's standing on.

But then the nightmare begins. "A salamander scurries into flame to be destroyed," which is actually kind of weird, because in the old mythological tradition, salamanders were always thought to be fire-resistant. And here he is in this environment where the salamander is suddenly being destroyed by fire. So it's sort of letting you know, okay, this is not really what we expect. And, "Imaginary creatures are trapped in birth on celluloid" and "The fleas cling to the golden fleece/Hoping they'll find peace."

Okay, so what is what? I don't think these words are random. I mean, the fleas cling onto the fleece. In other words, it's a commentary on this whole idea that religion will set you free, that religion will give you the answers. And it's like, no, your behaviour, your conviction, that's what counts, right? Not a ritual. Not a mechanistic kind of formula.

And then these guys are crawling through the carpet and he says, "We've got to get in to get out." And everybody's sort of moving towards this chamber that they intuitively know is above them. But the question is, how do I get there? And the narrator, Rael, is just really confused. And you have all these great lyrics, like "Mild-mannered supermen are held in kryptonite/And the wise and foolish virgins…" that's calling back to William Blake. They "giggle with their bodies blowing bright." See? And there are these callers saying, "We've got to get in to get out." But it's a trap. That's not the way out at all, as they learn later, when they realise that their lifeblood has now been drained, and when they get to the fountain, the fountain is dry. It's just a really powerful song. It's powerful harmonically, it's powerful rhythmically, it's powerful lyrically.

Charlie: "The Carpet Crawlers" is another song that became part of their canon, and it refers back to "The Lamb Lies Down on Broadway" with its intro, with one of those old-timey '30s-type intros that's separate from the rest of the song. The arpeggiated keyboard thing you hear on the opening song is recalled or echoed on this song. And Gabriel is using that kind of choir boy voice where he's singing at the back of his throat. And then when it sweeps in, this is where the story is really being told by the music, this paradox about being trapped.

It's like there's hope and futility in this song as he's stuck in this chamber with these other people who are trying to get through.

It's funny that this song has become an anthem for them. Even though the story is obscure, everybody sings along and waves their hands with the, "We've got to get in to get out" part. With *Lamb*, Peter was reading a lot of Eastern philosophy, even around the time of *Foxtrot*. That's a real influence on "Supper's Ready." He was reading Zen and I think he was reading *The Tibetan Book of the Dead*. And there's a lot about the Buddhist concept of bardo in this record, where you're stuck in this purgatory. It depends on whether or not you clung to desire and fear, whether your memories of your previous life are nightmarish or beautiful. And this whole section of the record is like that.

Martin: Interesting. Next, "The Chamber of 32 Doors" is a full-on song, and even structured like a single, but it's pretty much overlooked. What's its function on the album?

Charlie: Well, it marks the pivotal point in Rael's journey where he must choose his next path. There's some beautiful songwriting in that song, almost like an old Bee Gees thing, with these beautiful dramatic stops and Gabriel doing some really honest, emotional singing. It's a well-written song, full of nice two-part harmonies. I'd like to add that there are plenty of great backup vocals by Phil on this record. With multiple listens, you start to notice how great the backup vocals are. Which is amazing, because they recorded the album in such a rush.

Martin: Side three of the original vinyl issue begins with "Lillywhite Lilith," which combines the album's groove and heaviness of arrangement with accessibility, notwithstanding the flub by Phil at 2:19.

Phil: Really? I gotta go hear that (laughs). Yeah, "Lilywhite Lilith" is fantastic, a brilliant rock song with some great stuff from Tony Banks. They only do it for a few seconds, but there's this kind of syncopated drum and bass groove that comes in right after the first chorus that is just perfect.

Luis: "Lilywhite Lilith" was a song that they had from a few years before they even sat down to do this and it was previously called "The

Light." It was a late addition to the record, as I recall. The other one like that is "Anyway," which had been called "Frustration."

Charlie: In general, I have to say the second half of the record isn't as strong as the first half, although "Lilywhite Lilith" is great, with a really strong melody. Phil and Peter sing it together. The end of it alludes back to "Broadway Melody of 1974," with the same bass and drum pattern and there are other little allusions to previous melodies in the outro as well. Peter is describing how he's being led into a new chamber, following Lilywhite Lilith.

Martin: All right, next is "The Waiting Room," half sound effects and half instrumental. It reminds me of Hawkwind.

Phil: Yes, this is where some people have said the album starts to lose some of its charm. "The Waiting Room" is certainly off-the-wall. It reminds me of "On the Run" by Pink Floyd from *Dark Side*. It's got that kind of feel to it. It eventually turns into an instrumental with real drive to it. I think it shows the seeds of where Phil Collins went with Brand X. There's an element of jazz fusion, perhaps, in the way that Phil Collins is playing on the offbeat here, during that long 3/4 section. As we move towards the end of the track, the rhythm goes into a more traditional 4/4 rhythm. There's a lot of stuff going on in this track where the band are progressing, literally, to where they were going to go next, especially Phil Collins as a drummer. I don't think it's a throwaway track at all. I think it's a very important part of this record.

Charlie: Yeah, "The Waiting Room" is a sort of crazy improv that build and then breaks down and then ultimate fades out as they are jamming away there. It's a clear break because "Anyway" starts with very formal and ornate piano. It's a beautifully written Banks tune, depicting where Rael is buried underground and he confronts his own death. It's a piano-driven song, like Beethoven meets Elton John. There's this big, dramatic break with a harmony guitar solo, which quickly cuts away, back to the piano and this nice, pretty complicated ballad.

Philip: I really like "Anyway." I like the last half of the album because it just seems more visceral, and this one, even though it's superficially a ballad, it's got some really intense parts. I love Phil's drumming on here. I feel like for a large part of the album, until halfway, Collins is not shining in the manner I'm used to with him. He's not particularly going to his toms and cymbals, not filling up the space with his usual licks. But there are moments on "Anyway" where things start to take off. It's the kind of playing, similar to Neil Peart, that's made him one of my favourite drummers of all time.

Martin: "The Supernatural Anaesthetist" is a nice full-band track, mostly instrumental except for that opening bit, kind of pompous and fanfare-like, maybe a bit like ELO. This takes us to "The Lamia," the next pretty important song.

Phil: Yeah, "The Lamia" is a great song because this is where Steve Hackett has a chance to step out further into the limelight, especially as we move towards the latter part of the track. It's some of his most beautiful playing on the album. He doesn't really stretch out much. But even here he's staying within the confines of what the song is about. He's playing some wonderful melodic lines. In the story now, this is the bit when our hero is with the Lamia and being turned inside out by them in a ball of translucent goo somewhere (laughs). But it's a great song, an important part of the story and the album.

Charlie: "The Lamia" is very much a Banks tune. Story-wise, now he's trapped in another underground chamber with sirens who then become vampires. Again it alludes to this bardo concept. Whether you see these things depends on how you lived your life, whether you see them as beautiful or horrific. And it's a really beautiful ballad. There's kind of too many cul de sacs in this song, but it's very affecting, and has another beautiful Hackett solo at the end that emphasises his woodwind-like phrasing; he sounds like a clarinet almost.

Martin: "Silent Sorrow in Empty Boats" is an atmospheric instrumental, so the band are stepping in it, with respect to people thinking they are running out of ideas as the album draws to a close.

Phil: Yeah, I feel like there are three parts of the album that have this Tangerine Dream quality, kind of dreamy, with Mellotron, which is fairly new to Genesis. Using Mellotron isn't new, but being this committed to sort of new age-type music is. "Ravine" is like this, plus the little bits at the end of "Broadway Melody of 1974." There are these very ethereal sound collages that have never appeared on a Genesis album up to this point. But it's Tony Banks who is at the forefront.

Martin: Next is "The Colony of Slippermen," the longest track on the album, easy on the ears musically, but quite a trip both lyrically and vocally, with Peter really digging into his thespian chops.

Phil: Yes, classic track, eight minutes long. This is when our poor hero ends up being castrated, isn't it? To bring him back into the real world, I think, which again, to many music fans back then, all of this is going straight over our heads. Unless we were sitting down and studying the story intently.

Martin: Don't sell yourself short, Phil. You seem to have a pretty good grasp of it. But let me ask you this; is there a moral to the story?

Phil: You know, if there is one, it's hidden. It's still hidden amongst the creatures living in that pool, I think (laughs). I don't know what the message would be. I know as we move towards side four, his brother John is in this story now. And we know towards the end of the story, he looks to save John, and he looks into his face and he realises it's his face and not John's. But that doesn't necessarily mean that we know where it's going. I think we feel that a lot of the songs represent a rite of passage for a young teenage kid, just going through life with a bit of attitude and trying to fit in. And for whatever reason, he ends up going through a different dimension and having these experiences.

In "The Colony of Slippermen" which has different sections, in "A Visit to the Doktor," that's where he's castrated. It's a great track. It starts quite differently, obviously, with all the sound effects and stuff, but it's one of the main songs on the album. At about the two-minute mark, we've got the synthesizers coming in, because actually the first 1:45 is sound effects, really, before the song starts. And then we get into the first part of the song where Tony is playing this great, melodic, hooky synth line. Like I say, besides Peter and the pretty overbearing story, Tony is the star of the show, because he seems to have complete first choice at whatever instrumental sections and performances and shows of musical prowess that are going to come out. It seems to always be him at the front of the queue.

Charlie: On the final half, I'm skipping over some of these beautiful interstitial pieces like "Silent Sorrow," but the final side opens up with a lot of exposition by way of "The Colony of Slippermen." It's a bit like "Get 'Em Out by Friday" from *Foxtrot* or "Battle of Epping Forest" from the previous album in that there's a ton of storytelling. It's a bit too much and too busy. But there's actually really good pacing in this song from a musical standpoint, great rhythmic drive, lots of cool changes, and actually a very catchy chorus and more great playing from the band. The character is castrated in order to make it out into the next thing, which is, again, a Buddhist concept of letting go of your earthly desires to move into the next phase of your being. But Rael wants to keep his junk, so he goes chasing after this bird that took his castrated dick away from him.

Martin: "Ravine" is purely a piece of ambient music, essentially two minutes of wind.

Phil: Exactly, it's one of these sections that sort of drifts by. It's weird, spooky music stirred up in a soup that sounds like sound effects mixed with Mellotron, but curiously, Tony isn't credited, nor is Brian Eno. It's Mike and Steve that are listed as the composers.

Martin: "The Light Dies Down on Broadway" is one of these smart concept album songs that references something earlier but not completely. I love the way they did this song; it might be my favourite on the album. The playing and the arranging is just action-packed, start to finish.

Phil: Yes, it reminds me of some of the things on *Quadrophenia*. It's got that kind of rock feel to it, the way it's sung in juxtaposition to the instrumentation. This is what I was saying. If you listen to some of these songs on their own, completely away from the story, some of them don't sound like Genesis at all. They certainly don't sound like progressive rock songs. And the referencing thing, when we get to *A Trick of the Tail*, they do that again.

Martin: Speaking of The Who, the beginning of "Riding the Scree" sounds like "Who Are You," which isn't coming around until 1978. This one aligns closely with "In the Rapids," in terms of the story.

Phil: Funny you say that because there's something about the way that the song moves towards the end, where there's a kind of Pete Townshend feel in some of the picking on the guitar, as well as the keyboards. Plus there's the fanfare stuff and the vigorous strumming in the song "It." But "Riding the Scree" features Tony Banks and his roaring kind of Moog synthesizer lines. And then "In the Rapids" is where the main character says, "Something's changed/That's not your face/It's mine!"

Charlie: Yes, Rael ends up in this river, and the river becomes this image that they use for the rest of the record. He eventually sees his brother in the river and follows him down. There's this moment where he sees this vision of New York City. He can jump back into it or save his brother, who he has been chasing this whole time. That's in "The Light Dies Down on Broadway."

And then we get to the end, and he decides to follow his brother and not jump back to the city. He pulls his brother out of the water and all of a sudden, he sees his own face. So individualities dissolve. And that's the big turn on the second to the last song, at the end, on "In the Rapids;" that's the big, dramatic moment at the end.

Philip: "Riding the Scree" is fantastic. You sense that the album is climaxing. It's really trying to take off. The musicality is very present, and you can feel the interchange between Hackett and Banks. The rhythm section at the back is really solid but energetic. It's not exactly metallic but adjacent to that. It's galloping.

Martin: The album closes with "It," which is a strange one, almost Allman Brothers-like, with those harmonies, although they are more of a guitar-keyboard alloy. But the drumming is like Allman Brothers as well, a little jazz fusion. There's a buoyancy and lots of melody, the sort of thing you want as a closing number at a Broadway play.

Phil: Absolutely (laughs). Off we go towards "It," the last track, which is a joyous, uplifting, totally different feel to most of the songs, which are often dark. They did this again later, with "Los Endos." Genesis seems to embrace this idea, closing with something upbeat and with a different sort of chord sequence. But you know it's the last song. "It" couldn't have been anywhere else on the album. It's just a cascade of beautiful melodic lines that are almost hypnotic. They're conveying the sense that somehow everything's come right.

Whatever's happened to us over the last four sides, everything's now going to be fine.

Martin: Which is a standard trick of a Broadway or West End play, to send everybody out onto into the street with a bit of a spring in their step, hopeful. We're getting in a cab. We had a fun night.

Phil: Exactly (laughs).

Charlie: Yes, it's a joyful, breezy song, where Peter talks about all the things that "it" is. It's also fast, with breezy major sevenths and winding lines over the top. Like you say, it's like a musical revue, to wind the musical up. I don't know, to me the climax of the story doesn't have the musical force of say, "Supper's Ready." It gets a little diffused in the second half. Even though the story has a climactic ending, it doesn't feel like it. It feels a little rushed. But still, so many of the songs are strong on the record. They've become so good at what they do. The challenge of expressing themselves in a more compact way, they really rose to it. Ultimately, *Lamb* has a toughness that's a little different from the last few records. That's really inspiring.

Martin: Yeah, tightness mixed with toughness. Like, they could be tough before, but it seemed like things were off in separate corners. Here it's like straight between the eyes, kind of thing.

Charlie: And it's that directness that really grabbed me at the time. It was 1975 or 1976 when I heard it, and I was already hearing Patti Smith and Bruce Springsteen. So to me, without knowing much about pop history, as a 14-year-old, I just thought it was another cool development in music, to have that directness and toughness mixed with a really dramatic prog rock aesthetic.

Martin: Sweet, all right. Does anybody have any closing thoughts, or extra points they wanted to make?

Phil: Yes, I wanted to mention that in context, the other thing going on at this time was *Tales from Topographic Oceans* by Yes, and that was a double album, of course, too. Totally different acceptance. That was seen as overblown as soon as it arrived, but there's more love for it now. But I do believe there was more love for *The Lamb Lies*

Down on Broadway instantly, and I think it's probably drifted a bit as of late. I know that Steve Hackett has gone around doing several tours where he's concentrated on 50 years of playing albums in their completeness, but he hasn't done *Lamb*. He does *Lamb* highlights. He's never played the whole album in one go. It might be because his playing on it wouldn't warrant that kind of presentation because he's not really involved in it quite as much. He's in the background on a lot of the songs, I feel.

Martin: Yeah, Phil, you are right. The tide has turned on this album a little bit. It's widely been assumed to be the best Genesis album, and now people are starting to complain about it more.

Phil: At the time, when I first got into Genesis, I found it was quite inaccessible to start with. Thinking about my listening habits now, we sit down and we enjoy a whole album. A lot of times back then, we'd get an album out the sleeve and play the track we wanted to listen to before we went out on Friday night. On *Selling England*, you could do that—the first track, "Dancing with the Moonlight Knight," you just played it. But with *Lamb*, a lot of the tracks in isolation didn't work as well, unless you took a handful and listened to them in sequence.

Martin: They're doing rock, like you say, mixed with soundtrack-y bits, some typical Genesis, some ballads, some instrumentals. But yeah, this one has less of the straight English countryside pastoral music on it.

Phil: That's right. When we get to the next album, with tracks like "Squonk," I think *The Lamb Lies Down on Broadway* is where that was born. This bass and drum groove that Collins and Rutherford put together, it's first coming together on *Lamb*.

Martin: Do you remember how this came off on tour?

Phil: Well, first off, they did the whole thing. When they first went out on tour with this, it was the whole album. So when they went out, people had to sit through 90 minutes of music they didn't know before they got to anything they did know. And this is in the '70s when people really didn't do long sets. But it was only a few months. They had lots of technical problems, because Gabriel wanted to have a proper screen show, and the technology wasn't around to support that, really. Also, a lot of the songs, when they pulled them together, they were improvised to start with, which I don't think Genesis had ever really done before. And so playing them live was a challenge.

And it was incredibly tiring for Gabriel, who was centrestage and quite busy. There are some instrumental parts for him to go and have a glass of water, but most of the time it's very lyric-heavy. It must have been an incredibly exhausting experience to pull this together. And in fact, when Genesis—they're one of the few bands where all the members are still alive—talked a while ago now about coming back together to do *Lamb* in its entirety, it was Gabriel that said I don't want to do that. It would have been such an undertaking. In the end, the tour pushed the personalities beyond where they could get on with each other. And obviously, Gabriel jumped ship after the tour, didn't he?

Philip: As a double album concept, I don't feel like *The Lamb Lies Down on Broadway* is a journey I can go through and effortlessly enjoy. The reason I bought this album—and it was the first Genesis album I actually ever bought—was because of the hype and communal pressure you start getting as a young man, as a young fan, as a teenager, to recognise its genius. If I'm a real prog fan, I absolutely need to get this seminal double album by Genesis and I have to like it. And I would obsessively listen to it when I was younger because I really wanted to like it in order to fit in with the consensus. Now that I'm much older, I can say that I like it, but it's definitely not the greatest prog albums of all time. People generally pick *Close to the Edge* and I'd say I have to agree with that.

Charlie: I love records like this. It's a band in crisis album. And I love band in crisis albums, like *Abbey Road* for example, where a band is completely struggling to stay together, yet they make a brilliant record anyway. Forces are conspiring to pull them apart, but they've achieved all the skills of working together. Perhaps because they're so determined to try to pull this last one together, it comes out brilliant in its own way, even though it's flawed in others. There was a real rush to finish *Lamb*. That creates some problems for the record, but in other ways, it makes them make decisions fast. And you can hear that there are a lot of ideas on this record that become part of the vocabulary of Peter Gabriel's solo music, and then also become part of the vocabulary of Genesis' later music, with the tighter arrangements and the ability to create contrast and excitement in shorter packages.

Martin: Luis, you had something to say on the relative popularity of this album now years later, right?

Luis: Yes, we've talked about this before. The typical Genesis fan is very, very square. They're limited in what they like. They like the weepy guitar solos and they like the layers of Moog and organ and Mellotron and all that. If you don't give them that recipe, they get frustrated. *The Lamb Lies Down on Broadway* is not catering to that. This record was actually trying to make many bold things happen all at once. To me, artistically it's a huge accomplishment. I'm glad that the traditional Genesis fans don't like it, because it means there's probably something really forward-thinking in it.

Entangled: *Genesis on Record 1969-1976*

A TRICK OF THE TAIL

February 13, 1976
Charisma CDS 4001
Produced by David Hentschel and Genesis
Engineered by David Hentschel and Nick "Haddock" Bradford
Recorded at Trident Studios, London, UK
Personnel: Phil Collins – drums, percussion, lead and backing vocals; Steve Hackett – electric guitar, 12-string guitars; Tony Banks – pianos, synthesizers, organ, Mellotron, 12-string guitar, backing vocals; Mike Rutherford – 12-string guitar, basses, bass pedals

Side 1
1. Dance on a Volcano (Rutherford, Banks, Hackett, Collins) 5:53
2. Entangled (Hackett, Banks) 6:28
3. Squonk (Rutherford, Banks) 6:27
4. Mad Mad Moon (Banks) 7:35

Side 2
1. Robbery, Assault & Battery (Banks, Collins) 6:15
2. Ripples (Rutherford, Banks) 8:03
3. A Trick of the Tail (Banks) 4:34
4. Los Endos (Collins, Hackett, Rutherford, Banks) 5:46

Entangled: Genesis on Record 1969-1976

An *A Trick of the Tail* Timeline

October 1975. Steve Hackett releases a solo album called *Voyage of the Acolyte*. Both Phil Collins and Mike Rutherford contribute extensively.

October – November, 1975. Genesis and producer David Hentschel set up shop at Trident Studios in London to work on the band's first album without Peter Gabriel.

February 13, 1976. Genesis issue *A Trick of the Tail*, the band's seventh album. It reaches No.31 on the Billboard charts and No.3 in the UK and eventually certifies gold in both territories, plus gold in France and platinum in Canada.

March 12, 1976. "A Trick of the Tail," backed with "Ripples," is issued as a single in the UK. America gets "Ripples" backed with "Entangled." Note, "Ripples" is stylised as "Ripples…" on the inner gatefold of the original vinyl, but is simply "Ripples" on the back cover and on the record label.

March 26 – May 9, 1976. The band conduct a North American campaign in support of *A Trick of the Tail*. Drumming is Bill Bruford.

June 9 – July 11, 1976. The band close out their brief *A Trick of the Tail* tour with dates in the UK and mainland Europe.

June 18, 1976. Phil Collins' jazz-fusion side-project Brand X issue their debut album, *Unorthodox Behaviour*.

Entangled: Genesis on Record 1969-1976

Martin talks to Phil Aston, Ralph Chapman and Pontus Norshammar about *A Trick of the Tail*.

Martin Popoff: Genesis begin a new era with *A Trick of the Tail*. How do they respond to adversity?

Phil Aston: Well, it's one of my favourite Genesis albums, if that counts for anything, even though Peter Gabriel has left the band. It really comes together here. Peter's a powerful personality that's not around now, saying "I want to do this" and "I don't want to do that." They've got something to prove.

Martin: Do you remember as a kid feeling surprised that Peter Gabriel has this really distinct voice and oh, look, our drummer sounds like him?

Phil: Yeah (laughs), and it's interesting because on *Lamb*, Gabriel sounds the least like Phil Collins that he ever did. I mean, there were some effects and inflections on Peter Gabriel's voice for some of the songs, where he was doing these characters. He sounds like an exaggerated version of Peter Gabriel, and that's only on *Lamb*. Whereas on *Selling England* and the prior albums, there's a kind of interchangeability between him and Phil Collins. But on *Lamb* he was developing a different aspect to his own voice. Once Peter Gabriel becomes a solo artist, he doesn't sound like Phil Collins at all. On *Lamb*, he's developing his theatrical voice and his songwriting techniques in a way that was moving away from Genesis. But yeah, for *A Trick of the Tail*, Phil Collins just sounds like we've moved straight on from the Peter Gabriel of *Selling England* and missed out on *Lamb*.

Ralph Chapman: Like Phil says, they do have something to prove. Let's talk about Phil first, because he's now central to things. This would have been recorded in the autumn of '75. Phil was very active. He had done the Steve Hackett album and Brand X had formed and he was recording *Unorthodox Behaviour*. There's the 1975 *Peter and the Wolf* album, which is Jack Lancaster and Robin Lumley, Lumley being in Brand X. There's Lancaster's solo album in '76, *Marscape*, with Lumley, which is brilliant. Both those records had guys from Brand X and they're snapshots of just how evolved Phil was.

He was always a great player, but if you listen to, say, that Peter Banks solo record that Phil plays on, *Two Sides of Peter Banks*, 1973, Phil is great, but he's still a pretty raw talent, an extraordinary player but raw. At the time of that record, his influences were more like Bonham and Ringo and Bill Bruford and Roger Powell from The Action. Other than his superlative talent, he was guided, I'd say, in part by those seminal influences.

By the time you get to '76, Mahavishnu Orchestra and Return to Forever have happened and his sphere of influence had gotten much larger. So now he's listening to Billy Cobham, and presumably he's listening to guys like Lenny White and Tony Williams, serious fusion players. When I interviewed Rupert Hine about going to see Mahavishnu Orchestra in London, Phil was there and afterwards he recalls seeing Phil just being gobsmacked by Billy Cobham. So Billy Cobham looms large. I believe he was into Santana as well.

So Phil's playing style was changing, and with the new production, the drums sounded great. All of a sudden, you were hearing all the intricacies of his bass pedal work and his cymbal work. As for his evolution, you start to hear it on *Lamb*, like on "The Colony of Slippermen" and two-thirds of the way through the title track and on "The Grand Parade of Lifeless Packaging."

The other thing I want to say about Phil is, it's hard to separate him from everything that he is, with everything he brings to the table as a singer and as a songwriter as well. There was a period where by his own admission, he was basically an arranger/drummer; his skills were as an arranger, including his own drum parts. And so he's evolving, much like Ringo did in The Beatles. People forget that The Beatles had three incredibly progressive songwriters. And you had a drummer who was just as progressive in terms of what ideas he could bring to this ever-increasing stylistic shift that was pushing forward. Phil's perhaps not as acute as someone like Ringo, but that's what he was doing.

Anyway, so by the time you get to *A Trick of the Tail*, there's so much happening. The role of the drums have shifted, forgetting about it being the first record without Peter. It's a masterclass. There's the keyboard break in "Robbery, Assault and Battery." With "Los Endos," he takes what is essentially a Hackett song and rearranges it and brings in this whole Santana and Airto sensibility, this Latin thing. These were new ideas for Genesis. And I would say, again, that's because Phil was evolving so quickly as a player. Lastly, Phil might have changed kits at this point. He started out as Gretch,

I think, and then moved to Premier. I believe by *Trick*, he was now with Pearl. There's that great picture of him from the *Lamb* era where he's surrounded by timbales. And I think possibly around '76, he was using either Syndrums or Rotos. He was increasing his game and his creativity was off the charts.

So the next bit, as far as the creation of *Trick* goes, with Gabriel leaving, the music press declared Genesis dead. It's on record that it really lifted the band in some sense because all of a sudden, they were confronted with very little in terms of expectation from the press. They were already written off, so the freedom that must have brought them was, I'm sure, a huge shot in the arm.

And the other thing was that Gabriel was such a massive artistic and personal force and now he's gone. It's a matter of history that although he was tight with Banks, they had a fractious artistic relationship that had sharply deteriorated during *Lamb*. Peter had alienated himself from the band for a number of reasons. But the upside of Peter's departure, beyond the expectation, was that now there's this void, one that Tony Banks mostly filled just because of the hugeness of his personality and how prolific and how extraordinary a writer he was. But without that kind of fractious element, the sessions were easy and fun. They were in a situation where anything they did will surprise people and not disappoint them. Plus everybody's getting along and bringing ideas and there's a new producer too. It was a rebirth, and you can't underestimate the power of the rebirth.

Also what's fascinating is that without Gabriel there—not that they weren't superb with Gabriel in the band—it's now four players and that changes the dynamic. There's no one sort of off to the side trying to write a set of lyrics to an instrumental passage. Now an instrumental passage can stay instrumental because there's no lyrics trying to muscle their way in. Sometimes those experiments where Gabriel did that were spectacular, like in "Apocalypse in 9/8." Other times it was a source of friction. Now there was so much freedom beyond just artistic clashing. They had a wider canvas to paint on, which is exciting.

Again, contextually speaking, progressive rock in '75, '76 was an interesting time, if you think about it. Genesis were suddenly, in some ways, the last man standing. Yes, although I don't think they'd officially split, '75 is when they started to do all their solo projects. And I think Moraz was gone at that point. So Yes were kind of in disarray. ELP were totally burned-out. Tull were moving off in another direction, into what was almost a progressive folk rock thing. I guess Van der Graaf Generator had just finished a long hiatus but was back. Fripp had broken up King Crimson. But there was a moment there when Genesis had an opportunity to step in to be the premier progressive rock band, which they indeed did and were successful in doing that. But for whoever was left, progressive rock was getting leaner. There are eight tracks on *A Trick of the Tail*. "Ripples" is the longest song on there, at eight minutes.

There's one other thing I want to say before we get into the songs. It's a bee in my bonnet. I hated that documentary, *Sum of All Parts*. I thought it was fucking terrible. But one of the things in there which I have never understood, relating to *A Trick of the Tail*—and I read it again in Mike Rutherford's book—is this revisionist history there's been about *Voyage of the Acolyte*, which is the first Steve Hackett solo album. Although Tony Banks is not on it, it feels like a bit of a dry run for *A Trick of the Tail* because it's got Mike on bass for the most part—John Gustafson and Percy Jones do one track each. And it's got Phil on drums. So you can still very much hear the vitality of Genesis without it being a Genesis record.

Anyway, the revisionist part is them now—Rutherford, and I think even Banks— claiming that they were irritated with Hackett. That in a moment of crisis, he goes off and makes his solo album. It's implying that somehow they would have used any of that material. And although I could hear Genesis perhaps working up "Ace of Wands," for the most part, they were never going to do "The Hermit" or "Star of Sirius." And that feels like revisionism to me. Maybe they've grown weary of Steve spending the last decade-and-a-half cashing in on Genesis after leaving them, possibly disrespectfully, all those years ago.

Martin: Great stuff, Ralph. Pontus, what is your perspective on *A Trick of the Tail*?

Pontus Norshammar: For me, it's a fusion album. *Lamb* is an outlier in the catalogue; it's almost a film on record, a musical, heavily narrative-driven. Peter writes the whole story and then he leaves. It's also darker and bleaker than *Selling England by the Pound*. There are hints of industrial and Krautrock to it, plus the Brian Eno effect, and Peter eventually touches on all that in his solo career. But Peter leaves the band and now we have a different group. We have the two Charterhouse guys still in the band, and then Collins and Hackett.

And I think that chemistry meant that the ideas from *Selling England* could be put to new use on *A Trick of the Tail*.

They get Phil to sing on the songs, but they also try to find a singer. They're almost there, but then they decide, oh, Phil can do it. Another important factor, Steve has done a solo album with two other members of the group, plus a host of other musicians, which has boosted his self-confidence. He has written a very good album, and also proven to himself that all the material he wanted to have in the group is worthwhile. It's quite telling that Tony Banks is not on Steve's album.

Another factor is Brand X. They form in 1975 and the first album was released simultaneously with *A Trick of the Tail*. So on the side, Phil is in a group that is very much into fusion and new synthesizer technology, and so we get an influence of that. *A Trick of the Tail* is a drum-centric album, very much rhythmic. And it's funny, because you've got a fast song, then a slow song, then a fast one and a middle-paced one, balanced with an epic at the end. Side two, you've got a fast song, slow song, a pop song, and then fusion at the end. So it's very clearly organised. It feels like a happy album. It feels like they're saying, we've found our way and we're very proud of it.

Martin: How does this album cover sit with you?

Phil: Over here in England, it was textured, for one, or mottled. Again, we're going back to a representation of English pastoral prog. All the characters look like they're from English history, and each of the little characters is based on the music that's inside the album. It draws you in.

Martin: As alluded to, there's a new producer that the guys are going to be happy with, and use again.

Ralph: Yes, it's David Hentschel and he does good things for the band. *Lamb* marked a breakthrough in terms of how the drums sounded, but with *A Trick of the Tail*, all of that was recorded at Trident and I suppose that again they've been liberated by new recording techniques.

If I can back up, as many young kids did when they discover a band, I immediately went back and bought the back catalogue. I started with *Abacab*, and my brother already had *Wind & Wuthering* in his collection, so the next one I bought was *A Trick of the Tail*. And not only did I buy the records, but I bought every book I could find on the band. Such was the passion that was immediately invoked by *Abacab*. And Armando Gallo, in his book *I Know What I Like*, said of *A Trick of the Tail*, "Finally you can hear the drums."

And so *A Trick of the Tail* is notable, in part, for what Hentschel and Collins were able to capture from a percussion point of view. I always felt up to that point that Phil's drums had been mic'ed carefully and properly but they were not necessarily part of the palette. He wasn't integrated into the painting all that well. He was from an arrangement and performance standpoint, but not the sound of it. Again, I always reference The Beatles with something like "Tomorrow Never Knows," or The Small Faces and "Itchycoo Park." Those are great examples of treating the drums as part of a larger picture, as opposed to simply providing rhythm. And I think that *A Trick of the Tail* marks the first time that element was captured in Genesis.

But yes, in David Hentschel, you've got a sympathetic producer, who's into drums, who has a history. That's the other thing that David brought to the table. He had done soundtracks. With Phil, he had done an instrumental version of the Ringo Starr album *Ringo*, called *Startling Music*. Phil is the main drummer. So David and Phil had this new artistic partnership. Together they get great clarity from the drums. There's the cymbal work on "Squonk" and also the high-hats and the sound of the China cymbals on "Los Endos." On a song like "Can-Utility and the Coastliners" from *Foxtrot*, you could hear how good Phil was with his bass drum foot. But the clarity you get on "Los Endos" was exciting. As much as I love John Burns' production, especially on *Lamb*, this was a huge step up. Certainly as huge—but in a different way—as when Hugh Padgham joined after *Duke*.

Plus, contextually speaking, drums were shifting in the mid-'70s. They had gone through this whole period in the early '70s with what's called the dead Ringo sound, although I don't agree with using Ringo's name like that. But there was certainly a lifeless sound to the toms and we're back to that now. Drums sound terrible these days. Just wretched. This weird, awful, dead, Nashville sound is fucking terrible. But anyway, *A Trick of the Tail* was part of this new sweeping movement where drum sounds became fully explored again. Listen, for example, to "Better Off Dead" by Elton John with Gus Dudgeon and Nigel Olsson—it's an incredibly forward-sounding recording in terms of drums.

Martin: Into the record, as is the case with many Genesis albums, this one's opener becomes a famed classic.

Phil: Yes, we start off with "Dance on a Volcano," and it's not like *Selling England*, which was more quirky. This is at the rockier end of prog. It's determined, it's confident and the production is so different to what has gone before. It's still theatrical but it's bigger and bolder. We talked before about turning the dial from Gentle Giant on one side to Yes in the middle and Pink Floyd on the other side. They're more in the Yes world here. Plus Steve Hackett has come forward in the mix. He's more involved and prominent; it's more apparent that he's there. Tony Banks is obviously still doing his thing, but he's not taking all of the accolades. In fact "Dance on a Volcano," to me, is where Phil Collins becomes one of the best drummers in this field. He's working hard and he's produced great. It's a strong rock opener. It's got aggressive moments and, like I say, it's confident.

Ralph: We begin with bass pedals and sort of McGuinn-esque 12-string guitar and layered-in Mellotron choir. Other than "Watcher of the Skies," no Genesis record has started with such power. Sure, "Abacab" is pretty explosive, as is "Behind the Lines," but when I put on *A Trick of the Tail*, it's visceral. All the rest of the Genesis albums tend to start quiet and build. So this felt different. Let's come out of the gate baring our teeth.

You know, *A Trick of the Tail* is interesting because nobody would accuse that record of being a guitar record. You have to work to hear Hackett. And I don't think it's terrible; it's just a slight issue with the mix, with the balance. They were largely led by a keyboard player. But around 2:30 on the left channel of the original mix—and anything I'm going to say is about the original mixes and not the Nick Davis remixes etc.—the tone and the technique that Hackett uses… it's all about why they hired him in the first place. The texture, atmosphere, technique and variety in his playing is exciting and unique and what makes that record stand out for me.

And then because you've got this big drum sound, you're more encouraged to try something interesting with it. They're clearly recording in stereo, but there are some interesting panning effects. It also sounds like there's Syndrums involved. But at the break around 2:20, the drums pan across the stereo spectrum like rolling thunder. It's such an extraordinary moment.

Another thing that strikes me about "Dance on a Volcano" is that it's particularly adept at balancing the tension of the verses and the release of the chorus. So if you follow those lyrics in the music, it's an absolute match made in Heaven, so to speak. It represents that intoxicating feeling of moving closer to either Heaven or Hell. And that's just so unique to that song.

I don't know whether it's an unconscious autobiographical moment, but I love that passage near the end, where Phil goes, "The music's playing, the notes are right/Put your left foot first and move into the light." And then at the very end we get, "Let the dance begin," which tells you that the band has arrived, in my mind. I know we often project our own ideas onto the lyrics, but I've always found that similar to Queen's "Let Me Entertain You." They're demanding that the audience pay attention because the band has arrived. That's "Dance on a Volcano" for me.

Pontus: Like the album at large, I think of fusion when I hear "Dance on a Volcano." You have the drumming from Phil. You have that very memorable opening and sort of syncopated fill. You have interesting phrasings from Banks, who plays lots of Mellotron and ARP on this album. Plus it's just amazing that Phil is so convincing and projecting as a vocalist on these songs. The last time we had a solo vocal from Phil was "More Fool Me," which is a bit by the wayside for me. He's far more convincing here.

And you know what? It sounds like he's never done anything else other than lead a band. He comes across and he delivers those lines. As for his drumming, the rhythms are all over the place with lots of time changes. It's jazzy, frenetic, almost psychopathic. And when we get to the end, with "Let the dance begin," they double down on the fusion and you suddenly have all these synths and it's just beautiful. Oh, I love it so much. You even get a whistle. There's this powerhouse passage and you get this whistle and the energy just explodes.

It's an air-drumming song for me. The first time I heard his song was on *Seconds Out*, and of course it goes into "Los Endos" there (laughs). And the ending was weird. I was like, "You're gonna end it like *that*?! Everything comes down on an organ chord. I don't know, the songwriting here is just so good. The band is still mysterious. They're still telling fantastic stories and it's not mostly love songs yet. It's weird, it's quirky, it's very English but also incredibly lively—action-packed, as you would say.

Martin: "Entangled" is very much old-school Genesis in terms of ballads that sound 400 years old. With one difference—that's a hit song chorus right there. But mostly, it's just beautifully structured Genesis Renaissance music.

Phil: Yes, perfect sort of melancholy fairy tale-type music, which is a place, actually, that they go to several times on this album. On the back cover, we've got a picture of a nurse holding a lamp up, which goes with this song. Thy lyrics are well thought-out, and they evoke a distant time. The instrumentalists are almost breathing the words and that effect carries into Tony Banks' synthesizer solo, which unlike *Lamb*, where every time he did his solo it was right in your face, this one is really dialled back, lurking above the rest of the instrumentation. And it's very slow as he moves from one note to the other. It adds to the lush and ambient feel of the song.

Is it a ballad or more of a mood piece? Whatever it is, "Entangled" is one of my favourite songs off the album, because of how it draws you in, especially in the instrumental section. We're two songs in and it's already really accessible, really exciting, and you're thinking, what's going to happen next? Whereas with, say, *Selling England*, the tracks are all great but there's less of a curiosity factor. There's something about the way that *A Trick of the Tail* is moving where it feels like you're hearing a new and maybe unpredictable band.

Ralph: "Entangled" is a rare Hackett/Banks collaboration. I believe it was an unfinished Hackett song where he just had the verses and Banks came in with the chorus. The way the Mellotron drifts in and out at the verses is really lovely. It's a creative bit of arranging with an instrument that is largely known for washes and atmosphere. Here it's active.

The other thing I noticed is that Peter was obviously a great singer, and emotive. *Lamb* is an album where he really comes into his own. In that sense, it was such an extraordinary loss to have him leave, because he had evolved so greatly as a singer. But he left and Phil takes over. Phil sang "More Fool Me" and did a great job, as I believe Steve has acknowledged. He also did "For Absent Friends." And if you listen to his old band, Flaming Youth, he takes two or three leads. So he wasn't a completely inexperienced singer, although maybe he had a ways to go. Still, he was such a musical person, so that could only help. I believe Tony and Mike say he totally arrives on the *And Then There Were Three* album, or maybe *Duke*.

But in something like "Entangled," that guy understood harmony, and understood how to create and how to layer his voice. "Entangled" is so powerful because of how Phil's voice is used. You'd never in a million years think that this guy is their lead singer because they couldn't find anyone else. Mick Strickland auditioned, but he couldn't sing "Squonk" in the original key, so they just had to go with Phil. And apparently they were still looking for a new singer after they recorded *A Trick of the Tail*, which I'm not sure if that's apocryphal or not. So you started with "Dance on a Volcano," which was quite an aggressive vocal. He pulls that off and then you get "Entangled," which is a pastoral piece of work, and they use his voice differently and that also turns out extraordinary. One final thing, anybody who thinks they are somehow trying to hide Phil by layering his vocals so extensively here, I think that's a misnomer, or a fallacy.

Pontus: "Entangled" provides dramatic contrast to what came before with "Dance on a Volcano." It's interesting. If we go to *Selling England by the Pound*, we get "Dancing with the Moonlit Knight," which starts as a ballad and goes into a frantic sort of fusion song and then goes back to the folk music scene again. Here, we do get the frantic song in "Dance on a Volcano," and then we get the traditional British ballad, concentrated to one song. Their songwriting has developed to the point where they are saying, let's write a complete song in this fashion. Let's write a song in this mould.

I love "Entangled;" it's one of my all-time favourite Genesis songs. It's got the beautiful guitar lines, the thick harmonies, the smaller bits where they have the vibes coming in, put to the back of the sound picture. It's got the two melodies; one is Hackett and one is Banks—it's Banks for the chorus. In the end it's a beautiful dreamscape, maybe some kind of therapy through trance or hypnotism. After all, we're in a hospital and we're talking about a patient. So we're talking, perhaps, about Freudian things, psychoses, but it's couched in a very beautiful song.

It's very much tongue-in-cheek British humour. It's like, "If we can help you we will." But then it closes with "You'll have no trouble until/You can catch your breath/And the nurse will present you the bill!" It's so beautifully written and beautifully played. It's this sort of Crosby, Stills, Nash and Young feel to it, like people sitting around fires and strumming guitars but singing very well (laughs). And I love the production. It's very warm and inviting; you're in the music. You're in that dream state.

Martin: Next we have what is possibly the album's most famous song, another exercise in streamlining the songwriting.

Phil: Yes, absolutely. "Squonk" brings a heavy rock feel based around bass and drums, unlike any songs that have gone before. On the back cover there's this little creature that's crying, which must be the squonk. It's a song that contributes significantly to *A Trick of the Tail* being one of the band's harder, rockiest albums, in terms of what we think of as traditional rock. But you've got "Dance on a Volcano," rock, "Entangled," pull back, "Squonk," jump forwards again. Great lyrics, great vocal phrasing and great production on the voice as well as he moves out into the chorus, powered by the instrumentation behind it.

Martin: And it's all very *Alice in Wonderland*.

Phil: It is, indeed. But I think for people that didn't like Genesis, people who were into Sabbath, Zeppelin and Purple, this was the one that you could say to your friends that didn't like Genesis, you want to listen to *A Trick of the Tail*. Because it was consistently accessible. *Selling England* was accessible but there were parts that maybe some people would think, ah I'm not sure about that. I'm not sure if I want something that's 12 minutes long. These songs weren't overly long, but they had all the traits of Genesis within them, including lots of experimentation.

Ralph: A lot has been made of "Squonk," that it was Phil putting on his John Bonham hat, and that Mike and Tony were listening in the car and "Kashmir" came on and that's what they were looking for. And that indeed set in motion the embryonic moments rhythmically of that song. But there are some great drum moments on that song apart from all that. Around 4:16, Phil does a pair of flams that are just perfectly placed. I often wondered why Chester never reproduced those; I never understood that. I understand Chester making something his own. I don't think Bruford did them either, but he was kind of a maverick. But it's just one of those moments of creativity and power which was Phil at his best—4:16, check it out.

But what makes "Squonk" so fantastic is the ability of Banks and Rutherford in terms of writing such fantastic lyrics, in this case about this mythical creature who is so unfortunate to look at that he would dissolve into tears sort of thing. But the boys in Genesis had such a streak of humanity in them, that even in a song that was ostensibly about a mythical creature, you end up, certainly as a young person, young boy, I was identifying with these lyrics. The poetry of them, the humanism, the humanity, you say to yourself, somebody gets me. I have always resisted the idea that Genesis is one of those bands who wrote about dragons, when almost every single song they wrote in those solid years of the '70s had some element that rattled at your heart. And with "Squonk," you've got this beautiful set of lyrics contrasted by such a heavy track. It's that masterful approach to dynamics and contrast that makes them the second greatest band of all time, behind only The Beatles.

Pontus: As Ralph says, "Squonk" is always framed as their Led Zeppelin moment. They wanted to write their own "Kashmir." It's a fun albeit heartbreaking song, quirky, well-organised and Phil sings it well. It has some oomph to it, and also what I call the Little Feat ending, with the weird time signature at the end. "Squonk" works very well as an opener on *Seconds Out* as well. If we compare it to what the band were capable of on *Trespass*, we're in a different state of being now. Everybody knows where they're going.

Martin: It's not particularly Zeppelin-esque either, is it?

Pontus: No, it isn't. But they said they wanted to do something like that. I believe Phil mentioned something about Bonham's approach to high-hat. It's inspired by Led Zeppelin but it's done in its own way.

Martin: Hard to believe, but we're not even at the end of side one yet. Last track is "Mad Man Moon," which I suppose is another ballad, but unlike "Entangled," this one is propelled by drums.

Phil: Yes, and it's also distinguished by Tony dropping back to traditional piano. And actually, there's some lovely playing from the whole of the band. But it's interesting, because despite the dynamics between them, all of the songs so far have had the same kind of emotional feel to them, with a kind of angst behind the vocals, but not teenage angst, more like unease.

Ralph: To reach back to "Entangled" and how they layer the vocals with double-tracking and stacking, the thing that strikes me about "Mad Man Moon" is that it's a singular vocal, for the most part. There are brief bits of harmonies introduced, but they recognise that not every song needed or wanted or required that kind of approach. So "Mad Man Moon" features just a plaintive, single-tracked, almost lonely vocal, again, for the most part.

Looking back and thinking about the situation, it proves that they weren't concerned about whether Phil could pull it off. Somewhere at that point they must have known that this guy's as versatile in his own way as Peter was, that we can use this voice any way we want. "Mad Man Moon" is the last track on side one and we're getting a new side of Phil as a singer, or a new use of the singer, without making it obviously Phil-centric. It just meant that they had a lot of room for vocal arrangements and sometimes they could go big and sometimes they needed nothing.

Of course, the great thing about "Mad Man Moon" is the instrumental break in it, and the choice of instruments. I don't really know if that's a marimba, or if those are vibes, but there's this percussion element as that break starts that is fresh for them. There's the bass pedals and the layered-in ARPS and above all, there's Tony's quite sober piano guiding the whole thing. It's just masterful record-making and arranging. Again, it's an extraordinary act of arrangement over this beautiful, sprawling melody.

As compact as *A Trick of the Tail* is, comparatively to something like *Lamb*, they were getting better and better. And you see this later on, this skill with respect to jamming a lot of ideas in a rather finite amount of time. Now, "Mad Man Moon" is over seven minutes, but it never feels like it. I know that's a cliché, but it never feels like seven minutes. It's such a journey piece, which is emphasised by the way the instrumental part kind of winds down. Maybe that's not the right word. But out of that instrumental section, now a completely new piece of music emerges out of it. There's the "Hey, man, I'm the sandman" line and that really quick, almost double-time section, and then the song resolves. Other than Lennon, McCartney, Pete Townsend and Peter Gabriel, I can't think of a more accomplished songwriter than Tony Banks, and "Mad Man Moon" is an incredible example of his abilities.

Pontus: "Mad Man Moon" is essentially a ballad, but it somehow becomes the epic of the album for me. It's another storytelling song, and then we've got the sort of Spanish middle section. It's one of Tony's songs and there's beautiful piano playing by him and everything sits very well together. It's quiet, it's subtle and there's not much bombast, with Phil playing soft and jazzy but distinctive during the song. But for much of the song there are no drums.

Martin: A lot of different keyboards are utilised.

Pontus: Yeah, lots and lots of keyboards; it's like his whole stash is burned into this. You have Mellotron, a dozen synthesizers, organ and piano, which dominates. Everything is based around this chord sequence in the middle there. I mean, if Peter had stayed, that sort of first phrase (sings it), that would have been played on the flute, because the setting on the Mellotron is a flute setting, right? So they said, "All right, he's not here; let's use the Mellotron."

Martin: Now that King Crimson is gone, is Tony Banks the most senior maintainer of the Mellotron in popular music?

Phil: I would say he is, yeah. Because obviously Floyd have dropped it. And Genesis are the most accessible prog band leaning towards the potential of having hit singles, which is going to come very soon. But yeah, I would say they're the last man standing. Barclay James Harvest are probably still waving the flag at this point, but they're a few miles behind in the rearview mirror. They're not in the same division as these other bands. Van der Graaf is an interesting case. They're becoming more difficult for your average rock fan to get into. Whereas Genesis are becoming more accessible, but at the same time harder around the edges. But you're right, Tony Banks still loves the Mellotron.

Martin: Nice, Over to side two, and Genesis is still quirky, only now they're perky as well, skipping their way through "Robbery, Assault and Battery."

Phil: Yes (laughs), it's quite upbeat and poppy, isn't it? It's certainly a different emotional feel on display. It's probably my least favourite track on the album, and not because I don't like it. It's just if I was having to rank them all, then this one would sit at the bottom. It's a lift in energy from "Mad Man Moon," isn't it?

Ralph: With "Robbery, Assault and Battery," for me, the obvious thing is that Phil is able to play a role, a character. That's a Collins/Banks composition. There's a lot of runway being eaten up by the lyrics on this song. But also, one of the things that has always struck me is how Hackett is used, and how sparse and strange and idiosyncratic his lines are in the verses. And then in the chorus, it's so heavy and driving.

There's a lot to be said for Steve as a soloist, because he's one of the greatest. And I would say the same thing about Phil and certainly Mike as well, but there's a lot to be said in the rush to sort of crown these guys as the greatest ever because of their chops. You forget just how intuitive they were in just creating parts. It's almost like, you can love Tennessee Williams or David Mamet, or any of these playwrights, for the stories they tell, but sometimes what reveals them as the brilliant people they were, is in a single line, or a handful of lines or a moment in a scene.

And I would say that's often the case with Genesis. "Robbery, Assault and Battery," you wouldn't necessarily think about the guitar because there are so many other things that have been talked about. But I love the guitar on that song. Although I never copped to the notion that Genesis was diminished by his departure. I just think they changed. But those moments were harder to find in the post-Hackett era because he was a painter himself, and you don't have that artist anymore. It's different. You get a facsimile, but you don't get Steve.

Martin: How would Tony tend to write versus Mike?

Ralph: Musically, Tony has said that he's the guy who always adds one extra chord that kind of kills a song's commercial possibilities. Lyrically, as far as being explicit and simple, people always point to Phil. But Rutherford, to me, "Your Own Special Way" was a real breakthrough moment. There's also "More Fool Me," which again, is a simple song lyrically, and a great piece of lyric. The official credit there is just a blanket band credit, but it's considered to be Mike on the music and Mike and Phil on the lyrics.

Anyway, to answer your question, I think not so much with *Trick*. Because there's no solo Rutherford songs on *Trick*, right? That doesn't happen until the next record. So you really don't know what Rutherford is contributing lyrically. He's an enigma at that point. The first time you really hear a Rutherford lyric, like I said, is "Your Own Special Way," which is as sentimental and as passionate and as explicit as any love song. That lyric is, in part, inspired by a Christina Rossetti poem from the 19th century. Mike, very early on, is willing to put his heart on his sleeve.

With Banks, it's not that he didn't do that—and I'll talk a bit about that again on the *Invisible Touch*—but I would just say that Rutherford was more immediate, quicker, that he was really the first guy in Genesis to embrace the idea of a straight-up love song before Phil got involved with it at all. So that's how I would contrast them. But it's not really relevant in my mind on *A Trick of the Tail*. It doesn't happen until *Wind & Wuthering*.

Martin: There's mostly a 4/4 feel in "Robbery, Assault and Battery," but they make up for it with the break section, which is quite nutty. It's like fusion running headlong into prog.

Ralph: Phil was a drummer who could play a myriad of time signatures. But he had such a fantastic feel and sense of melody, that he could build these things in, in this melodious and groove-oriented way and that's what you get here. You hear it on later tracks like "Turn It On Again" and even later with "Fading Lights." This break, I believe, is in 7/4, something like that, maybe 11/8. I don't know if you notice, but Mike and Tony rarely talk about the how potent that band was in terms of veering off the 4/4 and jamming in these different time signatures. It usually comes down Phil and his ability to make things musical. He wasn't a math drummer. I love Neil Peart, but often you were really aware that you were straying into different time signatures. But if you're just a person who loves music like Phil does, he makes it seamless.

Martin: But "Dance on a Volcano" is pretty math rock, and as a result, you can't really say it grooves all that well.

Ralph: Well, yeah, fair enough. I mean, you can find anomalies. See, I don't know the development of that song. I know it developed in a jam before Hackett arrived. And Hackett's main contribution, I believe, is the coda to that song. But that song seems to be about atmosphere. But even "Robbery, Assault and Battery," where you all of a sudden find yourself in some crazy place, there are pyrotechnics, but it's so smooth and deftly performed. So the chops are there, but never at the expense of the melody and never at the expense of Tony, which I love. "Turn It On Again" is the most potent example of a song that sounds like it's in four, but it's not in four. But you'd never know it unless you tried to clap along to it.

Martin: Pontus, thoughts on this one?

Pontus: Here's the thing with Genesis. From *Nursery Cryme* on, there was always a humorous track. Or a topical track, right? You have "Harold the Barrel," you have "The Battle of Epping Forest," you have "Get 'Em Out by Friday" and things like that. And here comes "Robbery, Assault and Battery." We're back into fusion, right? And the funny thing here is that Phil gets to revisit his childhood acting prowess—remember that Phil was a working child actor. He gets to play all these roles, the policeman, the robber, etc. There's a conversation going on.

Martin: It's almost disco.

Pontus: Yeah, disco! And Phil really likes his high-hat on this album. It really works for him. His drumming is set in the middle of the sound picture and he's such a powerhouse.

Martin: Next, we always talk about Renaissance music and medieval music but how about Elizabethan music? Is that what "Ripples" is, at least sometimes? I'm half-joking, of course, but man, this is a space that Genesis owns. Or if anybody else ever attempted it beyond the British folk boom realm, it was with about one-tenth the effort. There is so much happening in this song.

Phil: Yes, and after a more upbeat track, we then drift back into another laid-back mood piece. I agree—this song is a tour de force. For me, it's one of the absolute highlights of their career because it's a song that everybody in the world grows into, whether you are aware of the song or not. It's about being in your 20s or your teens and about ripples never coming back. It's about growing older. You know, to write that song from the perspective of how young they were was a huge thing. But the way Phil Collins sings it, the way that the chorus builds, this is Steve Hackett's moment to come forward with notes that just drift and pop onto the kind of feel that the lyrics have given you. And that's just a great line, "Ripples never come back." It's about a woman looking at herself in the mirror and how she'll never look as good as she does today. And now, of course, the whole Genesis audience can sit and live in that song too, and think to themselves, yeah, I know exactly what that's about.

Ralph: Here's a story about "Ripples." Use it if you want. When I listen to "Ripples," the first thing I think of is high school. When I was just at the peak of that early phase of my fanaticism, it was hard to find other people who were into Genesis. But I did have a friend, Charles Jones, his name was—not the animator—who was this kind of goofy but very charming dude. He liked Genesis, but not in the way I liked Genesis. But he had a surprising depth about him and he loved that song "Ripples." And we were talking about it once and he said to me, I asked him, "Why do you love 'Ripples' so much?" And he was in a relationship with this very, very pretty girl named Cathy Thompson. Go with this. And he would say that him and Cathy would put that song on—I think it was in her basement—and slow dance to it.

And for whatever reason, that affected me. I didn't have a girlfriend and I didn't seem to be in any rush to get one (laughs). But it was just such a romantic notion, tinged with regret and mortality and better days gone. That song swept me up. When he created that image, it just stuck with me. All of a sudden, I could see the shag carpet and the panelling and the Electrohome stereo and that bright yellow Atco label of the Genesis record spinning as these two teenagers were entwined with each other for over eight minutes. And so "Ripples," to me, evokes youthful romance.

The other thing that "Ripples" did for me immediately, and still does, is linked to the illustrations that Colin Elgie did for the cover. The image that is matched with that lyric is of the old woman staring at the mirror. And when you're 17, or even when you're 37, that's a cool image. It's neat artwork. The whole album is stacked with examples of people being ambitious. I hesitate to say that it was the best cover so far, but it seemed to be the most ambitious. You had the Paul Whitehead stuff and then you had Betty Swanwick, who did the painting for *Selling England* and then *The Lamb* was something different.

But *A Trick of the Tail*, which was Hipgnosis with Colin Elgie artwork, it was so ambitious and so story-based and so part of an experience, so very formidable. But that specific drawing of the old lady staring at the mirror, again when you're in your late 30s even, it doesn't really register. But when you get to your mid- and late-50s, you look at that and you think about how it's really the beginning of the dying of the light.

That's the thing about *A Trick of the Tail*. You get these records when you're 16, 17, and because of the incredible ability of the artists to be prescient to see into the future, to want to create something either consciously or unconsciously, they're from a time where they're writing something for the ages. That kind of intention and this kind of record will never age. In other words, it will stay relevant. Pete Townsend is another guy and Paul McCartney is another guy—they can write lyrics like that. That's what I said long ago about *All the Best Cowboys Have Chinese Eyes*. That record, for a 16-year-old who's so shy and has acne, it's such a security blanket. And "Ripples" is that kind of security blanket too. I can't remember the term that means never falling out of relevance. I think it's a season expression.

Martin: Evergreen?

Ralph: Is that the right expression? I think it is. If I ever met Colin Elgie, I'd fall at his feet and say, "What an inspiring piece of work." That little illustration is completely and stunningly matched to the music and the artistic expression that the band was going for.

Pontus: "Ripples" is a two-part song. It's a straightforward ballad with a beautiful melody, and it's sort of a spooky love song. I think it would have made a good single. What happens is in the middle of it, you get another section. The first section fades out and the next section comes in. That rhythm that's full of hi-hats, it's disco but it's not disco (laughs).

Martin: Do you mean the double-fisted high-hats, beginning at about 5:20?

Pontus: Yeah, double-fisted. And Steve Hackett shines here, because it's essentially a guitar solo section. We haven't talked about him very much. Steve is a cross between David Gilmour and Steve Howe, in a sense, because he plays those long notes. But he plays them quirky. They're not bluesy. And he has this tone of his own.

Martin: Here comes that question again, but can you tell when it's him on 12-string versus Mike on 12-string?

Pontus: It's pretty tough. And Tony Banks even played some 12-string in the past, plus I believe he plays 12-string on "Entangled." But if they don't tell us in the credits, it's hard to tell because it's layered. Plus that was the trademark of Anthony Phillips, so his tradition lives on through Steve and Mike in the '70s. And by 1976, they really got the hang of it. So you can't really know who's playing what. You're sure that it's Tony Banks playing keyboards, because, as Peter Gabriel said, he didn't allow anybody else to touch the keyboards, right? Which was quite funny.

But they are very good arrangers. One thing that Phil Collins brought to the band was that he could organise stuff. He could be the one to say, "Oh, we have a section here; put it over there with the others." He's a type of co-producer. You see that these albums are produced by Genesis and David Hentschel or John Anthony or whatever. It's very much Phil, I think (laughs). He'd be the one to say, "I want it that way." Because he produced lots of stuff afterwards, and that was one of his trademarks. But I think that with this album, they really master the type of progressive rock they wanted to achieve way back when they did *Trespass*. Here is the apex of that. And it doesn't matter that Gabriel is gone because they are carrying on anyway. Because I think if Peter had been with them, it would have been more in the vein of the *Lamb* soundscape. It wouldn't be as fusion-oriented as this was.

Martin: Next we have a rare title track for this band, and they kind of flub the occasion. "A Trick of the Tail" isn't exactly one of the band's celebrated classics.

Phil: No, and it was issued as a single too. I know I called "Robbery, Assault and Battery" my least favourite track on the album, but this is pretty close (laughs). The other songs have got huge personalities. This one, although it's the title track, feels to me like a lesser song, especially surrounded by such greatness. You're also coming out of the other side of "Ripples" and the way that song ends. Whatever was going to follow that was probably going to struggle.

Martin: It's a bit Elton John or The Beatles piano-wise.

Phil: Yeah, it is. It fits on the album but then again it kind of doesn't. It's a breather before what happens next. But the way the album is sequenced, "A Trick of the Tail" had to be where it is. And "Los Endos" obviously had to be at the end. But by putting "A Trick of the Tail" before "Los Endos," the scene is set.

Ralph: Regarding "A Trick of the Tail," I've complained to you about this before, about the groupthink that Led Zeppelin *III* stinks because of fill in the blank or The Who's *It's Hard* because nothing after Keith Moon can be any good. You get this kind of groupthink when you enter the world of fandom. And "A Trick of the Tail," even though it was the title track, was kind of dismissed. It's the shortest song, it had a goofy video and it was an old song that I think Tony brought back just because they needed the material. And people, especially idiot prog snobs, dismiss things like hooks. But Genesis is one of the hookiest bands there ever was. So it means nothing to say I love it. But context is everything. On a record like *A Trick of the Tail*, which is such a journey, it's a nice sidestep.

Pontus: I definitely hear The Beatles in this, especially with the Ringo Starr-like drum beat as well as the piano. Plus you've got sort of Beach Boys harmonies in the back and there's these other small, glittery sounds, especially keyboard sounds, that float around in the song and create texture. So yes, it's the record's Beatles moment.

Martin: We close with "Los Endos," which is like the exit music of a Broadway play. In that respect, it serves the same purpose as "It" on *The Lamb Lies Down on Broadway*. "More of that Jazz" on Queen *Jazz* kinda does this too.

Phil: Yes, and I think it's genius. It's where all sorts of little traits from different parts of the album are all pulled together as a sort of crescendo. As you say, it's an affect used on *Quadrophenia*, bringing together threads at the end of the album. There are no lyrics because none are needed. It's one of the most moving and exciting endings of any album I know, the way it builds with the different parts. It demonstrates the aggressive aspects of Steve Hackett's playing and of Phil Collins' drumming.

And that part at the end when it kind of pulls back, it's like you're climbing up a hill and you don't know what's on the other side of it. And as the song reaches that climax and comes into that really wonderful chord sequence and playing in melody, you're at the top of a hill and you see this wonderful vista in front of you and this music just comes pouring over your head. That to me is "Los Endos."

And of course, it became one of the highlights of their live show with Chester Thompson playing dual drums with Phil Collins. It's definitely my favourite. Well, I say "Ripples" is, but "Los Endos" is up there. We can talk about the prog of "Dance on a Volcano," "Moonlit Knight" and "The Lamb Lies Down on Broadway," but "Los Endos" really shows how this band has developed as musicians. All of the aspects are there and all of the band are on fire. Instrumentals don't normally have this much significance. But the way it's sequenced, you've had all the lyrics and all the songs, "Los Endos" just sits there at the end with purpose. It's not random. It's an instrumental that's scooped up all ingredients of the album as it's gone along.

Ralph: "Los Endos" is this triumphant and swirling and extraordinary instrumental piece that may have started out as a little doodle of a musical idea, but it's transformed mostly because of the rhythm section, I suppose, and the band's willingness to just go with these ideas and influences. The other thing that I find so interesting about Genesis is that in terms of these prog rhythm sections, we hear a lot about Squire and Bruford, and to a lesser extent Squire and White. We hear a lot about Geddy and Neil. But I remember—and not to name-drop—talking to Geddy once about Mike Rutherford, just where he rated him. And Geddy, in that moment anyway, sitting in his music room surrounded by all his instruments, he was very like, meh. And I thought, okay, well, not everyone's perfect. Even Geddy can't hear what I hear. What made Rutherford so great as a bass player is that he found bass similar to the way McCartney found bass, which is he started out as a guitar player, and they needed a bass player. He was already confident on *Trespass*, but here, he's a seasoned bass player.

Plus, like Phil Collins, the other guys had chops just coming out of every orifice and "Los Endos" is an example of that. But when they just needed simplicity, they could do it. They didn't have to tell you over and over how good they were. And I don't mean just chops. I mean, the choice of tones they selected and what instruments to play. What makes Rutherford such an amazing bass player, to me, is he played the song. He didn't play his ego. But then again, "Los Endos" isn't the best example of what I'm talking about, because it's more an example of heavy chops. The fact that these 25-year-old guys, with their English upbringings, could create something like that is pretty incredible; it's a sublime moment. And some of the drum fills are otherworldly.

Pontus: I agree, "Los Endos" is fusion heaven, right? It's a tribute to everything Mahavishnu, everything Weather Report. A lot of Chick Corea goes into this. I'm pretty sure they listened a lot to those things. It's frantic but it's also lovely. There's even Brazilian rhythm.

It's called "Los Endos" and it's almost like a samba. Plus that title works as a bit of a pun for "loose ends" as well. You get "Squonk" in the end and you get the first riff from "Dance on a Volcano." There's even a sort of reference to "Supper's Ready" at the very end. The only sad thing for me is that it fades. Because it closes the fourth side of *Seconds Out* with more force. That's the perfect side. It's their fusion moment. You get all that energy with the siren at the end. They just go for it. They go boom! And we walk out to "There's No Business Like Show Business," right? It's very British and tongue-in-cheek. That's what we get on *Seconds Out* and it's exhilarating.

Martin: In the end, it's remarkable how much each of these guys, beyond their chosen instruments, are arrangers and producers and constructors of songs. As you guys have alluded to, it's actually hard to tell who is doing what on these records. Everything is such a collaboration, once all the parts are added. All three of them are builders.

Ralph: Yes, absolutely. And you know what I think, too? You could break it down and say, at this point, Phil was the arranger of the band, or that was his strong suit. I talked about this with *Invisible Touch* and *Trespass* too, but Genesis, from its inception, was a songwriting collective. And I'm not saying every songwriter has the abilities that you just laid out. But those guys, at the earliest of ages, were keenly listening to what they loved, and incorporating it. And you really start to hear it on *Trespass*. *From Genesis to Revelation* is really a Jonathan King record and him trying to make them sound like the Bee Gees, as legend has it, and them going along with it, because they're 17 years old.

I think part of what you're describing is because they were almost like classical composers. When you break down a classical piece, or when *I* break down a classical piece, the thing about classical composers is, they're just not writing melodies. They're writing specific melodies for specific instruments at different times, or writing in tempos or writing in arrangements. It's this massive, massive undertaking that just blows my mind. Keith Emerson, I suppose, would be another guy in this space. But what makes Genesis so superlative is their ability to craft great, great songs, but as you're saying, produce them in such a way... I can't think of the right words, but they're textured, layered and inventive.

But yes, in terms of Tony, Mike and Phil, what makes Genesis so magic is the collision of these talents. And again, other than The Beatles, I cannot think of a group of individuals who had so much variety in their abilities. And that was on display on virtually every record—but also evolving—up until *Invisible Touch*.

Martin: Sweet. So now that Phil is the front man, what is the drumming situation moving forward?

Pontus: First, when they decided Phil is going to do it, when he decides that, oh, I'm gonna sing, so now we have to have another drummer. First off, it's Bill Bruford for the 1976 tour, and the idea is that we have double drumming live, so that Phil can jump behind the kit and play drums during the instrumental breaks so he doesn't have to just stand there. It becomes their trademark to have two drummers, and it's a full-throttle percussive machine they've got going.

And that carries on through the rest of the career with Chester Thompson, of course, replacing Bruford. Thompson had been with Zappa. Famously, Phil Collins had heard *Roxy & Elsewhere*, which Chester was on, where he plays as one of two drummers. He plays with Ralph Humphrey. He had also been in Weather Report, who were very cool. And Bill Bruford, at an early stage, was part of Brand X as well, as a percussionist. Phil and Bill knew each other, of course, because they'd been on the road with King Crimson and Yes. So by this tour, it's Bill Bruford and it's very clear that you hear him playing the Crimson sort of things that he came up with on drums through the *Red* period, to fit into the Genesis material. And I think Phil is thinking, oh, I can sing now because I'm very secure. Drum-wise, it's not going to be a train wreck behind me. I've chosen the right guys.

Martin: So that's it? Nobody else drums for Genesis ever again? It's just Chester?

Pontus: No, I don't think so. Nir Zidkyahu is the drummer on the '97 tour, but that's a small and oddball part of the story (laughs). And of course, when they did the 2007 tour, Chester was back and so was Daryl Stuermer, who would replace the departing Steve Hackett, but only live. He comes in from the Jean-Luc Ponty band. The Genesis guys wanted to work with very good musicians. It's funny, because when you look at the interviews on those DVDs, they say, "Oh, we were a writing band that learned to play." But the way they play is so

A Trick of the Tail

virtuosic that they had to have jazz musicians playing with them live. They weren't another pub band. They just excelled. And this album, *A Trick of the Tail*, is very much like, let's get down and play. Let's show everybody what we can do.

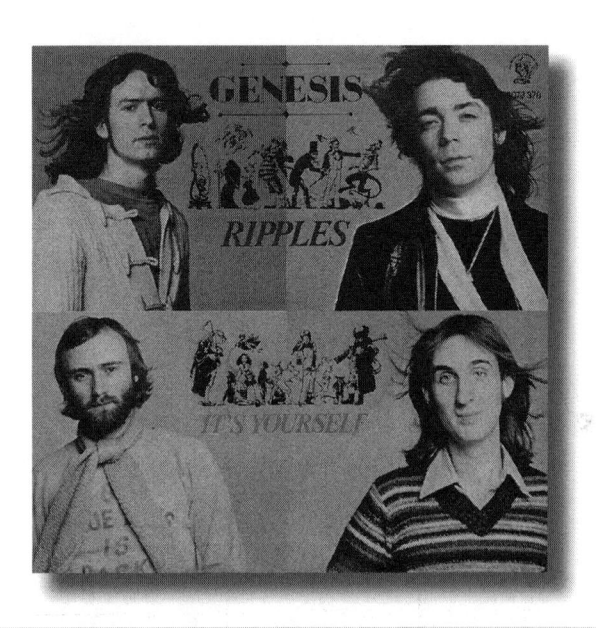

Entangled: Genesis on Record 1969-1976

WIND & WUTHERING

December 17, 1976
Charisma CDS 4005
Produced by David Hentschel and Genesis
Engineered by David Hentschel; assisted by Pierre Geofroy Chateau and Nick "Cod" Bradford
Recorded at Relight Studios, Hilvarenbeek, Netherlands; remixed at Trident Studios, London, UK
Personnel: Phil Collins – vocals, drums, cymbals, percussion; Steve Hackett – electric guitars, nylon classical, 12-string guitar, kalimba, auto-harp; Tony Banks – Steinway grand piano, ARP 2600 synthesizer, ARP Pro Soloist synthesizer, Hammond organ, Mellotron, Roland RS-202 string synthesizer, Fender Rhodes electric piano, 12-string guitar, backing vocals; Mike Rutherford – 4-, 6-, and 8-string bass guitars, electric and 12-string acoustic guitars, bass pedals

Side 1
1. Eleventh Earl of Mar (Banks, Hackett, Rutherford) 7:39
2. One for the Vine (Banks) 9:56
3. Your Own Special Way (Rutherford) 6:15
4. Wot Gorilla? (Collins, Banks) 3:12

Entangled: Genesis on Record 1969-1976

Side 2
1. All in a Mouse's Night (Banks) 6:35
2. Blood on the Rooftops (Hackett, Collins) 5:20
3. 'Unquiet Slumbers for the Sleepers... (Hackett, Rutherford) 2:24
4. ...In That Quiet Earth' (Hackett, Rutherford, Banks, Collins) 4:50
5. Afterglow (Banks) 4:11

Entangled: Genesis on Record 1969-1976

220

A *Wind & Wuthering* Timeline

September – October 1976. The band work once again with producer David Hentschel, this time at Relight Studios in Hilvarenbeek, Netherlands, on tracks slated for their next record.

November 13, 1976. Mike Rutherford marries his girlfriend, Angie. The couple have three children, born 1977, 1980 and 1986.

December 17, 1976. Genesis issue an eighth album, entitled *Wind & Wuthering*. It will be their last with Steve Hackett. It reaches No.26 on the Billboard charts and No.7 in the UK and certifies gold in both territories. It also goes gold in France and Canada.

January 1 – 23, 1977. The band play the UK in support of *Wind & Wuthering*. Chester Thompson joins as the band's new touring drummer, replacing Bill Bruford.

January 31, 1977. A 45-minute concert film called *Genesis: In Concert* is issued; it captures the band's live performances over the closing dates of the *A Trick of the Tail* tour, in Stafford and Glasgow.

February 2 – April 3, 1977. The band conduct a North American tour.

February 4, 1977. "Your Own Special Way," backed with "It's Yourself," is issued as a single. The song manages a No.43 placement on the UK charts and No.62 on the Billboard 200.

February 25, 1977. Peter Gabriel issues his first solo album. Peter's got a bit of a hit on his hands, with ballad "Solsbury Hill." The track reaches No.13 in the UK and No.68 on the Billboard Hot 100, propelling the album to No.7 in the UK and No. 38 in the US.

March 1977. Anthony Phillips issues his first solo album, *The Geese & The Ghost*. Both Mike Rutherford and Phil Collins participate in the project.

April 1977. Brand X issue a sophomore album, called *Moroccan Roll*. It seems that it's not just Peter Gabriel that likes a good pun. Phil is credited with drums and lead vocals, plus acoustic piano on one track.

Entangled: Genesis on Record 1969-1976

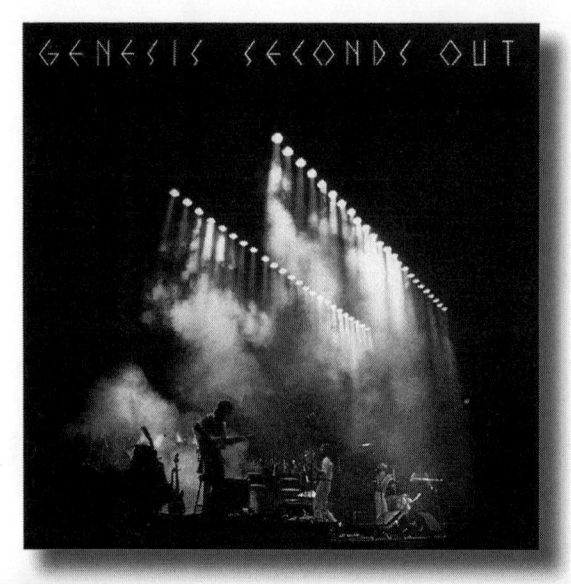

May 10 – 22, 1977. The band play South America for the first time, with all shows taking place in Brazil.

May 20, 1977. Genesis sees the release of a three-track EP called *Spot the Pigeon*, in the UK and in Canada, but not the US. Side one features "Match of the Day" and "Pigeons" while side two consists of "Inside and Out."

June 2 – July 3, 1977. The last leg of the *Wind & Wuthering* tour finds the band playing mainland Europe, along with three nights at Earls Court in London.

October 14, 1977. Genesis issue a second live album, a two-LP package, called *Seconds Out*. The version of "The Cinema Show" on the album dates back to the *A Trick of the Tail* tour, with the rest of the album capturing performances in Paris from June of 1977. Bill Bruford and Chester Thompson drum on "The Cinema Show," with Chester sharing drum duties with Phil on the rest of the album. The tracks chosen for inclusion on the album are as follows: "Squonk," "Robbery, Assault and Battery," "Dance on a Volcano" and "Los Endos" (from *A Trick of the Tail*), "The Carpet Crawlers" and "The Lamb Lies Down on Broadway" (from *The Lamb Lies Down on Broadway*), "Afterglow" (from *Wind & Wuthering*), "Fifth of Firth," "I Know What I Like (In Your Wardrobe)" and "The Cinema Show" (from *Selling England by the Pound*), "The Musical Box" (from *Nursery Cryme*) and "Supper's Ready" (from *Foxtrot*).

November 18, 1977. Brand X issue a live album, called *Livestock*.

Entangled: Genesis on Record 1969-1976

Martin talks to Tate Davis, Todd Evans and Charlie Nieland about *Wind & Wuthering*.

Martin Popoff: Well, we arrive at the last album of our book, due to the exit of Steve Hackett after the record. What do you make of *Wind & Wuthering*?

Tate Davis: So *Wind & Wuthering* is a continuation of... it's not even a continuation of what they were doing on *A Trick of the Tail* (laughs). I guess I think of *Wind & Wuthering* as *A Trick of the Tail* but not as good. And I say that lightly, because *Wind & Wuthering* is great. But I think you're getting a bit more commercial here than on *A Trick of the Tail*, because on *A Trick of the Tail*, it's still, for the most part, very Gabriel-oriented. On here, the song structure is definitely getting more compact, more realised and more commercial, maybe simpler, while still being interesting to listen to.

I don't think Steve Hackett has nearly as big of a role on here as he does on *A Trick of the Tail*. So it's this kind of purgatory, in a way, where they still want to be progressive because Steve's in the band and he's still exerting his influence on it, even though by this point, I think his songs are starting to get rejected for the more commercial, more straightforward direction that Phil, Tony and Mike want to go in, especially on songs like "Your Own Special Way."

So it's kind of like the Deep Purple *Stormbringer* situation, where Coverdale and Hughes want to go in this more funky, soul-driven direction and Blackmore wants to stay within a bluesy, hard rock and classically-inspired direction, and *Stormbringer* is an amalgamation of all that because Blackmore is still kind of fighting. Similarly on *Wind & Wuthering*, you have that sort of thing where you can feel the musical tug-of-war going on between Steve Hackett and the rest of the band. And then before you know it, he was out, although first he did the *Spot the Pigeon* EP and then the *Seconds Out* live album. And then there was that whole controversy surrounding him because he left while that live album was getting finished. They were fiddling around with his guitar parts, and kind of turning them down in the mix as a special FU to the fact that he left.

Todd Evans: I stop shy of calling it *A Trick of the Tail* part two, because I think it has a bit more going on. It's busier and kind of thicker. I've always felt like *A Trick of the Tail* is kind of a tight album. They had what they had, and I feel like with *Wind & Wuthering*, they had more than what they put on the record. Some people say that *Wind & Wuthering* could have been changed or trimmed or re-sequenced. I guess we'll talk about that when we get into the tracks.

But I feel like *Wind & Wuthering* is a "more of the same" record. Historically, in my personal view, I've always thought of *Wind & Wuthering* as better than *A Trick of the Tail* and for a long time it was my favourite. It probably is still a contender for my favourite, but as I spend more time with it as I get older, I feel like *A Trick of the Tail* is more cohesive and more elegant in its sequencing than *Wind & Wuthering* is. But I think there are a couple of things on *Wind & Wuthering* that should be considered Genesis classics by the people who are old Genesis snobs who only like old proggy Genesis. There are songs that should be elevated a bit higher in the echelon of what people consider to be their classic tracks.

Charlie Nieland: I saw the *Wind & Wuthering* tour. And that was actually the first time I saw them. I was 15 and this was coming very quickly off the heels of *A Trick of the Tail*, which came pretty quickly off the heels of *Lamb*, when you consider that Peter left. *A Trick of the Tail* is a spectacular record. They really consolidated a lot of what they were developing through *Selling England* and *Lamb*. And *Wind & Wuthering* has got wonderful layering and a lot of depth of sound. As for the writing, they were trying to step into the future and keep their foot in the past at the same time. So there's some awkwardness to that. But at the time, I loved it; I thought it was great. Both of these records are produced by David Hentschel, and he went on to produce several more records by them. He was really essential to the wonderful sound of these records, the big, clean, detailed picture, including the beginning of the ambient drum sounds and very colourful keyboard landscapes. David Hentschel was the guy who played synth on "Funeral for a Friend" on Elton John's *Goodbye Yellow Brick Road*, so he's a great musician in his own right. He stayed with them as a producer all the way through *Duke*.

Martin: I feel like you start to hear Phil's future identity and identifiers here, in terms of drum sound and his more aggressive playing style.

Tate: I would push more toward *Duke* for that, and I think it really arrives with *Abacab*. But I do agree with you that you can hear elements of that here and on *And Then There Were Three*.

Martin: How would you describe his drum sound on this?

Tate: I would describe it as great (laughs). The toms are almost Mutt Lange-y, but the kind of Mutt Lange drum sound that you would get on maybe a City Boy album, on like *Young Men Gone West*. On that album they had a session drummer, Tony Braunagel, and it was ringy, rather than gated. Mutt Lange was just starting his journey in the producer's chair when he was working with City Boy on those five albums. He was still experimenting and trying to figure out drum sounds. So it reminds me of that, and that goes for *And Then There Were Three* too. It's City Boy, rather than where he'd go with *Pyromania* and *Hysteria*.

Martin: Phil loves his ride. He loves his crashes and splashes and open high-hat. There are cymbals everywhere.

Tate: Yeah, and he loves his ghost notes too, because there's a lot of funky grace note-type patterns that he's playing here and on *A Trick of the Tail* too.

Todd: On *Wind & Wuthering*, his drums sound bigger. He's not using the gated sound like he uses later, you know, on purpose, but I definitely think it's fatter than it was on *A Trick of the Tail*. So yes, I do think this is where it starts. It's a little less so on *And Then There Were Three*, and then picks back up with *Duke*. But on *...And Then There Were Three...*, there were so many things going on. The story about that album is how good of a Steve Hackett impression Mike Rutherford is doing. But yeah, I think *Wind & Wuthering* is a great drum album, but it really goes crazy on *Abacab*. As for cymbals, I love the way the ping of the ride cymbal was always mixed so loud. Which I love about *Abacab*. You could listen to "Keep It Dark" just for the ride cymbal, which is in-your-face the whole time. Basically all of these Genesis albums from this point on are really good equipment demonstration records because of the drum sound.

Martin: Well, opener "Eleventh Earl of Mar" pays great dividends when you listen to it for the totality of the drum performance, and it's also an example of what I'm talking about with the cymbals.

Tate: Yeah, great way to start the album. Steve Hackett also makes his presence known. Here he's doubling what the synth is playing. I think this song could have fit on *The Lamb Lies Down on Broadway*; it has that sort of feel to it. Phil Collins has some really cool overdubbed percussion parts on it. Tony Banks has some nice keyboard flourishes throughout the song, especially in the middle, where he really shows off. Lyrically, it discusses a young kid and his father being the guests of royalty, with these amusing spoken word vocals from Phil during the chorus. Great ending as well, with these long, lingering notes and a return to the opening theme.

Todd: I think "Eleventh Earl of Mar" is one of Genesis' upper-tier songs. The way the Mellotron swells in the first part, and then the reprise of that part towards the end, is spectacular. I don't think it ever sounded more effective. This song has a lot of energy and starts the album with a bang. Steve adds a lot to the song. His guitar tone and the way that the guitar parts are used, it's kind of like lead guitar and part of the arrangement as well.

I actually have some pretty strong opinions about what happened here with Steve Hackett. There's a lot of revisionist history going on amongst diehard early Genesis fans that somehow his departure is the reason why Genesis shifted their focus and that they lost so much when they lost Steve Hackett. His contributions to this album are fantastic and he makes it a better album, but I also think it could have been made without him. Tony Banks is the star here. That's not surprising coming from me. When we get to "One for the Vine," that's where I'm really feeling that. But I think "Eleventh Earl of Mar" is fantastic. I liked the way it sounds, the arrangements, how dense it is. I like the Mellotron and the organ and I like Steve's playing on it.

Charlie: I agree, a wonderful opener. "Eleventh Earl of Mar" is so energised and multi-dimensional with the guitar and the synth and the Mellotron and there's a big crescendo that is so cinematic. You can hear on this record that they're being a little more layered. It's organ-driven, but at the same time, there's a piano doubling the organ part. They're not trying to make it so they could just reproduce this live. I mean, they did reproduce it live, but these are studio constructions. The story of "Eleventh Earl of Mar," from what I understand, it's a Rutherford lyric about a Scottish king and about war. And the kid's saying, "Daddy! You promised, you promised," meaning please take me to this thing.

And the tone is so jaunty and joyful. There's no menace. And this is where we see what they've traded away by losing Gabriel. Peter could bring, to a childlike scenario, some kind of darkness. And once Phil led the band, these things lacked a certain depth sometimes. But by this album, Phil was experimenting with different vocals and different voices and starting to do the stuff that Gabriel did with storytelling. But I don't know, the music doesn't quite match the tone of the story. But there's great, tough *The Lamb Lies Down on Broadway*-type bass on it, and Steve's solo is multi-tracked with harmonies, so there are numerous cool details. That ethereal middle section, that beautiful transition, which apparently was written by Hackett, the "Time to go to bed now" part—that's really cool. It ends with a big dramatic restatement of the beginning theme (sings it); that sort of diminished scale theme. It's got a beautiful prog sweep to it. In hindsight, something's a little off there, but I know I loved it at the time.

Martin: With "One for the Vine," I feel like given the same level of arrangement and volume as the opener, and the same textures, it's a continuation. Obviously a slow one, a kind of epic ballad, but I'm hearing parts that could have been swapped in to "Eleventh Earl of Mar."

Tate: Fair enough, but in isolation, it's a top-tier track. Tony writes it, and he continues to prove he can come up with great intros. The beginning reminds me a lot of "Ripples," and as a whole, it's the second cousin to "Ripples." It wouldn't have sounded out of place on *A Trick of the Tail*. Because it's still pretty and rooted in that proggy Gabriel-era sound. The lyrics speak of a chosen hero who doesn't want to be the chosen one. He's going on a quest to defeat a foe and is dealing with the loss of his companions along the way. As a person who plays Dungeons & Dragons somewhat regularly, I can relate to that. I find it interesting that they would write a D&D-type lyric to that sort of music.

And another thing, referencing what we talked about with *Trespass*, you have this theme of ice and snow in their lyrics and their ability to write good lyrics based around that. Because the hero is journeying up a mountain and their ultimate goal is to get to the top of the mountain and to vanquish his enemies. There's Mellotron on it too, which adds depth. And the instrumental bit in the middle is kind of like the soundtrack to the journey to the top of the mountain. Great song.

Todd: "One for the Vine" is my favourite Genesis track, kind of tied with "Cul de Sac" on *Duke*. There are things going on here that are just on another level compositionally. Lyrically, I'm not crazy about it. I mean, it's kind of cool. There's a really good analysis of this song by Doug Helvering, who is the "classical composer reacts to whatever" guy on YouTube. He goes through it, and he has the sheet music up, and he's talking about what's happening with the chord progressions and stuff. He really get into the weeds about the nuances and the things that are so great about the song.

Lyrically, I didn't ever think much of it. I just thought it was a bunch of medieval nonsense. But there's a character in it who's sort of Christ-like. He develops his following, he's always strived to be the person who's the leader, and then he gets the opportunity to be the leader. And then he's disillusioned with the whole process of what it's like to lead people in war and politics and stuff like that. So when you really dive into it, it's actually not bad.

But the thing that's crazy about "One for the Vine" is there's so much going on. And it's so focused around Tony, which I think is a good thing. But at the same time, it's got that percussion breakdown in the middle that's quite strange. Steve does some interesting things there. When I first heard that, that absolutely blew me away. I was like, what are they doing?! And then the arrangements from that point of the song until the end are just fantastic.

I've said this about "Cul de Sac" too, which is my other top Genesis song. The last minute, minute-and-a-half of "One for the Vine," I used to think that in the build-up towards the end of the track when it slows down again, that that was a bunch of key changes. But it's actually one key and Tony is introducing all of these other tones to it that makes it sound like it's changing in a more significant way. And then it does change keys at the end, and he's just throwing a whole bunch of unusual notes into the chords that make it feel like it's continuously modulating. Pretty amazing. "One for the Vine" is one of the best examples of Tony's genius, and yes, I am going to give him all the credit for that track (laughs). Even though Steve, sonically, provides some pretty cool detailing.

Charlie: When you look at it from a distance, *Wind & Wuthering* is very much a Tony Banks record, and "One for the Vine" is a perfect example of that. It's a ten-minute song and it tells this really elaborate story of a character who's in a war. He's leading the charge, and he wanders up into this mountain-like glacier because he's confused. He's confused about whether he wants to do it. And then these people there find him and turn him into a new messiah. And then he wanders his way back down into the valley. I don't know; it's a very Tony Banks story. He wrote a song like this on *A Trick of the Tail* called "Mad Man Moon," which is really wonderful. And you hear how Phil becomes a great interpretive singer for Tony's stuff, in a way that maybe Peter wasn't the perfect singer for Tony's more melancholy material.

Martin: What is Tony's personality?

Charlie: I love Tony's personality. In the interview videos, he's this combination of arrogant and self-effacing in this very British way. Both he and Michael Rutherford have this quality when they talk about the older material. They're like, "Well, that was a bunch of rubbish" (laughs). They're very dismissive of their earlier material in this way that you're like, wait a minute, I love that song! Tony was very controlling, but also, obviously, a great musical collaborator, because they all stayed working with him. My understanding was that Tony and Peter had a very interesting collaboration. There was lots of conflict there, but they were deeply connected. Which was probably one of the reasons Gabriel just bounced out of it after a while. He's like, I can't do it anymore with the Tony thing.

So Tony makes this very elaborate composition and it has all the signatures of Genesis with all the sections and a big instrumental break in the middle. And Phil's doing lots of stacked harmonies. There's incredible drumming, a big rhythmic section in the middle after a kind of a maudlin series of verses. But there's little mistakes that they make, like in the final chorus. Finally, when they get to the chorus, after all this sort of storytelling, Phil sings in this super-high falsetto octave. When I think about it now, I'm like, why didn't you just sing it an octave lower? It would've sounded much more authoritative. I don't know. And the middle section is kind of weirdly goofy. Like I said, sometimes it lacks the menace that the storytelling would imply. It's a good song, but I don't love it as much as I used to.

Martin: I suppose this is a leading question, but what function does "Your Own Special Way" serve on this album?

Tate: Well, it's the first real preview of where they were gonna go in the '80s. It's a great song and it also does a perfect job of being a radio single. It's got a catchy chorus and holds your interest throughout, with inventive synths from Tony and straightforward drumming throughout. And of course, they had to add in that 6/8-time bridge to add prog value.

Martin: One could imagine the verses being on any previous Genesis album, but the chorus is some new AOR thing, maybe even a bit maudlin.

Tate: Yeah, and I believe Steve Hackett was not a fan of the song. Think about it. He'd put out *Voyage of the Acolyte* already, which was built out of songs that had for the most part had been rejected for use in Genesis. And he's trying to write new ones for his solo album after that and he's still getting rejected. Then he's like, my songs are getting rejected for things like this?! I don't like this at all.

Todd: I think you're seeing the beginning of Michael Rutherford's pop sensibilities. And "Your Own Special Way" is kind of important. It really is the first kind of straightforward ballad and straightforward love song and I think that's super-important for a band. I'm gonna go on a sidetrack, if you don't mind. I saw Genesis in 2021 and there was a family sitting next to us. They were maybe a little less well-off, I would say, and generationally from about age 14 to about age 65. It was like grandkids to grandma.

And I remember sitting next to them and thinking, oh, what are they going to think of this show? And every single one of those people knew every single one of the words to the all of the songs, including grandma. So it's interesting when you think about who wants to see Genesis in 2021, and then you go to the show. You wind up thinking, okay, well, they did something, right. Because they were able to get everybody in a family to appreciate them. And for me, "Your Own Special Way" represents the beginning of that. Songs like that shouldn't be discounted, beginning with the fact that they don't take up that much space on the album, although this goes on over six minutes.

Martin: Yeah, crazy. When this came out, it was a 51-minute album on a single piece of vinyl. I'd say Genesis turned out to be the single most successful band at being able to make a long album sound acceptable.

Charlie: Yeah, they get away with it. It doesn't sound like those Todd Rundgren records back in the day. He'd put almost 30 minutes aside on his records, and they tended to sound crowded, a little squelchy.

Todd: Yeah, absolutely. And I can remember being frustrated that Genesis albums wouldn't fit on one side of a C-90. But yeah, that's true. I'd say *Duke* comes the closest to sounding like there's too much crammed on there. But even that one sounds okay. Yeah, I don't know how they did it.

Charlie: When I think about "Your Own Special Way," I think about "More Fool Me" from *Selling England by the Pound*. That was a ballad that Rutherford wrote and Phil sang and this is another one of those. But it's just really dragged-out. There was another song made for this record that Steve was much more involved in called "Inside and Out" and you can hear it on the *Spot the Pigeon* EP plus the Genesis *Archives* collection. They played it live at some shows, and it's a much more interesting song. It's more proggy with some great guitar breaks at the end and I always wondered why they didn't use that song instead of this song. Except somebody probably thought, oh, maybe this has more commercial potential. I don't think they hit their stride with respect to writing commercial ballads until the next couple of records.

Martin: Would you agree with my assessment that the chord changes at the chorus are a little too uncomfortably mainstream?

Charlie: Yeah, and while I think they pull that off very well on songs on *And Then There Were Three* and *Duke*, here it's a little tentative. And again, it goes on forever and Phil hasn't quite found his voice yet. It sounds a little uncertain when he's singing high and quavering. It doesn't grab me.

Martin: Side one ends with "Wot Gorilla?," a zesty instrumental clocking in at a brief 3:12.

Tate: "Wot Gorilla?" reminds me a lot of Brand X, especially "Nuclear Burn" from the first album. Phil and Tony put on a clinic, but I wish that Steve had more of a chance to shine. He could have ripped a great solo on a song like this. And I wish it was longer too, although the album is so long already. They had to keep in line with the limits of vinyl. And if you won't let Steve solo, why not bring John Goodsall over from Brand X for a guest slot? Because it's his type of thing.

Todd: When I first heard this album, "Wot Gorilla?" was a standout track. Before Phil Collins starts writing songs, it's an opportunity to give him a showcase. It's got great energy, it's the perfect length and it's a good side-ender. I've always had really positive feelings towards it. It's got a lot of the instrumental elements that would become a part of their later prog-ish things, in the rhythmic elements from Phil and the repeated patterns that Tony is doing. I don't want to disparage this song, because I think that it has value. It's kind of like "Who Dunnit?" done right.

Charlie: It's a bit of prog fluff, "Wot Gorilla?," and very Weather Report. It reminds me of this song called "Nubian Sundance" on *Mysterious Traveler*; the drum pattern's like that (sings it). And the guitars and keys swirl around. It's all very late-'70s Weather Report.

Martin: Brand X too?

Charlie: I think so. Yeah, he was bringing some of that influence into it. It's a fun little piece to end with. It's weird, these vinyl sides. There's no time for another song like "Inside and Out," so here's a three-minute instrumental.

Martin: You wonder if they even had a proper three-minute song with verses and choruses in them at this point. Okay, speaking of sides, flip over to side two and we have "All in a Mouse's Night."

Tate: Yes, and once again Tony puts on a synth clinic. Like "Eleventh Earl of Mar," I think this also would have fit on *The Lamb Lies Down on Broadway*. I like the point of view of a cat trying to hunt down a mouse and then the synths and the guitar texture is adding to the narrative of that mouse and that whole operation very well. The ending is like this triumphant theme music to where the cat finds that this mouse is this gigantic mutated beast that is eventually defeated. Or is he? It's actually hard to tell who loses the fight because the language is imprecise. With the clever switch from 4/4 to 6/8 time, it's like the two different perspectives from the two opposing points of view.

Todd: I had a lot of negative thoughts about this song for a long time. When I heard the album when I was in high school, I thought it was cool. I just missed out on it for a really long time in my adult life because of these kind of ridiculous lyrics. But there's a lot going for it. I've heard rumblings from people who are Steve Hackett fans that say that should have come off and "Inside and Out" should have gone on in its place. I'm not sure I disagree with that. But "All in a Mouse's Night" is pretty good. Instrumentally there's a lot going on and Tony provides these layers and textures. I like that kind of stuff, so I generally feel positive about it. But it's definitely my least favourite track on the album.

Martin: How would you describe the story?

Todd: Well, I try not to think about it much (laughs). But like I said, I was really too hard on it. It's okay for an album like this, and an album that looks like this. You have to have something on it that's a little lighter. I've given it some slack. I don't think that it's badly written. It's not cringey. It's kind of dumb, because it's about a giant mouse. But other than that, I don't think it's badly done.

Charlie: "All in a Mouse's Night" is another one of these dramatic opera pieces from Tony. It's about this couple, these lovers, trying to catch a mouse, and at first they think about getting a box. Then they send a cat, at the end of the song, to do the job, and it seems like the fight ends when the cat gets knocked out by a jar while pouncing. That seems to mark the end of the action. It's fine (laughs).

But again, there's great music in here. There's this sweeping, fanfare-like intro with swirlies keyboard and these descending fills. Once it kicks in, the drumming is in sort of flipping time signatures or meters; it's quite inventive. It sort of jumps in between the sections and there's a lot of contrast between the sort of tight parts and the washy parts. And there's a big, majestic guitar outro. So we have a lot of signature Genesis things in this song. Again, they've got their foot in the past and the future at the same time, but they're equivocating and it's a little fluffy. But it's fun and it's well recorded.

Martin: Next we have "Blood on the Rooftops," and it's incredible that in 1976 they can still sound this historic and pastoral, and yet by the turn of the decade, they are so transformed. This could have been on *Trespass*. It's so *Alice in Wonderland*.

Tate: "Blood on the Rooftops" is a song that reminds me of Jethro Tull or particularly The Kinks, albums like *The Kinks Are the Village Green Preservation Society* or *Arthur*, with themes of old England and village greens and croquet and stuff like that. There's lush, almost Renaissance music acoustic guitar at the beginning of the song, great arrangements of guitar with keys. It feels like a folk song but once the chorus hits, it crosses over into a pop song.

Todd: I've heard people call "Blood on the Rooftops" the centrepiece of the album. I really don't think it is, but I appreciate it for being able to showcase Hackett's nylon-string acoustic guitar playing, which was something that was truly his. There weren't that many people doing that and it's really beautiful. But song-wise, I think it's on a slightly lower level than "One for the Vine" or "Your Own Special Way."

Charlie: This is a Hackett and Collins composition, and really, Hackett's last stand, his signature song on the record, basically one thing he gets to write. With repeat listening, you really get the depth of it. It opens with the nylon-string guitar but then they transform into this different band. It's like if there was a Hackett Collins album, it would sound like this. It has this lush but dark quality, and Tony and Mike add great touches to it, Banks with synths and Mellotron and wonderful bass playing by Rutherford.

There's an irony to it with this old man watching TV and kind of shaking his fist at the clouds. He's describing the world and its horrors through being trapped at home and watching the television set. Coupled with this is a sort of bland celebration of the holidays. There's a sense of irony or amused cynicism to his reaction, when there's not a lot of irony in some of the other songs. Banks' approach is usually romantic and melancholic. But there's bitter irony in this song that's really neat. I think it's a great composition and kind of a road not taken if Hackett had stayed in the band.

Martin: Next—and of course it's cited inconsistently between back cover and label on the record—we have one song, or two, called "'Unquiet Slumbers for the Sleepers...'" and "'...In That Quiet Earth'," annoying single quote marks included.

Tate: Yeah, I know that stuff drives you crazy (laughs). Whatever it's called, the first bit is like "Wot Gorilla?" and it's a song that I wish could have been a bit longer. It's a really spooky instrumental with great Tony synths and great guitar from Hackett. On the second piece, you get this Brand X drumming from Phil, while Tony's synths continue on from the last song. It shows that Genesis could still do the Gabriel-era prog when they wanted to, even though Gabriel had long left by that point. But again, I wish I heard more Steve Hackett throughout the song and not just in the second half. He really makes his presence known on the second half. I imagine part of the purpose of this piece was to keep Steve happy.

Todd: Yeah, despite the confusing titling, I like these two tracks. It's got a complicated prog rock instrumental section that really goes somewhere. But at the same time, it's simplified compared to some of the other stuff going on prior. I mean, nobody would ever consider the guitar part to "…In That Quiet Earth'" to be metal, but it's certainly relatively heavy for them. And they themselves like that part. They've played it a lot throughout the years. It makes its way into the medleys in the later years and I'm pretty sure in 2021 they still played that little bit with the guitar riff. Yeah, the way those two songs go into "Afterglow" is genius. It's what for a long time made me think *Wind & Wuthering* was better than *A Trick of the Tail*. Because in the realm of instrumentals, it's as great as "Los Endos" is. The end of this album is really emotionally satisfying.

Charlie: It's two cool instrumentals connected to a great song at the end. And the first of the instrumentals, "'Unquiet Slumber for the Sleepers…" is this dreamy and eerie soundscape. I'm hearing Cocteau Twins in it; it reminds me of *Victorialand* or even parts of *Treasure* or something. It's got these humming, arpeggiated guitars, plus the synths. It's drenched in this atmosphere that creates anticipation that something's coming.

And then with a sort of formal occasion snare roll, it kicks into "…In That Quiet Earth.'" Besides the main melody, it's this great, super-fast thing in 6/8 with tremendous drumming and a strong guitar and keyboard melody. You can hear that Hackett got his teeth into this one. And then it kicks in this angular slower part, where there's these slashing chords by Rutherford on the 12-string. There's this slower, funky drum beat and Tony Banks is creating these mysterious Eastern melodies over the top. They call back to the intro melody of "Eleventh Earl of Mar." That gets liberally used in this part of the song, connecting the album back to the beginning in that brave prog rock way. It's what "Los Endos" did at the end of *A Trick of the Tail*.

Martin: Except it's not at the end. Weird. Last song is "Afterglow," and it's another slow, panoramic ballad.

Tate: Yes, and I think it could have been a hit single, maybe not on AM radio, but FM radio maybe could have played this to death. It would be a concert staple for the band going forward. Great synths from Tony here, and lyrically it's a preview of where we're gonna go in the '80s regarding lyrics of love and relationships. It's perhaps the reflection of how the protagonist could have been a better lover to his or her partner. As great as the studio version is, like what I was saying about "The Knife," I feel like the live version on *Seconds Out* is leagues better and more grandiose than the studio version. But it's still a great way to end a really good Genesis album from the Phil Collins era.

Todd: There's a great story about "Afterglow," where Tony Banks talks about how they were working on it, and when he was driving home, he went, "Oh my God, I just wrote 'Have Yourself a Merry Little Christmas' again." So he went back to the studio and told them, "We can't do 'Afterglow,'" and they were like, "Oh, you're being too hard on yourself—it's fine." But one of the things that is so great about "Afterglow" is that it's really simple. And what happens at the end of it is really emotionally satisfying. I mean, that's where those lights on the front of *Seconds Out* come in, with the lights that came down and then go over the crowd. It made for a really great visual moment in their concerts that they re-did over and over again as the technology changed. "Afterglow" is just an absolutely stunningly good ending to an album, one of their best album closers, in my opinion.

Charlie: Agreed. There's this sense of epic melancholy. I teared up listening to it even this week. When I first heard this, I was in high school with my band and I had my share of crushes gone wrong. And I remember singing this song to the stereo with the door closed. I love that line, "And I would search everywhere just to hear your call." It's a really beautiful song, and kind of Beatle-esque. Phil does a nice lead vocal and there are stacks of Phil's voice doing harmonies, doing "aah"s.

That's true of a bunch of songs in this record. Phil is doing an increased amount of stacked harmony backups and things like that and working on more arrangement ideas. But a lot of it isn't as emotionally direct as "Afterglow" is. And boy, this song is even better on *Seconds Out*, that live album that came out right after this. Phil kills that song on that record with a lot more emotion. He's starting to discover that much more powerful part of his voice that he was only just dipping his toe into on this record. But that's a great song and a great ending for the album. I don't know. It's like their notion of prog and storytelling was getting a little literal on this record. It's missing Pete's surrealism a little bit and his kind of rock star moves. There was no sex to these songs, whereas Peter's songs always had an undercurrent where there was something going on below the waist in those songs (laughs). And there's not really that here.

Martin: It's like the polite and upper-class version of the old band. And I do mean that while thinking about the famous British class system. It had been building for me all along, but I'm really feeling it here. This record sounds like old money.

Charlie: Yes (laughs). And you know, in some ways that works great on certain songs here. It works great on *A Trick of the Tail*, notably "Dance on a Volcano." What a signature song; you're not really missing him there. But as you get through the entirely of *Wind & Wuthering*, it floats by in a way that doesn't dig in emotionally. On later Genesis albums, Phil finds an emotional centre that is more authentic.

Martin: All right; thanks for ending on a hopeful note (laughs). As we know, Genesis manage to issue three more new songs before we lose Steve. What are your thoughts on the *Spot the Pigeon* EP?

Tate: Honestly, I really don't like much of it. It felt like a contractually obligated release of leftovers. "Match of the Day" and "Pigeons" are these bright, jangly kind of tunes, but at least there are some cool contributions from Steve Hackett.

Martin: They remind me of City Boy.

Tate: Yeah, and the problem with that sort of dancehall music thing, this quirky type of rock music, is that it comes across either really well like City Boy or 10CC, or it's badly done. You have to know what the hell you're doing in order to do a song like "Pigeons." City Boy could make that fun, but hearing Genesis do it doesn't sit right. It doesn't come across as very memorable to me.

Todd: The way I've always felt about *Spot the Pigeon*—and listening to it again the last couple of weeks has solidified this—each song has some things in it that are unique and every song has something wrong with it (laughs). "Match of the Day" is really cool because of the way it sounds. It's a little ahead of its time, the way the synth and the synth bass is, and the way it bounces along. But man, when Phil doesn't like lyrics to something, he has the power to stop it. So when they did that second Genesis *Archive* box set, it has "Pigeons" and "Inside and Out" on it but it doesn't have "Match of the Day." And Phil said in interviews that it's not there because he doesn't like it. He said the lyrics embarrass him and the song meant nothing to him. And it's funny, back then, we didn't have soccer in the US, so I just thought they were talking about something British that I didn't understand (laughs).

Martin: "Pigeons" has an interesting back-story to it.

Todd: Yeah, it's pretty cool because it's got a musical element that I really love, where the same note and the same pattern is repeated throughout the whole song, but the chords change under it. There's an interview with Steve Hackett where he talks about how they were trying to see if he could play the same thing from start to finish, and if Banks could play as many different things as he could under it and make all the changes fit. And I think they succeed. But you know, the song starts with the lyric, "Who put 50 pounds of shit on the Foreign Office roof?" I mean when you start like that... the whole song is really kind of dumb lyrically. It's not really about anything. So yeah, it's the good and the bad together.

Martin: I hear Queen's sort of "knees up" music in it, or Wings. Paul McCartney has talked about how he'd occasionally go to that place because it reminded him of his parents' music.

Todd: Yeah, I totally agree. I like it more than I dislike it, but I think it has problems.

Martin: *A Night at the Opera* has two of those, "Seaside Rendezvous" and "Good Company."

Tate: Yeah, exactly, and I'm not really big on those songs either. There's a group called Postmodern Jukebox that does jazz ragtime covers of pop songs. I could see them doing a version of "Pigeons" and just knocking it out of the park. But I don't want to hear Postmodern Jukebox cover Genesis. As for your Wings comparison, yeah, it sounds like Wings but not *good* Wings (laughs).

Martin: "Inside and Out" is substantial, but it sounds like one of those cases where it's good enough to make the album, but it's too similar to other songs that are there already, to make the album.

Tate: Yeah, "Inside and Out" is a great song, and sure, it could have fit on *Wind & Wuthering*. It's got pretty guitar and piano and it reminds me of "Your Own Special Way." Tony Banks puts on a synth clinic as part of the song, as well as Steve Hackett having a terrific solo. It's the best song on *Spot the Pigeon* by far.

Martin: Yeah, when they slam into that fusion part, it's like Tony is trying out everything in the keyboard store. Another thing about "Match of the Day," Phil is singing super-high and not really hitting the notes. He's a bit imprecise.

Tate: Yeah, Phil is—or was—a phenomenal singer. That's definitely not one of his best vocal performances. "Match of the Day" is sort of a preview of where they were gonna go on *And Then There Were Three*. I can sympathise with Steve Hackett leaving the band shortly thereafter.

Todd: "Inside and Out" is almost 100% perfect, except for the lyrical content, which is a little risky. I've heard it described as a story about somebody who goes to prison because he's wrongly accused of rape. That's the inside part. And then the outside part is jubilant, an instrumental interpretation of what it feels like to be free. It's effective in that way, Mike Rutherford is just a monster on the bass during that whole second half and it's a good showcase for Steve Hackett. It's amazing how Steve's solo sounds so much like Steve Howe. It's almost like he's doing it intentionally.

It's a fairly long song too. Something would have to be removed from *Wind & Wuthering* if it gets put there. I've read that Tony and Mike were disappointed at the time that "Match of the Day" and "Pigeons" didn't get on *Wind & Wuthering*; they kind of felt like they should have. And that was one of the reasons why they focused on short-form stuff on *And Then There Were Three*, because they thought they had something there with the shorter songs and they wanted to develop it further. It's interesting that Phil gets blamed for that. And I like your Wings analogy for the other two songs; I agree with that.

Martin: Nice, all right. Well as our tale draws to a close, what kind of band did Genesis ultimately become? What is the personality of the band that is projected on, say, *A Trick of the Tail* and *Wind & Wuthering*? Which I'm about to affirm that I think they're a pairing.

Tate: That's a good question. Genesis and Yes share a similar identity around this time, because by 1977, the golden age of prog is definitely in the rearview mirror. Everybody in the UK really likes The Sex Pistols and The Clash and the other punk bands that would be coming around soon after, followed by the post-punk and new wave bands. Genesis are kind of seen as prog dinosaurs that are out of touch with what their audience is feeling. But they're still able to make arguably some of the best music of their career.

Yes comes out with *Going for the One* the year after *Wind & Wuthering* and that's my favourite Yes album—it's perfect. They're able to do more straightforward songs like "Parallels" and "Wonderous Stories," while doing the full-on prog thing on "Awaken."

Martin: But they are quite modern compared to Genesis, no? *Wind & Wuthering* is an album that could have come out during Victorian times, although there'd be no point because there were no stereos.

Tate: No, there weren't (laughs). You could say the same thing about Jethro Tull's *Songs from the Wood*, especially the way that Ian Anderson sings, "Let me bring you songs from the wood." Punks don't wanna hear that. Punks could give a give a hoot about sitting down around a campfire and listening to a guy with an acoustic guitar telling stories about the woods. They want to spit and pogo and shout about how pissed-off they are.

And then ELP, they just don't know what they want to do, really, because the whole *The Works* saga is continuing on at this point. They can't figure out where they fit in these modern times. And then we'd get *Love Beach* from them and *Tormato* from Yes. Even though I love *Love Beach*, it's objectively not a good ELP album and it's just a reminder of how lost they would be in around that time. But no, Genesis, like Yes, were demonstrating that they could deliver old-school prog of a high standard, but at the same time, they're able to do the straightforward thing, and you would get more of that as time went on. While Yes would fracture a bit on *Tormato* and then on *Drama*, too, for totally different reasons.

Martin: Nice. Charlie, any final thoughts?

Charlie: I don't know, I just have a great memory of this *Wind & Wuthering* record. You know when you first get into a band and you buy their records, how magical that can be. In '76 I got *Lamb* and then I got *A Trick of the Tail*, which I loved. And then I got Genesis *Live* because that was in all the stores. The earlier records weren't really available. But there was this album put out by Buddha Records, which was the American version of Famous Charisma, the label they were on in England. That was called *Best of Genesis*, and it was basically *Nursery Cryme* and *Foxtrot* on this record with different cover art, a double album. And kind of shittier sounding; it wasn't a good pressing. I listened to that album a lot.

And then I went and got the import versions of those two records and I was in love. But *Wind & Wuthering* was the first new record for me, my first new release as now this huge Genesis fan. When you get into a band and get to buy their first new record after you've discovered them, that's a revelation. I was like, oh my god, I'm so excited for this. And I really was. I lived in Milwaukee at the time and I remember it was so cold that winter. It was so cold in Milwaukee, and Lake Michigan, which was across the street from where I lived, froze for as far as… it looked like a mile out. And it was like 10° below zero every day and there were these giant clouds of steam rising from the lake during the day. And I associate all that with *Wind & Wuthering*. The record has this icy, cold brilliance to it. So I have lots of great associations for this record and I can put it on and enjoy it. Now, having produced and written a lot of songs, I can hear the cracks in it. But I still like it.

Martin: Good stuff. Well, having gone through this exercise, I think what I've learned the most is just how British and aristocratic and regal and, yes, old money, this band sounds. I can picture those grand rooms in manor houses all over England with all the portraits hung and a harpsichord in the corner, and all of these Genesis songs playing quietly all day in the background (laughs).

Todd: Yes, funny, it's definitely exceedingly English, isn't it? To close up, I'd like to add that in my evolution of trying to discover and figure out prog bands when I was growing up, it was always that Yes was the easiest and Genesis came next and then King Crimson comes after that. It's like Yes, along with things that are really mainly art rock— Moody Blues, Alan Parsons Project—that's the easiest to appreciate. And then Genesis is on a slightly more cerebral, advanced level. After that, you go on to other things that are even more difficult to learn and appreciate. But yes, I like the way you frame that—Genesis are the most British of all of them.

It's really interesting what's going on with lyrics in this particular period of Genesis, because you had Peter Gabriel writing stories that were odd and sometimes uncomfortable. And then you have Tony and Mike and Phil and Steve. I've had discussion with people about prog, and there's the concept that progressive rock bands, when they stopped doing drugs, they had to figure out what they were going to write about (laughs). And these guys, they were family men early; they had wives and kids early. So they didn't really have as much of a period of mayhem and debauchery to go on. In fact, it feels like there was none of that at all sometimes, when you listen to these very structured records. Which is why, maybe, that they tended to write about fantasy and mythology. And while all that is going on, I feel like Tony Banks is always thinking, what is a progressive rock artist? What am I supposed to write about?

Martin: Sweet. That's a good place to leave it, because both of those questions are going to be explored intensely in the next book. Surprisingly, and somewhat counter to Tate's assessment there, Genesis don't turn out to be as out of fashion as the punks claimed them to be. Instead, they morph and modernise significantly, and in the process become insanely successful beyond anybody's wildest expectations.

Contributor Biographies

Phil Aston
Phil has had a lifelong passion for music, ignited when he witnessed Deep Purple live in 1974 at the tender age of 14. This transformative experience set him on a path deeply entwined with music, marked by his early days playing in local bands around Birmingham. Phil's career evolved notably as he became the lead guitarist for the NWOBHM band The Handsome Beasts, signed to Heavy Metal Records. His journey continued with stints in Rogue Male alongside Chris Aylmer of Samson and Tantrum, where he contributed music to a film featuring Lindsay Wagner. Phil's songwriting talents were further showcased with London-based Lionheart Music. In 2004, Phil relocated to Cornwall and founded Genius Loci Media, a digital marketing agency tailored to serve the music and creative industries. The agency also ventured into music production, releasing albums for violinist and composer Sue Aston. A pioneer in live streaming, Phil produced a notable performance in the USA featuring members from the bands Survivor and Halford. Currently, Phil runs *Now Spinning Magazine*, which he founded in 2020. The magazine has quickly built a reputation for its honest video reviews, in-depth music features and interviews with many famous artists. Through *Now Spinning Magazine*, Phil continues to share his passion for music, drawing on his extensive experience as a musician and marketer to enrich the music community.

Daniel Bosch
Daniel grew up in a musical family, with a father who was a professional double bass player in a folk band and a mother who played piano, guitar and sang. Listening to everything from classical, jazz, folk and rock from a very early age, he started collecting records at age ten. He now runs a small music-themed YouTube channel called *bicyclelegs*.

Ralph Chapman
Ralph's most recent project is scripting the very first official feature documentary on that "lIttle ol' band from Texas," ZZ Top, in collaboration with Banger Films. Previously, he served as writer and associate producer on the VH1 series *Rock Icons*. Prior to that, he served the same roles on the critically acclaimed 11-part series on heavy metal, *Metal Evolution*. Ralph was also part of the creative team behind the Juno award-winning documentary, *Rush: Beyond the Lighted Stage* which took the Audience Award at the Tribeca Film Festival in 2010. Ralph also continues to work with Iconoclassic Records as a project producer notably overseeing the reissue campaign of The Guess Who catalogue. He continues to develop projects with Banger Films, and on his own with his production company, Wesbrage Productions, while contributing to various music-related websites in his spare time.

Tate Davis
Tate really got into music after he heard Led Zeppelin's "Heartbreaker" on the radio for the first time at age 13. After he graduated high school, Tate spent time as an on-air personality at 88.3 WMTS in Murfreesboro, Tennessee for two years before becoming a part-time member of *The Contrarians* YouTube show. His favourite musician of all time is Keith Moon.

Todd Evans
Todd used to sit in front of the stereo in Buffalo, NY and watch the records spin. After moving to Atlanta, Todd was active in his high school band and attended the University of Georgia to study Music Education. Changing majors to Journalism, his DJ shift at UGA's WUOG 90.5 FM kept the music alive. Todd contributes to the YouTube channels *The Contrarians* and *Rushfans*, where he discusses classic rock, progressive, symphonic and classic alternative rock music.

David Gallagher
David was, like most musos, bitten at a young age and made a nuisance of himself long enough to work in a record store in Scotland through the 2000s. While he always maintained the passion, overly sharing his (sometimes) informed opinions via his YouTube channel *@flicksnpicks*, the pandemic gave him licence to unleash his almost impossibly lo-fi channel onto others.

Rand Kelly
Rand has been immersed in music since he can remember, going back to the mid-1950s. He has acquired quite a collection of recordings and musical instruments over the years including guitars synthesizers as well as a Mellotron. He was born in Eureka, California in 1952 and was raised on radio hearing Elvis Presley and The Beatles, which made a huge impression towards his goal of becoming a musician. Today he performs improvised music live on YouTube for anyone interested, recording on a mobile phone and sometimes overdubbing using YouTube and his TV as a studio. Favourite bands include Yes, King Crimson, ELP, Gentle Giant and Pink Floyd.

Jamie Laszlo
Jamie was raised in Pittsburgh, Pennsylvania and listened to the local radio station, WDVE, which helped teach him a lot about popular music. Even though the facts he learned at school faded from memory just days after each exam, the facts he learned about rock music seemed to stay embedded in his head. These days, Jamie is a YouTube music commentator and moderator, regularly contributing to *The Contrarians* and *Sea of Tranquility* music review channels. He's recently been awarded his own show on *Sea of Tranquility* called *The Review Crew* and he also commandeers a thriving Facebook page called *Let's Get Physical*, singing the praises of physical music media.

Luis Nasser
Luis is a bassist, composer and music lover, founder of Sonus Umbra and an active member of Luz de Riada, Might Could and The Devil's Staircase. He is also a member of *In the Prog Seat*, a show on all manner of progressive rock featured on Peter Pardo's YouTube channel *Sea of Tranquility*. Think of Luis as a mathematical metalhead with a prog-rocker alter-ego. Indeed, Luis is also Professor of Physics at Columbia College Chicago, teaching and doing NSF-funded research on the thermodynamics of musical harmony. Luis loves touring, writing, recording, collaborating with other musicians and helping incredible yet relatively unknown bands reach a larger audience.

Charlie Nieland
Charlie has been creating an atmospheric mix of songwriting and sonic exploration for decades. He's produced music for Debbie Harry and Rufus Wainwright and is currently half of the literature-inspired musical duo Lusterlit and technical director for Bushwick Book Club. His latest album *Division* was released in 2021. "He balances shards of guitar noise, beguiling electronica and his imploring vocals," wrote *Dancing About Architecture*.

Pontus Norshammar
Pontus is a Swedish journalist based in Stockholm. A music geek and a major record collector since childhood, Norshammar contributes regularly to the YouTube channel *The Contrarians*, is a regular panel member on Scot Lade's Prog Corner live streams and has appeared on the British music podcast *The Epileptic Gibbon Music Show*. He is also involved with the Swedish concert scene. The first Genesis-related music he heard was "Sussudio" by Phil Collins. When Peter Gabriel's *So* was released a year later, he embarked on a journey that had him hooked on the Genesis back catalogue.

Pete Pardo
Pete is a writer and on-air personality from the Hudson Valley in New York, and has served as the Editor-in-Chief of the *Sea of Tranquility* webzine since 2001 and the Host and Program Director of the *Sea of Tranquility* YouTube channel since 2014. With over 24,000 reviews and articles on the webzine, and over 5100 videos, 98,000 subscribers and over 60 million views on the YouTube channel, *Sea of Tranquility* has been a constant source of information and entertainment on all things hard rock and heavy metal, progressive rock, classic rock, and jazz fusion for over 22 years. Visit *Sea of Tranquility* at seaoftranquility.org and youtube.com/@seaoftranquilityprog/.

Philip-Edward Phillis
Philip is a lecturer in Film and Media Studies at SciencesPo, a.k.a. The Paris Institute of Political Sciences. He has a PhD in Film Studies and has published extensively on respective topics. His passion for cinema can only be rivalled by that for music and especially for rock and heavy metal music. His first ever foray into this universe was thanks to his older sister who played for him a bootlegged best of Metallica back in 1997. The song in particular was "Seek and Destroy." After that, like a domino effect, came Iron Maiden, Helloween, Blind Guardian and especially Dream Theatre, who became his gateway band to the world of progressive rock and metal. Since 2017, Philip has been a steady contributor to the online version of *Rock Hard* magazine in Greece. He has interviewed many of the important and upcoming bands of the expanding Greek heavy metal scene and provides reviews of numerous different international bands. Since 2023, he has been a Patreon supporter of *The Contrarians* on YouTube. The channel has hosted a number of discussions with Philip as a guest, on topics ranging from grunge music to progressive concept albums and the legacy of classic albums by superstar bands.

Bill Schuster
Also going by the name of Howler Monkey (founder of infamous music forums, *The Monkey House* and *CryNet*), Bill is a regular contributor to *The Contrarians* (co-commandeered by the author of this book), *Rock Daydream Nation*, *Grant's Rock Warehaus* and *Ryan's Vinyl Destination* among others.

Special Thanks

A hearty appreciation goes out to Agustin Garcia de Paredes who applied his eagle eye to a copy edit of this book. Agustin is also the moderator of the *History in Five Songs with Martin Popoff* podcast Facebook page.

About the Author

At approximately 7900 (with over 7000 appearing in his books), Martin has unofficially written more record reviews than anybody in the history of music writing across all genres. Additionally, Martin has penned approximately 130 books on hard rock, heavy metal, classic rock, prog, punk and record collecting. He was Editor-in-Chief of the now retired *Brave Words & Bloody Knuckles*, Canada's foremost heavy metal publication for 14 years, and has also contributed to *Revolver*, *Guitar World*, *Goldmine*, *Record Collector*, bravewords.com, lollipop.com and hardradio.com, with many record label band bios and liner notes to his credit as well.

Additionally, Martin has been a regular contractor to Banger Films, having worked for two years as researcher on the award-winning documentary *Rush: Beyond the Lighted Stage*, on the writing and research team for the 11-episode *Metal Evolution* and on the ten-episode *Rock Icons*, both for VH1 Classic. Additionally, Martin is the writer of the original metal genre chart used in *Metal: A Headbanger's Journey* and throughout the *Metal Evolution* episodes.

Then there's his audio podcast, *History in Five Songs with Martin Popoff* and the YouTube channel he runs with Marco D'Auria, *The Contrarians*. The community of guest analysts seen on *The Contrarians* has provided the pool of speakers used across the pages of this very book. Martin currently resides in Toronto and can be reached through martinp@inforamp.net or martinpopoff.com.

A Complete Martin Popoff Bibliography

2024: Entangled: Genesis on Record 1969 - 1976, Run with the Wolf: Rainbow on Record, Queen Live!, Led Zeppelin: A Visual Biography, Honesty Is No Excuse: Thin Lizzy on Record, Van Halen at 50, Pictures at Eleven: Robert Plant Album by Album, Perfect Water: The Rebel Imaginos

2023: Kiss at 50, The Electric Church: The Biography, Dominance and Submission: The Blue Öyster Cult Canon, The Who and Quadrophenia, Wild Mood Swings: Disintegrating The Cure Album by Album, AC/DC at 50

2022: Pink Floyd and The Dark Side of the Moon: 50 Years, Killing the Dragon: Dio in the '90s and 2000s, Feed My Frankenstein: Alice Cooper, the Solo Years, Easy Action: The Original Alice Cooper Band, Lively Arts: The Damned Deconstructed, Yes: A Visual Biography II: 1982 – 2022, Bowie @ 75, Dream Evil: Dio in the '80s, Judas Priest: A Visual Biography, UFO: A Visual Biography

2021: Hawkwind: A Visual Biography, Loud 'n' Proud: Fifty Years of Nazareth, Yes: A Visual Biography, Uriah Heep: A Visual Biography, Driven: Rush in the '90s and "In the End," Flaming Telepaths: Imaginos Expanded and Specified, Rebel Rouser: A Sweet User Manual

2020: The Fortune: On the Rocks with Angel, Van Halen: A Visual Biography, Limelight: Rush in the '80s, Thin Lizzy: A Visual Biography, Empire of the Clouds: Iron Maiden in the 2000s, Blue Öyster Cult: A Visual Biography, Anthem: Rush in the '70s, Denim and Leather: Saxon's First Ten Years, Black Funeral: Into the Coven with Mercyful Fate

2019: Satisfaction: 10 Albums That Changed My Life, Holy Smoke: Iron Maiden in the '90s, Sensitive to Light: The Rainbow Story, Where Eagles Dare: Iron Maiden in the '80s, Aces High: The Top 250 Heavy Metal Songs of the '80s, Judas Priest: Turbo 'til Now, Born Again! Black Sabbath in the Eighties and Nineties

2018: Riff Raff: The Top 250 Heavy Metal Songs of the '70s, Lettin' Go: UFO in the '80s and '90s, Queen: Album by Album, Unchained: A Van Halen User Manual, Iron Maiden: Album by Album, Sabotage! Black Sabbath in the Seventies, Welcome to My Nightmare: 50 Years of Alice Cooper, Judas Priest: Decade of Domination, Popoff Archive – 6: American Power Metal, Popoff Archive – 5: European Power Metal, The Clash: All the Albums, All the Songs

2017: Led Zeppelin: All the Albums, All the Songs, AC/DC: Album by Album, Lights Out: Surviving the '70s with UFO, Tornado of Souls: Thrash's Titanic Clash, Caught in a Mosh: The Golden Era of Thrash, Rush: Album by Album, Beer Drinkers and Hell Raisers: The Rise of Motörhead, Metal Collector: Gathered Tales from Headbangers, Hit the Lights: The Birth of Thrash, Popoff Archive – 4: Classic Rock, Popoff Archive – 3: Hair Metal

2016: Popoff Archive – 2: Progressive Rock, Popoff Archive – 1: Doom Metal, Rock the Nation: Montrose, Gamma and Ronnie Redefined, Punk Tees: The Punk Revolution in 125 T-Shirts, Metal Heart: Aiming High with Accept, Ramones at 40, Time and a Word: The Yes Story

2015: Kickstart My Heart: A Mötley Crüe Day-by-Day, This Means War: The Sunset Years of the NWOBHM, Wheels of Steel: The Explosive Early Years of the NWOBHM, Swords and Tequila: Riot's Classic First Decade, Who Invented Heavy Metal?, Sail Away: Whitesnake's Fantastic Voyage

2014: Live Magnetic Air: The Unlikely Saga of the Superlative Max Webster, Steal Away the Night: An Ozzy Osbourne Day-by-Day, The Big Book of Hair Metal, Sweating Bullets: The Deth and Rebirth of Megadeth, Smokin' Valves: A Headbanger's Guide to 900 NWOBHM Records

2013: The Art of Metal (co-edit with Malcolm Dome), 2 Minutes to Midnight: An Iron Maiden Day-by-Day, Metallica: The Complete Illustrated History, Rush: The Illustrated History, Ye Olde Metal: 1979, Scorpions: Top of the Bill - updated and reissued as Wind of Change: The Scorpions Story in 2016

2012: Epic Ted Nugent, Fade To Black: Hard Rock Cover Art of the Vinyl Age, It's Getting Dangerous: Thin Lizzy 81-12, We Will Be Strong: Thin Lizzy 76-81, Fighting My Way Back: Thin Lizzy 69-76, The Deep Purple Royal Family: Chain of Events '80 – '11, The Deep Purple Royal Family: Chain of Events Through '79 - reissued as The Deep Purple Family Year by Year books

2011: Black Sabbath FAQ, The Collector's Guide to Heavy Metal: Volume 4: The '00s (co-authored with David Perri)

2010: Goldmine Standard Catalogue of American Records 1948 – 1991, 7th Edition

2009: Goldmine Record Album Price Guide, 6th Edition, Goldmine 45 RPM Price Guide, 7th Edition, A Castle Full of Rascals: Deep Purple '83 – '09, Worlds Away: Voivod and the Art of Michel Langevin, Ye Olde Metal: 1978

2008: Gettin' Tighter: Deep Purple '68 – '76, All Access: The Art of the Backstage Pass, Ye Olde Metal: 1977, Ye Olde Metal: 1976

2007: Judas Priest: Heavy Metal Painkillers, Ye Olde Metal: 1973 to 1975, The Collector's Guide to Heavy Metal: Volume 3: The Nineties, Ye Olde Metal: 1968 to 1972

2006: Run for Cover: The Art of Derek Riggs, Black Sabbath: Doom Let Loose, Dio: Light Beyond the Black

2005: The Collector's Guide to Heavy Metal: Volume 2: The Eighties, Rainbow: English Castle Magic, UFO: Shoot Out the Lights, The New Wave of British Heavy Metal Singles

2004: Blue Öyster Cult: Secrets Revealed! (updated and reissued in 2009 with the same title; updated and reissued as Agents of Fortune: The Blue Öyster Cult Story in 2016), Contents Under Pressure: 30 Years of Rush at Home & Away, The Top 500 Heavy Metal Albums of All Time

2003: The Collector's Guide to Heavy Metal: Volume 1: The Seventies, The Top 500 Heavy Metal Songs of All Time

2001: Southern Rock Review

2000: Heavy Metal: 20th Century Rock and Roll, The Goldmine Price Guide to Heavy Metal Records

1997: The Collector's Guide to Heavy Metal

1993: Riff Kills Man! 25 Years of Recorded Hard Rock & Heavy Metal

See martinpopoff.com for complete details and ordering information.

Entangled: Genesis on Record 1969-1976

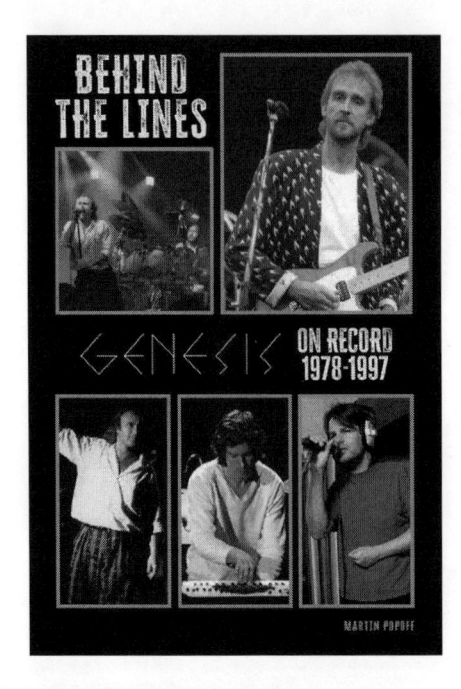

Behind the Lines: Genesis on Record 1978 – 1997

ISBN: 978-1-915246-64-6

In this revelatory follow-up to *Entangled: Genesis on Record 1969 – 1976*, Martin Popoff, also author of multiple books on Yes and Pink Floyd, re-assembles his team of progressive rock experts to tacked the second half of the Genesis catalogue, namely:

> *And Then There Were Three*
> *Duke*
> *Abacab*
> *Genesis*
> *Invisible Touch*
> *We Can't Dance* and finally...
> *Calling All Stations*.

And defying possibility, the angles and opinions and concepts on offer are even more fresh and intriguing than those suggested in the first book. Perhaps that's because the second half of the Genesis catalogue has never been discussed this fervently and sincerely, given the band's embracing of pop conventions and the smash, multi-platinum success Phil Collins, Tony Banks and Mike Rutherford enjoyed because of it.

But the bottom line is this: if you were looking the have the art across these records highlighted and validated for you, then Popoff's panel of progressive pronouncers are at your service. Indeed, Martin is confident that after you read what these guys have to say, you'll be scurrying back to the albums looking for any number of the hundreds of details celebrated in these Q&A chapters of yummy music talk.